F. v. Erhart

THE ROLE OF THE LAITY IN THE CHURCH

THE
ROLE OF THE LAITY
IN THE CHURCH

by

Msgr. GERARD PHILIPS, S.T.D. et M.

(Chair of Dogmatic Theology, University of Louvain)

Translated by

JOHN R. GILBERT AND JAMES W. MOUDRY

of the

LOUVAIN AMERICAN COLLEGE

FIDES PUBLISHERS ASSOCIATION
Chicago   Illinois

First Published in U.S.A. in 1956 by
FIDES PUBLISHERS ASSOCIATION,
Chicago,   Illinois.

Imprimatur: ✠ HON. VAN WAEYENBERGH, rect. Univ. deleg.

Lovanii, die 14 februarii 1955.

Acknowledgement

*The translators are deeply indebted to Mr. Bernard McMahon,
S.T.L., George Stanley Winders, B.A., Oxon., and to Mr.
Maurice Carroll of the Louvain American College who read the
manuscript with painstaking care and made many valuable
corrections and suggestions. They also wish to express their
sincere appreciation to all those who in any way assisted with
preparing this translation.*

Ash Wednesday, 1955
Louvain

*Printed in the Republic of Ireland
by The Kerryman Ltd., Tralee.*

CONTENTS

CHAPTER I

THE HOUR OF THE LAITY

A Present Day Phenomenon

LAY PEOPLE, today, are showing a growing interest in religious problems, and not only for their political repercussions.

This phenomenon is not limited to French speaking countries, but is noticeable throughout the whole Catholic world, and even beyond on the oecumenical scale. It is an answer to today's general state of dechristianization. Large sections of the population have abandoned the practices of their fathers and even, it seems, all religious preoccupation. The proletariat masses are woefully ignorant of the Church. This defection does not date from the present day; it was effected for the greater part in the last century. But it is only now that we are becoming aware of its alarming proportions. A reaction is springing up; far from capitulating before the evil, we are seeking its remedy.

The 16th century underwent a similar crisis, but since then the accent has been changed. At that time, as now, the decadence did not begin with the birth of Protestantism. For a long time the religious sense of the Middle Ages had been decreasing. It still showed on the surface, but in its depths it was undermined by ignorance and simple conformity. The call for a reform, *in capite et in membris*, of the leaders and the members, resounded in vain. Luther's revolt was needed before reform was taken seriously. And, by the time the first attempts of the Counter-Reform were launched, it was already too late for the greater part of Christian Europe.

Our century seems determined not to repeat this lamentable experience. Refusing to view our time as the twenty-fifth hour, it chooses to see it as the first hour, the hour of resurrection and hope. In the 16th century the struggle served to strengthen the authority of the hierarchy. Today the layman is coming to the fore.[1]

Any cultural review worthy of the name must make a diagnosis of our times. Study weeks and the minutes of congresses or meetings give us only a transient literature. But in many recent works, religious sociology follows modern scientific methods.[2] Occasionally, the word 'revolution' has been flourished, but the general tenor is clearly constructive. It is the exception when the pessimistic view prevails. The Catholic world was shocked when, in the middle of the last war, Abbé Godin posed the troubling question: *France pagan?* A rigorous examination of conscience was the result, an introspection that went beyond the frontiers of the French speaking world and extended into Germany and England. Is Western Europe pagan? [3]

The question is directed not only to the Cardinal prefect of Propaganda, but especially to the Christian conscience. The layman finds himself at the very heart of the matter. If the Pope in person calls upon him, it is not to come to the aid of a floundering clergy, nor is it a frantic appeal for the layman to take up the yoke and free the clerical coach from the mire. It is not a question of saving the sad remnants of an outmoded theocracy; the very existence of the Christian world is at stake. It follows, then, that the simplest of the faithful must become aware not so much of his rights as of his duties, his apostolic responsibility. Many are the signs revealing this reawakening of the laity, this dawning promise of The Great Return.

What is the significance of this religious reaction?

One may wonder, now that Communism is threatening to submerge Western civilization, if Catholics are not simply following a defensive reflex. In doing so, their religious reaction would have in view primarily the safeguarding of their liberty and of their possessions. But while the psychosis of fear might provoke a flight to America, it could hardly evoke a religious revival. Political desperation can explain an interest in the Atlantic Pact and European Defence; it cannot explain the enthusiasm for the doctrine of the Mystical Body. Without a doubt, religious motives are the most powerful in this revival.

Among a good number of the laity, we are witnessing today a new interest in the profound mysteries of life in the Church. For a long time they have considered themselves as the passive subjects of ecclesiastical authority. But now this apathy is giving way to an active participation; they feel themselves living members of a community of salvation, a fact rich in promise in the face of a despairing dechristianization. We are in the presence of a great expansion of authentic Christianity, the Christianity of revelation and not of the pseudo-religion of enlightenment or romanticism.

Needless to say, many are still groping and searching. Many have become displaced persons in this 'supernatural' world. This is true not only of laymen, but also of priests and more than once of theologians.

Religious instruction of the simple should not impede access to the mysteries of grace which the Gospel can open to them. Lay people hunger for the bread of doctrine which the Church alone can distribute. Pius XII launched his encyclical *Mystici Corporis* in the midst of the horrors of war, convinced that the misery of souls was far greater than present material sufferings.

Doctrinal authority precedes and enlightens the spirit of Faith in the community. One could also say that the lay community precedes doctrinal authority, by demanding deeper instruction, if not always vocally, at least by their very real distress.

Between two world wars, *lay Catholic action*, the predilection of Pius XI, developed in scope. Some are inclined to believe that the brilliance of its early stages is fast fading. It would be more accurate to say that its real brilliance is yet to come. We must make a profound study of its theory and practice, its essence and its repercussions. It would be an injustice to drop it as just another near miss. It needs to examine and to purify itself. But its content is so rich that it already forms an integral part of Catholic life.

At the end of the first world-wide upheaval, the *missionary Spirit* saw a great rise. The forms of the apostolate, whether within the Christian milieu or among the pagans, are innumerable. Women have shown themselves equally ardent in being Christ's witnesses to the world. Thanks to the liturgical movement, the Church assembling in large numbers feels itself a communion of prayer before the living God, in Christ and the Holy Spirit. But that is not all. For the cultivated layman, the 'solicitude for all the Churches' has taken on a more real, a wider sense. Dissident congregations pose grave questions for Roman Catholics. We are urged not as much to a defence as to a more charitable self-commitment and a more disinterested zeal. On the occasion of the Amsterdam World Conference of 1948, a number of Catholics heard the word *ecumenism* for the first time; and strange as that word may be to them even now, it will never disappear from their vocabulary. [4]

THE ADVANCE OF THE LAITY

Non-Catholics have the impression that the Roman authorities frown upon this 'emancipation' of the laity and hesitate to endorse it. If they really favoured it, wouldn't they rather have taken the initiative? Have they not always tended to keep the 'flock' in a state of inferiority so that they could be more easily governed? After all, minors are more easy to control. Their emancipation would present many difficulties for their leaders. The only duty of the masses is docility.

This accusation is a complete deformation of the Biblical figure of the Good Shepherd. The devotedness of leaders, which is the lesson of the allegory, is transformed into a spirit of domination, and the well-being of the governed is effaced before the egotistical self-interest of those who hold power. In the course of her historic evolution, the Church has sometimes emphasized one value, sometimes another, depending on the opposition which she faced. But concerning principles, she has never known hesitation. Pius XII told the World Congress of Lay Apostles that in the Kingdom of grace, all are regarded as adults.[5] Only the ancient Israelites were under the yoke of the Law. For Christ has liberated us; from the day of our Baptism, we have been 'emancipated' by Him. Moreover, since the Reformation the pioneers among the Catholic laity have necessarily been anything but children or minors in the Church.

More than once the call to Catholic Action has come to the laity by the voice of the hierarchy. The development of the sacramental life, thanks to the decrees of Pius X, has stimulated their zeal. If the Eucharist is the bond of charity, frequent communion will stimulate the better Catholics to consecrate themselves to advancing the less favoured. The Scholastic is sometimes accused of having taught an individualistic conception of the Sacraments. For Saint Thomas, the primary effect of Communion is the unity of the Mystical Body in active charity.

The encyclical, *Mystici Corporis*, has duly apprised the laity of its duty not to leave everything which concerns the Kingdom of God to the clergy. It was not merely to extend the sphere of clerical influence that the Pope said:

> And so we would have all who acknowledge the Church as their mother carefully consider that, not only the sacred ministers, not only those who have dedicated themselves to God in the religious life, but in their measure also the other members of the Mystical Body of Jesus Christ, are under an obligation to work zealously and energetically for the building and increase of that Body. We wish this to be especially realised—as in fact, to their honour, it is realised—by those militant members of Catholic Action who are co-operating with Bishops and priests in the work of the apostolate, and by the members of auxiliary pious associations which work to the same end. It is evident that under present conditions this untiring activity of theirs is of the first and highest importance.[6]

In his address of February 20, 1946, to the new cardinals, Pius XII expressed himself still more clearly:

> The faithful, and more precisely the laity, are stationed in the front ranks of the life of the Church, and through them the Church is the

living principle of human society. Consequently, they especially must
have an ever clearer consciousness, not only of belonging to the Church,
but of *being the Church*, that is, of being the community of the faithful
on earth under the guidance of their common leader, the Pope, and the
bishops in communion with him. *They are the Church*, and therefore even
from the beginning, the faithful, with the consent of their bishops, have
united in associations directed to the most diverse types of human activity.
And the Holy See has never ceased to approve and praise them.[7]

Even many Catholics are surprised at this statement, 'The laity is
the Church!' Here are words they are unaccustomed to hear. We
have avoided this way of speaking for too long, hoping thus better
to avoid any so-called collusion with Protestantism. It is not a
question of attenuating the office of the bishops or priests. But besides
their office and under their direction, there do exist other responsibilities
in the Church, those of the faithful. We can speak of different degrees
or even, if you will, distinct dignities in the community; but nevertheless a hierarchy shut up within itself and nourishing a passive body
is inconceivable. The organism is a whole, and only as such, with
all its different members functioning, does it have its full vitality.
Otherwise, the hierarchy would be an obstacle; it would constitute
a wall of separation rather than a uniting force. Its mediation would
produce rupture instead of unity between distinct elements. The
sacrament of Orders does not set up a barrier which the layman cannot
even approach. In Christ, all divisions have been destroyed: the court
of the Gentiles and the court of the Jews exist no longer. All have
access to the sanctuary, even though all don't have the same function
to fulfil there.

Nor is the Church a mere association of worshippers. She is also
the vivifying principle of human society. If she is to make her spirit
penetrate the world, she cannot do without the ranks of thinkers
and poets, philosophers and journalists, workers and heads of families,
all of whom can be witnesses of the faith in all departments of life.

The collaboration of eminent lay people is not peculiar to our
times, but today we regard more highly than ever the contributions
of the simple and ordinary people, people whose names will never
be noted in history. Though called a mission country, France is
under the constant watch of contemporary Christianity as a land rich
in Catholic experience. Criticized and envied, her capital importance
is everywhere recognized. If her errors are regretted, her recoveries
are admired, unexpected as they may be. Her immense reserves of
generosity and evangelical enthusiasm cannot be disregarded. She is
the vanguard of lay apostolic activity. We wonder whether we
should qualify as 'lay' the theological genius of Pascal, at once mystical

and anti-Jesuit, when his was a priestly soul though without the priestly anointing. Again, Leon Bloy, fiery and explosive as an Old Testament prophet, has poured out his invectives upon the heads of the New Testament bourgeois who have transformed the Kingdom of God into a sort of insurance policy. Anti-papal and ultra-montane, he has formed perfectly orthodox disciples of the Scholastic temper of Jacques Maritain. Maurice Blondel, type of the Biblical patriarch, carries the wisdom of the philosopher to the portal of revelation, there to ask its Baptism. Paul Claudel, modern singer of the Canticle of Canticles, in the very exercise of his diplomatic missions for the Third Republic became an ambassador of Christianity. Charles Péguy, himself the incarnation of the prodigal son, was yet capable, fortified by his eminently evangelical consciousness of sin and hope, of sending a Protestant to do homage to Our Lady of Chartres. None of these virile temperaments, however, has been anointed with the oils of the priesthood. Yet, like the grandson of Renan, the centurion Ernest Psichari, they are all soldiers in arms. Nor can we forget Emmanuel Mounier, a fierce and wary fighter, bold in the purity of his faith.

By contrast, the noted German lay Catholics are generally historians. The most famous, after Görres, is Ludwig von Pastor. How many times has this celebrated historiographer of the popes been mistaken for a Roman prelate? The English are still less suspect of clericalism. In their broad descriptions of history as in their Sunday preaching at Hyde Park they are practical, concrete and realistic but not at the expense of their poetic sense or especially their sense of humour. G. K. Chesterton, knight of the Middle Ages and yet a man whose spirit rivals the moderns, is ready to duel for the honour of the Virgin. With scintillating humour and invincible optimism, he forces even the admirers of the Red Dean to listen to the Church. In Switzerland, as if from an observation tower, Gonzague de Reynold is studying the symptoms of the European tragedy and rebirth. In the countries of longstanding Christianity like Italy, sociologists and university professors are pre-eminent: Toniolo, C. Ferrini, and the artists emulating The Poverello, such as Lapira, mayor of Florence and orator of the Mass of the Poor, or Papini, the lay confessor of Celestine VI, the last Pope of history. Can anyone say that these characters of tempered steel are sacristy vergers or mere schoolboys under the rod of a master? Far from behaving like frightened and speechless little boys, they show the frank outspokenness of responsible adults in the Church.

In Flanders and the Low Countries, the level horizons offer no invitation to mountain-scaling ventures. The great voice of Hedwig, the mystic of the Middle Ages, is answered only with feeble echoes. Though there are few geniuses of pure thought in these regions, nevertheless capable and determined organizers of a new social order are on the march. The most noted authors are often converts. Pierre van der Meer, spiritual son of France as well as Holland, even if he has finally found rest in the monastery, has not forsaken his lay vocation as a writer. And from the mists of the North, the Catholic novels of Sigrid Undset, with their papal stress, come as a challenge to established Lutheranism. Everywhere, the laity awakens!

LAICISM, LAICITY, LAITY*

What is the source of this renewal, this rebirth? Without doubt it stems first of all from a sane reaction against laicism. We will better understand this reversal by examining the history of the word 'lay.' When speaking of laicism, we mean not only anticlericalism or opposition to the abuses of clerical power, but more often an anti-religious attitude. 'Lay laws' remain, in France, the battle cry of the Free Thinkers and Masons in their fight against Christian schools and convents. A recent declaration of Le Grand Orient de France confirms this idea: 'The idea of laicism is not for us simply an objective idea, it is our very substance.'[8]

The bishops of Belgium give the same meaning to the word in warning their faithful 'that baptized children are out of place in neutral or lay institutions that have no regard for their Christian education.'[9] This admonition is in no way aimed at the thousands of lay teachers who, with the religious, are devoting themselves to Catholic teaching. It condemns a spirit, an areligious neutralism which too often leads to disaffection and even to hostility.

It is significant that the Larousse defines the word 'laicize' as an 'exclusion of religious teaching from the scholastic programme.'

For the Italian Socialists, the word 'lay' has the same flavour of opposition to all religious influence. When de Gasperi formed his first cabinet, they implored him to appoint a 'layman' for the department of education. And when he answered that he had no intention of naming a priest or religious, they were forced to become more explicit: they wanted above all a non-Catholic.[10]

The over tones of the word 'laicity' are entirely different, and in connection with it, the word 'lay' has an acceptable meaning. Article I of the new French Constitution of June 29th, 1946, is worded as follows: 'France is an indivisible republic, lay, democratic, and social.' These qualifications can hide vastly different realities, as, for example, the term 'democracy' used on either side of the Iron Curtain. The

Fourth Republic calls itself 'social' and 'lay.' Is this to ward off the spectre of absolutism and theocracy? The precaution seems almost superfluous, but the constituents thought it useful to repeat even the obvious. Sentimental reaction, no doubt. The bishops wisely thought it best not to take offence. They preferred to exorcise in advance any evil spirits hiding behind these words. In a Declaration dated June 29, 1945, concerning the human personality, the family and society, they indicated their position regarding four different interpretations of the 'laicity of the state.' Here is the substance of this much studied text:

'1. If by these words is understood a proclamation of *the autonomous sovereignty of the State in its temporal domain*, we declare that this doctrine is in complete conformity with the doctrine of the Church.

'2. The "laicity of the State" can also be understood in the sense that, *in a country divided in belief*, the State must leave to each citizen the free practice of his religion. This second sense, if rightly understood, also conforms to the thought of the Church.

'3. But if the "laicity of the State" is *a philosophical doctrine* which contains *a materialistic and atheistic concept of human life and society*, if these words intend to define *a system of political government which imposes such a concept*, then with all our strength we rise up against this doctrine: we condemn it in the very name of the true mission of the State and the mission of the Church. . . .

'4. Finally, if "laicity of the State" signifies *the will of the State not to submit itself to any superior morality* and *to regard its own interests as the sole norm of its actions*, we affirm that this thesis is extremely dangerous, unsound and false.'[11]

We can well wonder if the politicians realized these theological niceties. They continue to masquerade under the name of 'laymen,' unaware of the thoroughly Christian origin of the expression. Its primitive accent can be rediscovered in the term 'laity' which still means 'of the Church.' Catholics would do well to reclaim for their own a term which is rightfully theirs. The word 'lay' originally meant 'sacred' or 'baptized.' To use it outside the Church is meaningless. We are now in the presence of a strange inversion, as a return to sources clearly demonstrates.

The word Λαός in the Greek bible which gives us 'laicus, lay,' designates the chosen people, the holy nation consecrated to Jahweh. *Laos* in the Septuagint takes on an explicit religious sense, especially with the prophets. God has graciously sealed a pact of friendship and fidelity with the Jewish people; outside are the Gentiles, confirmed in their sin of infidelity. Still the prophetic message, through its universal promises, dissolves national boundaries.

Sometimes in the New Testament, the word *laos* simply means 'the crowd'; but the Apostles, and especially Saint Paul, have taken up again the specific sense of the word in applying it to Christianity. 'God visited the Gentiles' (*ethne*), said Saint James at the Council of Jerusalem, 'to take from among them a people (*laos*) to bear his name.' (Acts, XV, 14), in order, finally, to realise the truly super-natural universality of Christianity. The honorary titles of Israel have become the right of the faithful of Christ: 'a chosen race, a royal priesthood, a holy nation, purchased people (*laos*).' (I Pt., II, 9). Now the faithful, children of light, who have come together from every tongue and tribe, are opposed no longer to other nations but only to those who, whether Jew or Gentile, remain obstinate in the darkness of their unbelief.[12]

Every member of the new community, sanctified by the faith and by Baptism, can be called 'lay.' But from the very beginning this community has been organized. Saint Clement of Rome about the year 96, distinguishes different orders: 'the high priest, the priests, the levites, and the *homo laicus*.'[13] In the Eucharistic celebration, the president (προεστώς) directs the public prayer to which the *laos* answer: Amen! Thus, about the year 160, Saint Justin describes the Eucharistic supper and the active part which the faithful take therein.[14] And so, by his membership in the group, the layman is a person 'consecrated' even though the holy things are especially entrusted to the clergy. This distinction was not to the liking of all. Tertullian, having joined the Montanist camp, violently rejected it: 'We laymen, are not we also priests?'[15] Going even further, it was in the charismatics and the 'illuminated' and not in the established authority that he recognized the spiritual power.

We have, therefore, the episcopacy, *numerus episcoporum*, and 'the others.' In these controversies, the word 'lay' referred more and more exclusively to those under authority. Soon it was opposed to 'consecrated.' The early Latin version of the Bible speaks of 'lay loaves' to distinguish them from the 'loaves of proposition' sanctified for use in the Tabernacle (I Sam., XXI, 4). During the high Middle Ages, professed religious who had charge of the manual labour in the monasteries were called *laici* in opposition to the choir monks. Hence, their state was sacred but their work was profane.[16]

In principle, Protestantism no longer recognizes the hierarchical priesthood, but nevertheless they use the word 'lay.' How do they define it? At the Amsterdam Conference of 1948, the question was vigorously debated. Some of the delegates wanted the word 'layman' to designate those members of the community who receive but do not distribute the sacraments; a catholicising tendency opposed by the majority. Finally they agreed to call laymen, those not having theological degrees.[17] Thus the word 'cleric' takes on again its Middle Age meaning of a highly educated man. What a strange fortune for the simple faithful at the heart of the Reformation!

Until recent times, theology hardly took account of the layman. The *Kirchenlexicon* of Wetzer and Welte, a twelve-volume encyclopedia, dismisses the word 'layman' with a simple reference to 'clergy.'[18] *Le Dictionaire de Theologie Catholique* does not even mention the word. Out of a total of 2,414 canons, the Code of Canon Law consecrates only 44 to the chapter 'De Laicis.'

Still we must not exaggerate the objection that the Code is exclusively clerical. The laws on the Sacraments, for example, concern the laity almost as much as the clergy. The Order instituted by Christ distinguishes the clergy from the laity (as being set apart) for the direction of the faithful and the administration of the divine cult (Canon 948). The laity have the right to receive from the clergy, according to the norms of ecclesiastical discipline, spiritual benefits and especially the indispensable means of salvation (Canon 682). This is the fundamental principle: it emphasizes the 'receptivity' of the faithful. But it acknowledges something more in them than obligations: they also have the right to the fulfilment of their needs. By their Baptism, they have the dignity of 'persons' in the Church, subjects of rights and duties (Canon 87).[19]

The existence of religious multiplies the distinctions. In theory, there is no difficulty. Clerics and laity can both enter religion. Still in practice it is no longer customary to number monks and nuns among the laity. The Code itself recognises their precedence over the 'laity', in the first paragraph of Canon 491; the second paragraph of the same article speaks explicitly of three categories: secular clergy, laity and religious.

There are many border-line cases and intermediary forms. A certain number of religious have access to the priesthood; they are called regular clergy. In the Catholic Church, women are always excluded from the priesthood but not from the religious life. Priests, on their part, can still tend to religious perfection and live together, even sometimes with public vows, without becoming 'regulars.' Men and women can practise the evangelical counsels and take vows without losing their lay status. Such, for example, is the case with the recently established Secular Institutes.

For our purposes, the reality is more important than juridical definition. No one, in practice, confuses the three principal categories enumerated above. It is now our task to determine more exactly their chief characteristics, their spirit.

Although in different ways, both priests and religious are consecrated by their state to the things of God; laymen, by their state, are in the world. The *Conclusions* of the World Congress of the Lay Apostolate, while emphasizing the fidelity of the laity 'to their vocation as God's people,' explicitly describe them as 'engaged in the life of the world.'[20] Father Congar attempts a more exact description with the following formula:

1. Laymen do not live exclusively for the realities of heaven; this is the condition of monks in so far as this life allows it;
2. While the laity are Christians in the full sense of the word, living a life in Christ, still they do not have competence, or at least their competence is limited, over the means to this life in Christ which are properly ecclesiastical, means which are within the competence of clerics.[21]

Except for a few slight differences, we are in agreement with the author. A religious does not live only *for* but also *in* the heavenly realities, no matter what his material occupation be. The layman, in his turn, can and ought to work in view of eternal values, at least having them as the ultimate goal of his activities. But he can not so act outside the conditions of his ordinary life. Neither materially nor spiritually does he enter the cloister. As the Congress has said, the layman is loyally 'engaged in the life of the world.' In the final analysis it is the 'situation' which determines the major classifications. The laity are to sanctify themselves in and through their work in the world. In our chapter on lay spirituality we will return to these ideas in order to determine them more precisely.

We would be wrong in limiting the Church's idea of the laity to her juridical texts alone. Canon Law is neither the sole nor the principal source of Theology. Furthermore, written law is generally behind the times. Although relatively recent, since it dates from 1918, the Code makes no mention of Catholic Action, a movement whose importance escapes no one today. Secular Institutes existed long before the Apostolic Constitution *Provida Mater* of 1947 recognized them officially and determined their status.

Catholics sometimes have complained of the 'ostracizing of the laity.' They are, said Edouard Le Roy, like the lambs presented to the Pope on Candlemas Day, whose wool is used to weave the liturgical pallium: 'they are blessed and then sheared!'[22] This slightly irreverent reflection is no longer applicable. During the last half-a-century we have made progress. Something other than money is being asked of the laity: the total consecration of their Christian personality.

DEVELOPING ECCLESIOLOGY

There is no better antidote for laicism than to recognise the full spiritual significance of the laity. But this realization of their worth is also the result of a further factor, namely, *our less antagonistic attitude toward Protestantism*. Each controversial reply emphasised and made more rigid the particular teaching which had been attached, relegating others to the background. The inevitable result of this, even for dogmatic definitions, is an impression of partiality, a one-sidedness which must be corrected through a more serene study of the problem as a whole. For example, it would be wrong to deduce the whole doctrine of grace from the decrees of the Council of Trent. The fathers of the Council were only interested in condemning heretical positions, and not in publishing a treatise on sanctifying grace. When the Reformation tried to suppress all hierarchical authority, the Church was forced to counter with a vindication of papal and episcopal authority. Most of our catechisms, especially in their original form, have been drawn up with this anti-Protestant motive. They rendered invaluable service, but succeeding generations have felt the blow of this rigidity. Today we realize better than ever before that, while rejecting many Catholic notions, Protestantism has still kept many authentic Christian values. These values are partially ineffective because they are emmeshed in a false framework, but they still retain their birthmarks. They belong to the dowry of the legitimate spouse, and even in the hands of the unfaithful, as Saint Augustine said, they do not lose their value. [23]

Our classical treatise on the Church in its systematic form owes its origin to the errors of Luther and Calvin. It was conceived as a reply to the Reformation. It stresses the chapters treating of the hierarchy and insists on the visible elements. From this point of view, the celebrated definition of Saint Robert Bellarmine is typical: 'The Church is the society of men united by the profession of the same Christian faith and participation in the same Sacraments, governed by their legitimate pastors and especially by the only Vicar of Christ on earth, the Pope of Rome.' [24]

This description, perfectly adapted to its particular end, passes over in silence the internally vitalizing infusion of Christ and the proper end of the community, sanctification. The faithful, it says, must obey. Moreover, they profess their faith and take part in worship. They are not purely passive, but what they should produce is scarcely elaborated. In practice, our ecclesiology has remained more or less a defence of the episcopate and the supreme power of the Pope, a doctrine of the hierarchy. Today, a new chapter is being elaborated;

somewhat barbarously it could be entitled *laicology*. This development touches the legitimate desire of Oriental Christians. The Orthodox churches have a high regard for their bishops, but their lay people are intimately connected with ecclesiastical life. To give only one example, the professors of the Theological faculties in the Orient are nearly always laymen.

Among all the Christian churches, we are witnessing today a larger participation of the simple faithful both in the propagation of the faith and in the temporal and spiritual works of charity. Preachers will forever complain of the sluggishness of the masses, and there will always be those who complain that the authorities want to have a hand in everything. Yet it is nonetheless true that in the face of today's widespread dechristianization there is an ever growing number of ordinary Christians showing a great interest in the Apostolate. Non-Catholic churches are naturally much broader in the activity they allow to all their members. They can more easily allow lay people to fill the gaps in the ranks of the clergy, and in some instances they even allow women to take charge of their programme of worship. On this precise point of the ordination of women, most of the churches are extremely cautious; the Orthodox completely opposed. Still, the question has been explicitly posed.[25] The important thing to note is that in consecrating women and giving them a larger share in directing official church activities, nothing but an indirect appeal to the laity is being proposed. Even though many of them pass into the ecclesiastical state, the status of the laity as a whole has not been changed.

The general line is clear. Among the members of a really living community, no one can remain inactive when the highest interests are at stake and many are exposed to catastrophe. Throughout the world, the laity is rapidly becoming conscious of its vocation, in view of the growing needs of the community and the increasingly obvious fact that the collaboration of all available forces is indispensable. In the eyes of unbelievers, Rome, usually very slow, seems to be closely following if not leading the trend. Since, according to them, this is rare, they should not be offended by it. But let us rather agree that the events and ideas of the day, even in the sphere of nature, are ruled by the Spirit of Christ, not only within the walls of Rome, but all over the world. Nobody who believes in Providence would dare deny it.

OUR PURPOSE

In the light of revealed truth, we will try as clearly as possible to formulate the *exact principles* concerning the place and the role of the laity in the Church. It would be equally irritating to say too much or too little about the subject; exaggerated boldness or pusillanimous timidity would be equally detrimental. It is not a question either of defending privileges or of producing a 'democratic' symmetry at the expense of revealed truth. A split-up of the social structure into its constituent parts would be disastrous for human society, and *a fortiori* for the supernatural organism whose shepherds and leaders have been established by Our Lord Himself. Our starting point is not purely sociological; we have no right to apply the categories of human society to the Kingdom of Christ. Only the word of God can decide the question. Before speaking, any believer must hear this Word.

Secondly, once the principles are recognized, our task is to advance their *faithful application* by the clergy as well as by the laity. Those subject to authority will hear subversive voices urging them on to revolt and independence; those with authority will be tempted to vanity and abuse of their power. A brief glance at history is enough to establish the fact. It could even happen that in theory authority would recognize the rights of the community, but in practice would stifle them. Clergymen should reflect on the warning of Christ about kings who tyrannise over their people and yet call themselves benefactors (Lk., XXII, 25). The only way to curtail anticlericalism is to spread the message and the spirit of the Gospel, and especially to live it. Our motive is far deeper than the mere desire to anticipate possible resistances. Because of our human weakness, we must be wary. Leaders and faithful, all of us will have to account for the light and the graces which have been so abundantly given to us.

---

* 'Laicism' and 'laicity' are merely transliterations of the French. 'Laicism' more or less corresponds to the English 'laicization.' The equivalent of 'laicity' does not exist in English. The meanings of both words are explained in the text. (Tr.).

1 See, for example, R. AUBERT, *Quelques études récentes sur la place du laïcat dans l'Eglise.* Coll. Mechlin., 33, 1948, pp. 674-691. J. DELFOSSE, *La Parole est aux laïcs. Rev. Nouv.,* 16, 1952, pp. 488-505. This article studies the results of an inquiry on the subject of the laity. R. M. SPIAZZI, O.P., *La Missione dei laici,* 2nd ed., Rome, 1952.

2 The research of Prof. G. LE BRAS is a model of this type: *Introduction à l'histoire de la pratique religieuse en France* (Bibl. Ecole des Hautes Etudes. Sc. Rel., 57), 2 vol., Paris, 1942-1945. Also, H. DESROCHE, *Domaines et méthodes de la Sociologie religieuse dans l'oeuvre de G. Le Bras,* in *Rev. Hist. Phil. Rel.,* 34, 1954, pp. 128-154. Since then, under his influence, the work has been extended. The international review *Lumen Vitae* (Brussels) published in 1951 an important collection entitled *Etat présent de la Sociologie religieuse.* Specifically for Belgium: E. COLLARD, *Commentaire de la carte de la pratique dominicale en Belgique,* in *Lumen Vitae,* 7, 1952, pp. 644-652. N. DE. VOLDER, *De godsdienstigheid der intellectuelen,* Bruges, 1947.—For Holland: N. G.M. VANDOORNIK, *Jeugd tussen God en chaos,* La Haye, 1948.—For Italy: P. DROULERS, S.J., and A. RIMOLDI, *La Sociologia religiosa in Italia,* in *Scuola Cattolica,* 80, 1952, pp. 169-193. —For Spain: F. DEL VALLE, S.J., *Sombras de una grande ciudad:* Barcelona, 1950, in

Razón y Fe, 1950, t. I, pp. 136-160, etc.—See also the current reviews, for example the special number of the *Revue Nouvelle*, of December 15, 1952, which is consecrated to the laity.

3 H. GODIN, *France Pagan*, Trans. by M. WARD, London, 2nd. ed., 1950. F. BOULARD, *Problèmes missionnaires de la France rurale (Rencontres, 16, 17, 18)*, Paris, 1945. G. MICHONNEAU, *Revolution in a City Parish.* (Blackfriars), London, 1949. To this literature of an excellent, apostolic frankness, E. R. MORGAN, the Anglican Bishop of Southampton, dedicates a sympathetic review in *Erasmus, Speculum scientiarum*, I, 1947, pp. 771-774. See also, J. V. LONGMEAD CASSERLEY, *The Retreats from Christianity in the Modern World*, London, 1951. M. R. LOEW, *Mission to the Poorest*, Trans. by P. CARSWELL, London, 1950.

4 Cf. J. GUITTON, *Vérité et charité. Souvenirs oecuméniques*, in the *Nouvelle Revue Theol.*, 71, 1949, pp. 673-686, on the oecumenical evolution and its necessary purifications. Also, R. AUBERT, *Mouvement oecuménique et Oecuménisme catholique*, in the *Vie Spir.*, 88, 1953, pp. 85-97.

5 PIUS XII, Address of Oct. 14, 1951. Cf. Eng. Trans., *The Lay Apostolate—Its Need Today*, N.C.W.C., Washington, nos. 6-17, esp. n. 16 or *Actes du Ier Congres mondial de l'Apostolat des Laïcs*, Rome, 1952, vol. I, p. 49.

6 PIUS XII, Enc. *Mystici Corporis.* Latin text in *Acta Apl. Sedis*, 35, 1943, p. 241. Eng. Trans. by Can. G. D. SMITH, *The Mystical Body of Jesus Christ*, Cath. Truth Soc., London, 1952 ed., n. 97.

7 PIUS XII, Allocution to the Sacred College, Nov. 20, 1946. Cf. *Acta Ap. Sed.*, 38, 1946, p. 149.

8 Declaration of the *Grand Orient de France*, Assembly of Sept. 17-20, 1951, cited in *Docum. Cath.*, t. 50, 1952, col. 794. All the documents of columns 787-826, among others dealing with the 'Laicity' of schools and of overseas territory, should be read.

9 Pastoral letter of the Bishops of Belgium concerning the Christian school, Aug., 1948.

10 G. BROM, *De Leek in de Kerkgeschiedenis; II Secularisatie; III, De term Leek*, in: *Kath. Archief*, 4, 1949, pp. 325-332. This publication gives information sometimes very picturesque, on the history of the words *lay* and *secular*. See also: Fr. GOGARTEN, *Verhängnis und Hoffnung der Neuzeit. Die Säkularisierung als theologisches Problem*, Stuttgart, 1953. On the subject of laicism in Italy, cf. the studies of E. PASSERIN and G. B. SCAGLIA, in *Studium*, Rome, 1952, n. V.

11 Declaration of the French hierarchy on the human person, the family and society *Doc. Cath.*, t. 43, 1946, col. 6-7. We will have to return to this subject of the 'laicity of the State.'

12 H. STRATHMANN, art. Laos, in G. KITTEL, *Theologisches Wörterbuch zum Neuen Testament* t. IV, Stuttgart, 1942. For the Old Testament, see pp. 32-39; for the New, pp. 49-57. Compare with St. Luke, II, 32 : 'Lumen ad revelationem gentium (ethnon), et gloriam plebis (laou) tuae Israel.' Acts. XXVI, 23; Rom., XV, 10; etc.

13 St. CLEMENT OF ROME, *Epis. to the Corinthians*, 40, n. 5. F. X. FUNK, *Patres Apostolici*, Tübingen, 1909, Vol. I, p. 151. Trans. by J. KLEIST, s.J., *Ancient Christian Writers: The Epistles of St. Clement of Rome and St. Ignatius of Antioch*, Westminster (U.S.A.) and London, 1949, p. 34.

14 St. JUSTIN, *First Apology*, 67, 5; P.G., 6. The Latin word *populus* is likewise opposed to the leaders in the celebrated Roman inscription S.P.Q.R.—senatus *populus*que romanus, even though the senators should not be considered as if they did not belong to the general population. The same development is found in the use of the phrase 'the faithful' for the laity; the members of the clergy have nevertheless the same obligation to believe and as such they too are included among the faithful. Cf. H. KELLER and O. VON NELL BREUNING, *Das Recht der Laien in der Kirche*, Heidelberg, 1950, p. 23.

15 TERTULLIAN, *Exhortatio ad castitatem*, 7: 'Nonne et laici sacerdotes sunt?' *P.L.*, 2, 922. While still a Catholic, Tertullian considered this pretension as exorbitant; see: *Praescr. Haer.*, 41; *P.L.*, 2, 54; *Bapt.*, 17; *P.L.*, 1, 1217.

16 See D. DU CANGE, *Glossarium mediae et infimae latinitatis*, s.v., Laicus. Tome V, Niort, 1885, p. 15.

17 For the report of this discussion, cf. *Kath. Archief*, III, 1948, col. 743.

18 WETZER and WELTE, *Kirchenlexicon* VII, Fribourg-en-Brisgau, 1891. col. 1323 : *Laien, s. Clerus.*

19   Cf. O. KOEHLER, *Der Laie im katholischen Kirchenrecht*, in *Stimmen der Zeit*, 146, 1950, pp. 43-53. This article gives some interesting historical information. —H. KELLER and O. VON NELL-BREUNING, o.c. —E. ROESSER, *Die Stellung der Laien in der Kirche nach dem kanonischen Recht* (*Würzburger Universitätsreden, Heft* 9), 1949. —R. MULLER-ERB, *Der Laie in der Kirche*, in *Theol. Quartalschrift*, 130, 1950, pp. 184-196. Canonists, it appears, are becoming interested in the question. The last article is rather superficial.

20   Cf. *Actes du Ier Congrès mondial pour l'Apostolat des Laïcs*, Vol. I, Rome, 1952, p. 83.

21   Y. CONGAR, *Jalons pour une Théologie du Laïcat* (*Unam Sanctam*, 23). Paris, 1953, p. 19 ff. According to A. CHAVASSE, *Eglise et Apostolat* (*Eglise Vivante*), Paris, 1953. p. 165, the religious prefigures the eschatalogical state of the Church. Fr. K. RAHNER unduly attributes to the clergy the full-time worker of the lay apostolate: *Das eigentliche Apostolate der Laien*, in *Grosse Entschluss*, 3, 1954, pp. 318-324.

22   E. LE ROY, *Dogme et critique*, Paris, 1907, p. xiii.

23   ST. AUGUSTINE, *De Baptismo contra Donatistas*, III, 19, 27; P.L. 43, 154 The principle here advanced by St. Augustine serves to demonstrate the validity, not the licitness, of sacraments confered by heretics.

24   ST. ROBERT BELLARMINE, *Controversiae*, II, Book 3. *De Ecclesia militante*, c. 2, Ed. of Cologne, 1619, col. 108.

25   Official Report of the First Assembly of the Oecumenical Council of Churches, Amsterdam, 1948. Paris-Neuchâtel, pp. 187 ff. on the role of the woman in the Church; pp. 145 ff. on the importance of laymen in the Church. These reports are very instructive. Certain sections would be completely acceptable even in a Catholic exposé. For example, p. 196: 'Solely by the intelligent and active witness of laymen can the Church *be present* in the modern world and bravely confront its practical problems.' The following pages of the report not only appeal to the 'royal priesthood' but also to 'the Church, the Body of Christ.'

CHAPTER II.

THE PRINCIPLES

In order that the dignity of the laity be clearly seen it must be viewed in its proper theological perspective, that of the mystery.[1]

THE CHURCH, MYSTERY OF FAITH

Unfortunately, the word 'mystery' is today perhaps even more enfeebled than the word 'lay.' We speak of murder mysteries, mysteries of politics and atomic secrets. Popular preachers, bent on apologetics, assure us that we can, without depreciating ourselves, admit the presence of mysteries in God, when we are prepared to accept their existence in the realms of natural science and history. But such analogy could lead us to a deplorable levelling.

The fact remains that a religious mystery is totally different and transcendent. Between the two categories religious and profane, there is only one common element: the hidden character. Furthermore for the one this character is provisional, for the other essential. In the realm of the profane, a mystery is a secret reality of a completely created order. A sharper or better informed mind could penetrate the hidden elements. More profound study would automatically produce a degree of knowledge capable of eliminating all obscurity, and by that very fact, the haze of mystery fades before the glaring light of science.

This is not the case with religious mysteries. For Saint Paul, the mystery *par excellence* is the wisdom of God, not lack of human knowledge. It is the plan of salvation conceived by Eternal Love, a plan hidden from the powers of the world, but revealed and realized in the Church. [2] This revelation has a two fold contradictory effect: it enlightens the faithful, but blinds the obstinate. Like every word of God, it makes a discrimination. We find ourselves in the presence of a supernatural reality: God the Father gives Himself to us by the mission of the Son and the Holy Spirit. The revealing word of God does not simply arouse our curiosity, it also transforms us in our very existence. It cannot be reduced to a series of abstract truths; it is far more; it is the divine action of salvation realized in history by the passion and glory of Christ and destined to be proclaimed

17

universally. It will never be a study which we will master; it is addressed to our faith and masters us. When the mystery is thus manifested and preached, it does not evaporate but rather it appears still more 'mysterious' and more inexpressible. Here the mystery is God Himself, God, the Father of Jesus Christ, making Himself also Our Father by the gift of His Spirit.

The object of faith is always a person: in the first article of the *Credo*, we profess our faith in *God*, Father and Creator. To be our Father, He created us. In the final article we express our faith in eternal life, which again signifies *God* giving Himself to us through Christ.[3] The articles inserted between this *alpha* and *omega* describe the outpouring of this life in God and outside of Him, through His only Son, Our Saviour, and through His Spirit. Immediately after the mention of the Holy Spirit comes that of the *Holy Catholic Church*. He is her soul, and through her He accomplishes the work of Christ. The Church is at the very heart of the mystery of Christ.

A recent catechism defines the Church as 'the visible and supernatural society of the faithful, founded by Jesus Christ to continue His work of redemption and salvation among men.'[4] As such she is the object of our faith. We *see* her; were it otherwise the mystery would not be manifested. We *believe* in her; if we did not she would possess no supernatural element for us. It is not enough to see in order to believe. One can see and still persecute as do the enemies of Christianity; 'the Turks and the Jews' according to the Catechism of Trent;[5] today, atheistic Communists. Yet we accept not only the doctrines taught by the Church, we believe in the Church herself and in her mysterious actuality as the organ of salvation. She descends from heaven as the New Jerusalem and the Spouse of the Lamb (Apoc. XXI, 2). In virtue of Her heavenly origin she brings to us from the hand of God, 'the forgiveness of sins, the resurrection of the body and life everlasting.'

Saint Cyprian has described the Church with remarkable theological accuracy in the following phrase: *de unitate Patris et Filii et Spiritus Sancti plebs adunata;*[6] a people gathered together, participating in the unity of the three persons. She is an assembly which is sacred in the strictest sense; an institution at once visible and invisible, but not duplicated. She is like Jesus Christ 'the great sacrament,' the bearer of life and, like Him, 'mystery,' and so 'scandal' for those who, lacking faith, cannot understand her. Saint Paul identifies her with Christ to the point of calling her His Body, or again, the Body of which He is the Head and upon which He bestows His gifts.[7]

By trying to apply to the Church the categories of ordinary sociology, we finish by misunderstanding her profound nature;

divine, or rather divine-human, hers is a union established by God's contact with us through the Body of Christ and the mission of the Holy Spirit; and, at the same time, a social phenomenon historically and locally concretized, the Roman Church governed by the Pope and the bishops.

The Church is not simply the organised collectivity and mutual co-operation of believers; nor is she the place where they assemble. If this were so, the faithful would 'make' the Church. *Materially* speaking, this is quite correct. Moreover, the members have to 'make' the Church in the sense that they ought to contribute to her life and increase.[8] But *formally*, the statement is false: it is for the Church to 'make' her members. In Christ she has existed before them and she brings them forth into spiritual life. She was never without members; at the very least she was incorporated in the apostolic group and the primitive community. In every sense she remains the Mother of the living.[9]

In oecumenical language, this conception is given the name of 'catholic.' The 'protestant' conception makes the Church the result of a meeting of believers entering into a social contract in matters of religion. Schematically the first notion gives us: Christ-the Church-the faithful; the second inverts the last two factors to: Christ-the faithful-the Church. For the latter, the Church would not be from above as it is in the Bible. It would be a result rather than a principle. Today, indeed, the 'catholic' concept is gaining ground in the majority of reformed churches.[10]

But, while the Church is the source of grace, at the same time she is incarnate in us, in sinners, and, thus, she finds *sin* inbred in her —sin which is not her own, but which is in her, at least materially, as a heterogeneous body, sin that she must fight, that she must uproot, but that she will never completely conquer before the end of her earthly travail. The antithesis is well-known and it is irreducible. The Church in all its beauty *has* no stain, no wrinkle, no such disfigurement (Eph., V, 27). That immunity is hers by virtue of her origin, of her profound nature and of her final glory. But, during the course of her earthly journey, in her empirical state, she comes into contact with evil. In fact, she is 'given' precisely to conquer evil; and this she does, not by remote skirmishes, but by fighting hand to hand. The devil, who has no command over her being, can attack and cut down her members and occasionally even her leaders. But the final victory will not be taken from her: Christ has already won and assured her victory.

The Church is in no sense a source of sin, but she must take into account the culpable weakness of her children. She must be alive to their faults and work to amend them. Fortunately, the power of grace to save is greater than sin's power to ruin. Moreover, sin comes from without, while grace comes from within. Thus, the Church, as the gift of God, has no guilt to acknowledge. She cannot fall into infidelity, for if so the mystery of salvation would be destroyed. Nevertheless her subjects, and even her leaders, as individuals, need to beg for pardon. But this is not all: the Church as a collectivity asks the Saviour to purify her.[11] Within the reality which is 'The Church,' all aspects do not perfectly coincide, and her unity will not become perfect until its final stage: The Church is a 'holy' society, in process of self-formation, and we might even say, in process of self-reformation.[12]

There is a further duality of aspects which coalesce into a single, higher unity, for each is already implied in the other. The Church is simultaneously an *organism* of grace and truth and an *organization* with a social character. We must not see these as two 'parts' of the Church, much less as two separate entities. The great sacrament of grace and the social structure are one reality, even though they do not coincide from every point of view. In distributing His gifts God is not tied to any juridical institution; the fact remains, however, that the ecclesiastical society is the sole institution of salvation, willed by Him. There is not an invisible group beside or beyond the visible one nor a perfect Church of the ethereal realm beside a Church terrestrial and deficient.[13] The visible body itself is supernatural; incarnation of the divine in the human penetrates thus far. She will transform all of humanity from within by a slow and progressive work.

To designate this double aspect, the Germans use the words *Heilsanstalt* for the social organization, and *Heilsgemeinschaft* for the vital internal relations. Father Yves Congar has analysed the distinction thoroughly.[14] The Church, he says, in so far as she is living interiorly and is in possession of her heritage, is a living organism, a royal, priestly and prophetic community without law: the *Mystical Body of Christ*. To the extent in which she is in process of self-completion, she reproduces the traits of the Old Testament, the Law and the Synagogue; as such she is *an exterior, hierarchical society*, to which is guaranteed the means of grace. Stuck by the first characteristic, Protestants have in great part ignored the second. Catholics, in reaction to the ideas of the time, perhaps even impelled by them, have insisted on the hierarchical mediation, on the elements of authority, magisterium, jurisdiction, as well as the efficacy of the sacramental signs. Thus all the sacred riches seem to be a treasure reserved to bishops and priests. Lay people have only the right to bow down in humble submission, an anonymous mass, well administered and well diciplined, but, in the final analysis, purely passive subjects before the will and power of a few masters.

But, continues Fr. Congar, in the living community there is, on the contrary, an uninterrupted exchange of spiritual goods. All the members work together, each according to his ability. In all difficulties, both material and spiritual, the members help one another. Each can assist the other, or each can be an obstacle to the other through sin. The faithful and clergy work together to build the same body. In the matter of personal charismata, clerics are not necessarily superior to lay people, even though it is fitting that, in virtue of their functions, they be spiritually richer and more generous than those under their care. In the communion of saints the last are, however, sometimes the first; the clergy has no monopoly in sanctity.

Father Congar's analysis is penetrating and his description of the passivity of the laity is as frank and uncompromising as any indictment. Doubtless it touches existing situations. But the Catholic doctrine is larger and better balanced. And though the author's view does not deny this fact still his distinction seems to us to be too rigid. Obviously, there will be no more ecclesiastical laws in heaven, no more pulpits, no more sacramental discipline. Once the end is reached, it is foolish to be concerned with the means. Nonetheless, salvation remains the reward of faith and obedience to the commandments and, more especially, the fruit of the redemptive sacrifice. True, in the kingdom of perfect liberty there will be neither constraint nor temptation, masters nor servants. The Heavenly City has no need of sun or moon: the glory of God will be its light, and the Lamb its torch (Apoc., XXI, 23); yet many pastors and teachers will shine there forever like the stars, a reward for fidelity to their tasks.

But for the present this eschatological possession has already been entrusted to the earthly community, confided to its social organization. The heavenly principle already impregnates the material, so that matter becomes the 'sacrament' or efficacious sign of its influence. We are living an inverted history; the final situation, realized in Christ, lies behind and transfigures the passing moment. Our pilgrimage is a time neither of pure joy nor of simple waiting. We, too, live in the promise, and it is in hope that we are saved (Rom., VIII, 23). Though she does bear a likeness to the Synagogue the Church is no longer temporary as was the one of the Old Testament: she was born in the fulness of time and will never be replaced, she will simply develop. Her nature is completely different from that of the Law. We are no longer under the yoke, we are liberated souls eagerly accomplishing now the will of the Father. We love, and for love no burdens are intolerable (I Jn., V, 3). The commandments remain, but the spirit is changed. The New Alliance no longer looks to the letter but to the Spirit (II Cor., III, 6): it does not leave us with empty hands; it gives us the first fruits.

In this light, we can grasp the exact range of the church and its outpouring upon the religious régime organized about it. This influence can be reversed—and is not without the danger: the 'organization' could make us forget 'the life.' 'When in fact,' says M. Montuclard, 'anxiety for the Church is replaced by anxiety for the Christian society, Christianity tends to pass from faith to reason, from spiritual liberty to moralism, *from the community to the society*, from religious vitality to pragmatic action. The Christian finds himself little by little enveloped in an ideological universe whose elements manifest less pure Christianity than Christian humanism. In this universe everything is assigned its place: sociology, politics, as well as the mysteries of faith. When this happens, whether you like it or not, to be a Christian means not so much entering into the word of God and the Church, as meeting this ideological synthesis, holding it as true by the same mental process you use for any other teaching, and striving to make it incarnate in reality by all forms of activity.'[15]

This observation is not without foundation. But we must be careful not to go to the other extreme, concluding that Christians, adhering to the mystery, no longer need to be preoccupied with moral applications and concrete categories. The ecclesiastical society may indeed be incarnate in this world, yet followers of Christ ought to be ever conscious of its transcendence. It is in this same perspective that they will discover the significance of the Church's directive organ, the hierarchy.

THE HIERARCHY IN THE MYSTERY

A certain text of St. Paul (Eph., IV, 11-13) is of capital importance here:

> And he himself gave some men as apostles, and some as prophets, others again as evangelists, and others as pastors and teachers, in order to perfect the saints for a work of ministry, for building up the body of Christ, until we all attain to the unity of the faith and of the deep knowledge of the Son of God, to perfect manhood, to the mature measure of the fullness of Christ.

This is the principle: hierarchical functions are a gift of the Saviour to His Church. The leaders do not assume command on their own;

rather, Christ raises them up. Frequently the term 'Saints' in Saint Paul refers to all the faithful and sometimes exclusively to those of Jerusalem. Here, as well as in Eph., III, 5 and Col., I, 26, it indicates the leaders and the great missionaries of the faith.[16] Their task is to spread true knowledge, not a theoretical science; an interior vital force which shows its authenticity in the witness of charity. Thus the members are not a dead weight destined to be dragged along; a personal force seizes them and urges them to co-operate, with the greatest diversity, towards a perfect harmony:

> And this he has done that we may be now no longer children, tossed to and fro and carried about by every wind of doctrine devised in the wickedness of men, in craftiness, according to the wiles of error. Rather are we to practise the truth in love and so grow up in all things in him who is the head, Christ. For from him the whole body (being closely joined and knit together through every joint of the system according to the functioning in due measure of each single part) derives its increase to the building up of itself in love: (ibid., v. 14-16).

This remarkable passage, as so many others in Saint Paul, overflows with ideas. The principal factor is not the hierarchy but the body. Still, within the body the hierarchical structure is primary and essential. Protestants say that the Catholic laity is reduced to a state of absolute silence, passivity and slavery. Saint Paul says exactly the opposite: the hierarchy is instituted to lead all the members to religious majority, to virile activity, to a responsible and concerted action.

Every organ, from the highest to the lowest, has its own inalienable function. The function is one of charity, not one of pride or envy. Any desire for domination would prove destructive; any form of defeatism, any feeble resignation or faint-heartedness would be equally disastrous. Modern history teaches us that the desire for domination often corresponds to a desire to be dominated.[17] Only when the feeble give up the struggle can the tyrant impose his power. In a healthy society, authority and the free, vigorous co-operation of those governed balance one another. In the Church of God, all abdication, whether on the part of leaders or members, is a sin against charity, that is, against Christ Himself.

Will this work, this battle, this growth bear fruit in long-coveted peace? Certainly it will; but only when there is no longer any fear of error and wickedness, only when charity shall have reached its full flowering. This, however, is nothing other than ultimate glory. And in the meanwhile, as long as there are cunning seducers lurking among the simple, each one must remain vigilant and active, the shepherds and teachers in the forefront, but also all the members at their more humble posts, all under the aegis of the one Head.

The hierarchy exists to serve the body not the body to serve the hierarchy. For unless there is a body to support it the hierarchy cannot subsist, just as the body cannot develop without the constant care of the sanctifying hierarchy. Bishops establish and build the Church, but the Church must first make the bishops. Or rather, to return to Saint Paul, the Lord establishes the shepherds and teachers for the growth of His Body. The hierarchy cannot replace God; this would lead us to idolatry. Nevertheless, under the guidance of the Spirit, it exercises divine power.[18]

Authority creates rights and duties, the Spirit gives life. In the one Church the two meet one another. The Spirit institutes authority and by it He not only gives orders but He also diffuses life.

Authority cannot emancipate itself from the Spirit: it would become sterile. It is exercised by feeble men who are often beneath their task. Subjects, too, are not a collection of Saints. The inevitable result is continual *tension* and often uncomfortable situations. On more than one occasion interior aspirations have groaned under legal restraint. Which should we choose in such a case, the Church of authority or the Church of the Spirit? If we wish to remain Catholic we must choose both. Rather, without choosing, we must accept the word of Christ who gives the Church both the authority and the Spirit as well as a vital balancing tension, a balance how often shaky and unstable! At any moment, all seems ready to collapse and yet soon all is again level and ready to advance. The authority, experienced and mature, guards the tradition into which the Spirit breathes rejuvenation so that it may return to the sources to uncover new depths of richness. Sometimes the reverse is true: faced with insensibility, numbness and indifference on the part of the flock, the shepherds themselves rise as pioneers and progressives.

An oversimplified or extremist view would place all the weight on one side or the other: the Spirit embraces the two. In the Church, authority is not for commanding a group of automatons. Why transform the body into a machine? Our own technical civilization has chosen the machine and that is how it has stifled life. If the clergy degenerate into a corps of functionaries, they will sacrifice the Spirit to administration and so foster a veritable weariness and aversion among its members. That is also the way to dry up vocations: religious souls are seeking something other than a sanctified office job.

A purely juridical Church would maintain the community under tutelage and ensure its degeneration. Recall the state church of the Russian tsars. When the clergy lose their spiritual vigour, there is a great temptation to suppress them. Protestantism succumbed to the temptation.

History shows us that the Catholic hierarchy has not accomplished its rise at the expense of the community, but rather in defence of it. Its 'tactics' did not consist in crushing liberty of conscience, but in defending it. The hierarchy's battle against the whims of princes was an epic one. One of the volumes in Fliche and Martin's great Church History series is entitled: *The Church at the Mercy of the Laity*.[19] It names the tenth century, 'the century of iron,' when the German emperor made sport of the papacy.

This was 'laicism' of quite another kind. More than one prince became a protector of the Church.[20] Moreover, his power was sacred as deriving from God. In fact, anointing of kings was sometimes regarded as a sacrament. Barons and counts founded bishoprics, monasteries and parishes. They looked on them—and it should not surprise us—as personal property. They sold, rented and exploited religious property as they wished, joining political and religious interests to the serious detriment of Christian liberty. They did not want to suppress the Church, they wanted to batten on her. Again, at the time of the Reformation, the will of the prince determined the religion of his subjects. When we speak of the emancipation of the laity, it is not such a situation which we have in view.

The famous Roman centralization of the Church owes its origin partially to the repeated appeals the bishops and the people made to the Pope against the oppression of barons and dukes. But this concerns the supreme power. The task of episcopal authority is to guard the faithful against the spirit of independence and dissent. Throughout the Middle Ages, long before Luther or Calvin's time, the bishops had to fight against exaggerated subjectivism and illuminism. They had to shield 'obedience to the Gospel' against the unfortunate excesses of personal preference. Protestantism took a decisive step by leaving the original community. Its astounding success would be inexplicable had the prestige of the clergy and respect for its interior values remained intact. Many priests and bishops, however, had flung their dignity aside with their questionable moral lives and their culpable ignorance. Modern Catholic historians have thrown a startling light on this situation.[21]

Though it may be that Modernists of the twentieth century have not had leaders whose genius equalled that of the sixteenth century reformers, it is nonetheless true that they have had very capable men. If they have not been able to set in motion a great schism, it is because the spiritual value of the hierarchy, taken as a whole, is no longer questionable.

In Luther's age, it was extremely difficult to believe in a transcendent Church when confronted with the great lack of sanctity among her highest authorities. When the value of the priest is scarcely evident it is easy to discredit the entire priesthood and transfer everything to the hands of the laity. People often wonder if the hierarchy is sufficiently fore-armed against vanity, desire for power and formalism. The spontaneous resistance of free and upright men is there to warn, the lessons of history to instruct.

The nineteenth century favoured the juridical in every department of European life. The legislator was regarded as the sole creator of the society. Law and rights were placed above life, and legalism triumphed. Under such indirect influence, people could believe that religious society too, depended exclusively on authority. Thus we had an excessive secularization which did hurt the dignity of the Christian person.

Catholicism is reproached by some with having made grace a 'thing' when she should have emphasised man's personal relationship with God. Others go further and see the Church as a juridical apparatus whose various parts can be dismantled and later reassembled. Yet to do this, you have to put yourself outside the Church, treat it as an object, and see it as purely human. [22] Under these conditions, there is obviously no question of a living faith in the Church or grace. Permeating organizations, and going beyond the faults of those who direct them, living faith sees the supernatural redemptive activity of Christ.

THE LAITY IN THE MYSTERY

If the hierarchy is holy, at least in its essence, so too is the layman as member of the 'communion of saints.' If we look upon him merely as an inferior part of a well-organized society, we fail to recognize his true religious dignity. We would condemn him to passivity, and then would have no Christianity.

Here, the theology of the laity points out the sacramental signs which introduce the faithful into the supernatural society, baptism and confirmation. The sacraments of the new birth and consecration impress on the soul an indelible character, a concrete and spiritual reality by which the baptised is made a member of the Body of Christ, the confirmed a competent member, capable of bearing witness to the Body and assuring its propagation and defence. Of a social nature, the rites almost entirely lose their significance in such a spiritualised conception as the Protestant one. They are part of the corporal and spiritual means at the disposal of the dynamism of grace.

At the same time, they unite the Christian to Christ the High Priest by a number of personal relationships, and extend the non-functional priesthood to the whole worshipping community. In a word, they establish the existence of the Christian in the whole Christ, they bring him into the *laos* or people of God.

This supernatural realism must be translated into concrete experience; it demands a certain way of living. The Catholic layman will, then, have preoccupations which are catholic or universal. He will try to form a soul with a universal range, even if he still sins today by narrowness. He will practise obedience under pain of renouncing his Catholicism, but under the impulsion of grace he will develop a spirit of initiative: otherwise his submission will not save his orthodoxy. Finally, recognizing the Church as a mystery of faith, he will see the clear light of higher truths shining through religious authority, and finding diffusion in its very prescriptions. Only then will the 'hierarchical sense' be perfectly adapted to every authentic movement of the Spirit.

These, then, are the principal considerations which will give precision to a definition of the laity's role.

A Universal Solicitude

If the Church is composed of thinking members and not of mere puppets, then each must give proof of a genuine earnestness. First of all, he should *deepen his faith* by sober and serious reflection and this not to satisfy his intellectual curiosity, but to 'know' in the sense of the Gospel. From Augustine to Anselm, the *fides quaerens intellectum* does not lose its mystical impulse. To know, for Saint John, is to pass beyond pure knowledge, to choose, embrace, and love with the consciousness of having been chosen, embraced, and loved beforehand by God. In this sense, 'the sinner knows not God.' He neither receives Him nor respects Him as his Father and Lord, nor does he even 'understand' Him. Whatever he learns of God is for him a scandal and folly. And God, on His part, 'knows not the sinner.' He no longer sees in him the image of His Son and He rejects him. Yet Christ knows His own and they know Him. They understand whereas others are scandalized; they are 'in tune' with Him and their will supports the adhesion of their intellect. It is not man's personal preference which makes truth; it is his spirit, not his heart which must assent to it. Sincerity concentrates on the Truth alone and grace undertakes to unite them.

Efforts to develop one's religious knowledge prove one's loyalty. Indifference in this regard is a sign of wavering conviction. Brunetière once said: 'If you want to know what I believe, go to Rome and ask.' More than one parishioner has said the same thing: 'My pastor knows it all, and that's enough for me.' Obviously, it is *not* enough. The faith of a coalminer can be inspired by a praiseworthy sense of mystery, not by a disguised spiritual sloth.

To think as a Catholic means to think with a sense of universality. Catholicity is the expression of God's universal 'philanthropy' and the continuation of Christ's unlimited work. Each Christian shall love his brothers, even the wayward, with a love the Holy Spirit infuses in his soul, a love which participates in uncreated and creating Love. He shall show generosity, 'not only moral but also intellectual generosity because in the final analysis it is more difficult to understand someone than to be devoted to him, and too often Catholics believe that a good deed excuses them from charitable judgment.'[23]

John Wesley, founder of the Methodist Church, had this maxim: 'I look upon the whole world as my parish.'[24] A Christian cannot be satisfied with caring for his immediate neighbour. His horizon must extend beyond the boundaries of his parish. To be truly 'Catholic' is neither common nor easy. We are far removed from the times when the various churches assisted one another not only materially but morally. We have formed too many exclusive ecclesiastical circles. Individual egoism is repugnant to a conscientious soul. Yet collective egoism is often presented as a virtue. To remedy the evil by establishing branches of our own firm on every continent is no solution. Ten thousand chapels do not make a cathedral. And yet the smallest group in the smallest village can have an oecumenical sense if its members think and feel in harmony with the *Catholica*. Thank God, lay Catholics today are 'less easy-going, less pharisaical and, in a word, more evangelical.'[25]

A SPIRIT OF INITIATIVE

If the laity are awake they will be ready to respond whenever the Spirit calls. If they are slumbering then they will not give even passive heed to the hierarchy. Passivity is the worst resistance imaginable. You cannot say that passivity is 'just letting things go on;' it is opposition with all its crushing inertia to an activity that demands support.

The Spirit can issue a direct appeal to the laity when the Church is an inspirited supernatural society and not a mere rigid social institution. In modern industry each worker is a number; any initiative on his part would impede the manufacturing process. Modern technology, however, has no place in the sanctuary.

During the course of the Church's growth the hierarchy has more than once formulated extremely bold and fertile projects. Pope Gregory who sent the first missionaries to the Anglo-Saxons bade them return when they came home discouraged by their initial failure. Even orders coming directly from higher authority must be executed by human means. Certainly there is no question of an assembly line process here; rather the question is one of spiritual effort based on personal dedication.

History shows that great apostolic projects of the past often arose from the initiative of subordinates, priests, lay men and women. Neither fanatics nor proselytisers, they were receptive to the Spirit and so were in perfect accord with the dictates of a hierarchy born of that Spirit and ready to direct and purify them, and endow them with supernatural helps. In reality there is no contradiction here: for at the heart of the institution the Holy Spirit maintains His perfect freedom to act upon souls when and as He wills. [26]

If the Church were not to approve their work, it would soon wither and come to nothing. Without her backing no apostolic activity can hope to succeed. It is quite possible to mistake fantasy for heavenly inspiration while claiming a direct contact with Christ in the depths of the soul. Saint John discerned the Spirit of truth from the spirit of error by submitting the prophets to the authority of the Apostles (I Jn., IV, 1-6).

Bishops owe their name to their role as *episcopes*, or overseers. They must suppress pseudomysticism and sectarianism. By its very nature the hierarchy must maintain the divine deposit and help it mature. Theirs is a strict obligation in conscience to advance prudently and to govern carefully so that the community may avoid illusory success and attain its true goal. They are beyond temporary and local contingencies the better to safeguard eternal values. A parish assistant was in a much better position than a cardinal-archbishop for discovering the Y.C.W. method. No one denies that the fundamental inspiration came from Pius XI; still there was need of someone to put the idea into practice, to give it flesh and blood and to make it live among the people. Nor is this a reproach to an episcopate too far removed from the situation. It is for the authority to grant and consecrate the mission, to indicate the field of action, and to make the work fruitful by a steady flow of grace. Shepherds and doctors need collaborators who are more than lifeless instruments.

The fact that the Middle Ages saw a great flowering of Christian life is due in great measure to the fervour of subordinates, priests, religious and lay people, who were neither working outside the hierarchy nor against its will but in vital contact with its direction.

Thanks to them, the devotion to the humanity of Christ has been profoundly imprinted on our Western piety.[27] It is Christocentric and Trinitarian, yet also solidly anchored in the liturgical and sacramental life of the Church. It associates Eucharistic devotion with veneration for the Mother of God. In this field it is impossible to distinguish between monks and lay people.[28] The visions of Julianne of Cornillon and the prayers of Eve, the recluse, are at the origin of the feast of Corpus Christi. Devotion to the Sacred Heart, so characteristic of the Roman Church, did not come from Rome but from Paray-le-Monial.

Piety is not the concern only of those in authority, and mysticism even less. The initiative for the great monastic reforms, the Beguinage movement, and the Franciscan revival came not from the centre but from the periphery of the Christian community.[29] Although it did not start these revivals, the authority later sanctioned them. The Poor Man of Assisi was not a priest, and even though the great Teresa is often called a Doctor of the Church, nobody ever dreams of placing her among the ranks of the clergy. We may be surprised to realise how many women played important roles in the life of the Medieval Church, both in apostolic endeavours and mystical success. Bridget of Sweden and Catherine of Sienna are not isolated cases. Think of Gertrude, Mathilda, Lutgarde, and, at the frontiers of the terrestrial city, Joan of Arc. Christians of such mettle as these were not slow in showing the way to ecclesiastical dignitaries, and this in the name of hierarchical obedience itself. The violent fulminations of Ruysbroeck against the Cathedral chapters of his time do not brand him as a precursor of Protestantism. His Catholic sense gave him an unwavering fidelity to the hierarchical Church.

The Reformation did not succeed in stifling lay initiative in the Roman Church. How many are the charitable works and missionary undertakings which owe their origin to the laity, not to mention the great international Eucharistic Congresses? Nor has the hierarchy been inactive. The name of Pius X is linked with frequent Communion and the Communion of the young, Benedict XV with missionary expansion, Pius XI with Catholic Action. In this happy interplay of activity, it is difficult to separate the work of the hierarchy from that of the faithful. If superiors' sole concern were to restrain activity, they would indeed severely impede the Church's religious vitality.

Pius XII has appealed for the laity to show the *courage* of initiative. Now the clergy must be magnanimous enough not only to tolerate their personal ventures but to help them to flourish. 'The true concept,' says the Pope *a propos* of Catholic Action, 'will be incompatible with the mentality of groups who consider themselves as inert cogs

in a gigantic machine, incapable of moving unless the central force sets
them in motion. It will be impossible to consider leaders as
manipulators of a central electric system, only interested in starting
or stopping, regulating or chanelling the current in the vast network.'[30]
Who is the adult who would want to stoop to play this materialistic
and depersonalized role? That is not the way he understands his
part in the Christian fight, and he is right. 'In decisive battles,'
continues the Pope, 'it is often from the front lines that the greatest
initiative comes.'[31]

Should we look upon these initiatives as an aspiring onset of the
laity?[32] The exact contrary is the case: this movement is inspired
from above as is the activity of its leaders. The one Spirit is tracing
two converging lines. He inclines the hierarchy toward the spiritual
life of the humble, and he uplifts the latter in all their activities towards
their shepherds.

Paul was converted by a direct personal meeting with the Lord but
he received Baptism from the hands of the Church's minister (Acts,
IX, 18). Cornelius, the centurion, was graced with heavenly visions
but he had to ask Saint Peter for admission into the Church (Ib., X,
1-6). Peter, too, is a man (Ib., v. 26), and the Holy Spirit does not
wait for his advice before descending on the converted pagans
(ib., v. 44); rather, the Prince of the Apostles must humbly submit
to the Spirit and baptize with water those already baptised with the
Spirit (ib., v. 47-48). Thus, under the royal sceptre of Christ, the
two aspects meet and reinforce one another : the hierarchical institution
and the vitality of grace.

And so, pure passivity is out of the question for subordinates. A
sane and healthy personalism must replace automatism, authoritarian
decisions, and bland subterfuges. The clergy alone is not to blame
for such a mentality. One also meets among the laity tepid dispositions
which chill before responsibility and fail to accept the mystery of
the hierarchy as a gift of God to be received with vigorous collaboration.
A totalitarian state looks on personal reflection as a threat against
its safety and a crime tantamount to high treason. Such a régime is
consciously creating the worst type of slavery, slavery of the spirit.
Where the liberty of God's children reigns, thinking and conscientious
men use their minds and wills to serve the community.

Passive and, therefore, false submission to authority sometimes
reveals a strong tinge of egoism, a selfish desire to relax, at all costs
to avoid being disturbed. When the first difficulty comes along,
they bow their heads, remain silent and fade into the background,
with disastrous results for their leaders. Such an attitude, typically
pharisaic, is simply a cover for cowardice and spiritual sloth unrealised

or unadmitted. To wait for explicit orders often signals sloth or, still worse, a spirit of opposition. A subordinate as well as his leader must acquit himself of his responsibility and must not allow himself to be hindered by passing difficulties. St. Teresa, the reformer of Carmel, in the course of the many difficulties which she encountered in her foundations, saw her intentions constantly purified without for an instant losing the confidence or respect of her superiors. Docility should not degenerate into faint-heartedness, and still less into bitterness over imaginary wrongs.

In such circumstances pride, which more frequently afflicts the strongest personalities, whispers subtle temptations: Your work is not valued . . . resign yourself . . . give way to others. We must be on our guard against this false humility. To retire because one's self-love has been wounded leads to ill-will and the worst kind of defeatism. Genuine sincerity will not camouflage ill-feeling under the pious mask of literal obedience. As P. de Montcheuil has said, 'There would be more resentment and pride in this than true submission.'33

Besides, to do so is to leave oneself open to the sin of omission. Not to use one's capacities because men do not immediately recognize such generous efforts, is proof of a pitiable immaturity. A truly humble soul recognizes that he is not infallible even in a concrete case. Should his superiors judge his activity to be inopportune, they do not intend to discourage future effort. Generally there are many means to arrive at a particular end. To maintain enthusiasm in the face of failure is neither an easy nor a common thing. But if we are not prepared for this kind of sacrifice, we cannot claim to be whole hearted in our undertaking. Here simplicity will find quite otherwise. Hindered by the Spirit from going to Bithynia, the Apostle Paul was prepared nonetheless, to embark immediately for Europe (Acts, XVI, 7-10). God calls when or where He will and how He will; our personal preferences simply do not enter. For this reason the hierarchy does not claim monopoly of the spirit of initiative. Refusal to attempt a new effort is equivalent to disobedience, not only to the Holy Spirit but also to the established authority.

Sometimes we decide to keep silence when the Spirit enjoins us to speak. *The Summa of Alexander of Hales* has in this regard a question which is scarcely found among any of the later Scholastics; its title: *de peccato taciturnitatis*.34 We sin by silence when we refuse to give to our superiors the information and advice to which they have a right. Authorities, on the other hand, are not to suffocate this frankness under crushing harshness. Saint John of the Cross knew by experience how easily the touchy disposition of superiors could engender bitterness and unleash persecution. In his *Spiritual Counsels*, he did not hesitate to stigmatize the desire for mastery which, among the directors of the Order, was threatening to replace charity and justice: 'And this is clearly seen when nobody raises protests in chapter, but everything is ceded and allowed to pass, because everyone is intent on pressing his own interests. This causes serious harm to the common good and nourishes the vice of ambition.'[35] Opportunists feign a certain docility before influential persons, whilst dividing out the spoils. To keep silence in the face of authority for no other reason than to spare one's self unpleasantness, reveals a gross misconception of the hierarchical sense.

THE HIERARCHICAL SENSE

An unequivocal recognition of the dignity of the laity in the Church can only make respect for the hierarchy more keen. Assiduous Catholics have sometimes spoken of 'blind' obedience, thus hoping to put an end to all the subtle arguing of the unsubmissive. But there is nothing so clear-sighted as the obedience of a Catholic. The eyes of faith see in the hierarchy ambassadors and representatives of Jesus Christ. Often this is difficult to see. The more vigorous and enlightened his faith, the more loyal will be the co-operation of the layman. The authority of the Church will be seen in its sanctifying role; no sacrifice or effort will be too great a test of his fidelity. He holds conformism in horror and he detests the cringings of the slave which Péguy opposes to the royal liberty of the kneeling Saint Louis.

The primary virtue in Christianity is not obedience but charity. It is called theological because it has God for its object and end. Without it, obedience does not even merit the name of virtue. We must beware of lapsing into moralism as has been the case in the domain of chastity.[36] In the minds of some young Christians who have been reared and educated to purity of morals and submission, the first commandment has been pushed into the background. Insistence on discipline is explained as a reaction against both the Protestant revolt and the modern spirit of independence. The priest, the educator of the laity, often has to cope with the same bewildering arrivals as the parents of a teen-age son. So restless, unpredictable, and especially critical, in fact, the boy is only seeking to be of service. Seized by the fear that their faithful will slip or err, priests frequently counsel them not to do too much lest they encroach upon forbidden territory.

Such views, whilst being understandable, make poor advice. They blind us to a balanced view of the whole man whose education should not lead to stagnation but to an expansion of personality. If we are merely looking for security, we will perish for want of courage, fearlessness, and a sincere and trusting faith. Faint-heartedness will enclose us still more in a Christian ghetto. We must risk a break-through and must not cower fearfully. Only that way can we arrive at the necessary purification. Lay personality is not as yet entirely formed—a greater reason to help the laity discover not so much their rights but their duties, not their privileges but their responsibilities. There is no dishonour in serving and obeying. Authority itself bows before the Lord it serves in His disciples.

At any rate, conscientious objection to a formal decision of authority is unthinkable for a Catholic. At the Diet of Worms, in 1521, Luther would in no way modify his position, saying that his conscience was the prisoner of the word of God. His radicalism led him to the following declaration in his book on the Babylonian Captivity: 'Neither the Pope, nor the bishop, nor anybody in the world has the right to impose on anyone, without his consent, a single syllable; all else would be the spirit of tyranny.'³⁷

Such an attitude is not evangelical. The Catholic firmly believes that the Spirit has been promised and given to the community and particularly to its leaders. How is it possible to grant that one man is right when his words are contrary to the witness of the whole group? Even if he were in good faith, the Catholic would answer that he is in error. How could the Spirit of truth allow the whole Church to perish in error while He gave to one man, alone and against everyone, the absolute guarantee of truth? The mutineer always accuses his leaders of tyranny. By encouraging him in revolt, we open the door to anarchy.

If tomorrow a new reformer arrives on the scene, contradicting the old by appealing to his own personal lights, how can he be denied? There is only one alternative: let him, too, follow his own way. In this way, you arrive at a multitude of divergent and contradictory systems, all allegedly explaining the unique truth. The problem has no solution. Unless we want to founder in total relativism we must reject the premises. A recent and fervid apologia for heretics presents them as living a 'tragedy of conscience.'³⁸ Never must we joke about the very real difficulties of dissidents; but we must preserve our respect for the truth. Otherwise, it is altogether impossible to make a serious matter even of the words of heretics.

The objection could be raised that Luther was not alone, that there were many clever men with him. In fact, he took whole nations with him. When it was necessary to reform the leaders and the members, he changed doctrines and institutions. He raised a new Church against the old. In the name of the Spirit, he fought an authority which had degenerated into pure formalism among many of its representatives. Instead of revivifying it, he suppressed it. Psychologically, it is an understandable phenomenon; but nonetheless, an unjustifiable one. Meanwhile, it has provoked a catastrophe.

The precise point where Catholics and Protestants separate is faith in the hierarchical Church. In the eyes of the Reformation, 'the hierarchy has no part in the mystery. In fact it is only too 'intelligible' since it is arbitrary human domination and in no way an organ or mediatrix of God. The descending motion of grace is arrested when it reaches the human frontier. Recourse to the individual conscience, however, is a way without issue. In reflecting today on the dogma of the Incarnation, the Reformation is discovering Catholic tendencies in its own midst.[39] The Word was made flesh so as to make us, in His Humanity, participants of the divine plenitude. In continuing His Incarnation in the Church, He extends His redemption to all of us. As a final result it is not surprising to see the Counter-Reformation's insistence on perfect obedience. It points to a certain distress, an anxiety to forfeit no part of its indispensable authority. Under pressure of events, the fact that all the Church's declarations are not infallible was sometimes forgotten. These declarations are not infrequently measures of prudence, in no way irrevocable. Well informed Catholics have on occasion the duty to ask for precisions.

Nobody can free himself of such obligations by pleading for his personal peace. Courage demands that we go to the authorities, not to the uninformed masses. Thorny theological problems are not to be discussed in public forums: that only confuses matters. Nobody has the right to compromise the prestige which, for religious reasons and for the common good, should surround the magisterium. The Reformation delighted in mocking pope and bishops. Was it pure resentment or was it systematic planning? We fear the latter: an organized detraction from which Protestantism will separate itself with only the greatest difficulty.

Liberty of conscience won nothing. Obedience alone liberates, for it alone snaps the chains of obstinate individualism. For one who sees the hierarchy as the mystery's core neither illuminism nor autonomism can gainsay it. The Spirit does not build with one hand only to destroy with the other. Rather, He removes every obstacle to the knowledge of God, preached by the apostles and their successors (II Cor., X, 4-6).

To submit to apostolic power with a bow of the head and out of fear of sanctions is insufficient. The 'hierarchical sense' demands more. It consists in a spontaneous assent to be guided by faith as it is legitimately interpreted by the magisterium. The true believer adapts himself inwardly to the transforming light which dispels all the darkness of self love and egocentric judgment. And so there is created between him and the object of his act of faith a mysterious affinity which is none other than the revealing Spirit. He will 'comprehend' from within the proposed truth when the sensuous man of whom St. Paul speaks is often scandalised and irritated, and he will judge calmly and sanely on every pronouncement given him.

The greatest freedom is attachment to God. It is not given to us in its entirety once for all; we must win it and render ourselves worthy of it through constant fidelity. Newman, in his famous poem, does not ask to 'See the distant scene;' he relies on the 'Kindly Light' to illumine the next step for him.

Man does not suddenly become a criminal or a saint. Each one of his decisions flows from his entire past and each engages his entire future. Each augments or diminishes his spiritual liberty and his Christian personality. The hierarchical sense is a delicate thing. It does not take much to dull or sharpen it. If we wish to sound the depths of the ecclesiastical mystery within the hierarchical organization we must guard, with a jealous care, this 'clear eye' of which the Gospel speaks.

---

1 For the concept of *Mystery*, cf. D. Déden, *Le 'Mystère' paulinien*, in *Eph. Theol. Lov.*, 13, 1936, pp. 405-442. BORNKAMM, in the article *Musterion*, *Theol. Wörterbuch*, IV., Stuttgart, 1942, pp. 809-834. L. BOUYER, *Mystèrion*, in *La Vie Spir.*, Supplément, n. 23, 1952, pp. 397-412. H. RAHNER, *Mythes grecs et Mystère chrétien* (Bibl. Hist.), Fr. trans, H. VOISIN, Paris, 1954.

2 Here are some typical passages from St. Paul's epistles: *I. Cor.*, II., 7-10: 'What we make known is the wisdom of God, his secret, kept hidden till now; so, before the ages, God had decreed, reserving glory for us. (None of the rulers of this world could read his secret . . .) Things no eye has seen, no ear has heard, no human heart conceived, the welcome God has prepared for those who love him. To us, then, God has made a revelation of it through his Spirit . . . .'
Rom., XVI., 25-26: '. . . a gospel which reveals the mystery, hidden from us through countless ages, but now made plain, through what the prophets have written, and published, at the eternal God's command, to all the nations, so as to win the homage of their faith.' *Eph.*, III., 9-11: 'the plan of this mystery, hidden till now, brings to light and makes manifest in the Church,' the subtlety of God's wisdom. Cf.ib., I, 9-10. *Col.* I, 26-27, the mystery made known to the saints is 'Christ among you, your hope of glory.'
See also the hymn to the mystery, I *Tim.*, III, 16.
We could speak also of the metaphysical mystery, which, while remaining natural concerns itself with the profound meaning of being. This mystery sometimes manifests itself like a streak of lightning to the eyes of a philosopher or even the man of science who discovers the immeasurable dimensions of it in grasping beings in being. This call is an echo of the religious mystery and it can bring about a sort of ecstasy. We are then in the presence of a phenomenon of natural mysticism, an experience of high human value, but which runs the risk of substituting itself for a properly religious reaction in the face of supernatural revelation.

3 'Eternal life is knowing thee, who art the only true God, and Jesus Christ, whom thou hast sent.' *John*, XVII, 3.

4 Catechism for use in all the dioceses of Belgium, 1947. Question 106.

5 *Catechismus ad Parochos*. Pars I, art. 9, n. 117. Ed. Rome, 1924, p. 78.

6 S. CYPRIAN, *De orat. domin.*, 23; P.L., 4, 553, Corpus of Vienna, 3, A, p.285.

7 For example: I *Cor.*, XII, concerning the Church. *Eph.* I, 22, on Christ, the Head. The literature here is extensive and sufficiently well known. Reference should be had above all to the encyclical of Pius XII on the Mystical Body.

8 Y. CONGAR, *Rythmes de l'Eglise et du Monde*, in *La Vie Intell.*, 14, April, 1946, pp.6-22, in particular, p.17. —*Jalons*, p.461ff.

9 Y. CONGAR, *Vraie et fausse réforme dans l'Eglise* (Unam Sanctam, 20). Paris, 1950, pp. 442s., p. 454. An article taken from the conclusion of this work, trans. by B. GILLIGAN, appears in the quarterly review Cross Currents (N.Y.), Summer, 1951, pp. 80-102.

10 For the 'catholic' and 'protestant' tendencies amidst the Reform and Oecumenism, see *L'Eglise Universelle dans le dessein de Dieu*, Report of Section I for the Amsterdam Assembly, Paris,—Neuchâtel, 1949, pp. 304s.

11 See the frequently quoted Collect of the XVth Sunday after Pentecost: 'Ecclesiam tuam, Domine, miseratio continuata mundet et muniat . . .' The collective sense is manifest in these liturgical prayers. The 'purification of the Church' is understood to concern the whole body of its members. Compare the Collect of the XXIIIrd Sunday: 'Absolve quaesumus, Domine, tuorum delicta populorum . . .'

12 On the difficult question of the presence of sin and of sinners in the Church, see among others Y. DE MONTCHEUIL, *Aspects de l'Eglise* (Unam Sanctam, 18), Paris, 1949, pp. 64ff. –CH. JOURNET, *Nature du Corps de l'Eglise*, in *Revue Thomiste*, 49, 1948, pp. 122-205. ID., *L'Eglise du Verbe Incarné*, II. *Sa structure interne et son unité catholique*, Paris, 1951, pp. 910 f. and 1103 f. -J. SALAVERRI, S.J., *Lo divino y lo umano en la Iglesia*, in *Estudios Eclesiasticos*, 27, 1953, 167-201. (Good bibliography). On the need of reform, the work of Y. CONGAR, already cited, is particularly well documented. See also the study made by P. RAHNER, S.J., *Die Kirche der Sünder*. Fribourg-en-Br., 1948. Protestants are wrong in being scandalized over the fact that the Roman Church never pleads guilty. If the Church were simply 'collectivity' and nothing more, they would be right.

13 Pope Pius XII., in his encyclical, *Mystici Corporis*, speaks strongly against this imaginary dissociation. Cf. *Act. Apl. Sedis*, 1943, p. 224. Eng. Trans., ed. cit., *The Mystical Body*, nos. 62-63.

14 Y. CONGAR, *Sacerdoce et Laïcat dans l'Eglise*, in *Vie Intell.*, December, 1946, pp. 6-39. Published also in *Masses Ouvrières*, Dec. 1946, pp. 19-56. Cf. also, *Jalons*, p. 146 ff.

15 M. J. MONTUCLARD, *Eglise et partis*, in *Les Chrétiens et la Politique*, Paris, 1948, p. 160.

16 Cf. L. CERFAUX, *La Théologie de L'Eglise suivant S. Paul.* (Unam Sanctam, 10). Paris, 1942, pp. 105f.

17 G. SALET, *Le Mystère de la charité divine* in *Rech. Sc. Rel.*, 28, 1938, p. 28.

18 Cf. A. M. DUBARLE, *Prophétisme et Apostolat dans le Nouveau Testament*. In *Vie Spir.*, 1948, pp. 413-428.

19 E. AMANN and A. DUMAS, *L'Eglise au pouvoir des laïques* (Histoire de l'Eglise, sous la direction D'A. FLICHE and V. MARTIN, Vol. 7). Paris, 1948.

20 Some interesting indications in H. CARPAY, *L'Action catholique, Essai de justification historique et de précision doctrinale*. Tournai-Paris, 1948.

21 See especially the great work of J. LORTZ, *Die Reformation in Deutschland*. 2 vols. Fribourg-en-Br., 1939-1940. K. ADAM blackens the picture in his essay *Vers l'Unité chrétienne. Le point de vue catholique* (Les Religions, 5). Paris, 1949.

22 Cf. M. MONTUCLARD, *Vivre l'Eglise. La part des laïques dans la transformation des structures religieuses*, in *Jeunesse de L'Eglise*, 8, 1948, pp. 11-34.

23 H. DUMÉRY, *Les Trois Tentations de l'apostolat moderne* (Rencontres, 28). Paris, 1948, p. 97.

24 Y. CONGAR, *Sacerdoce et laïcat dans l'Eglise*, in *Vie Intell.*, 14, Dec. 1946, p. 31. *Jalons*, p. 515.

25 A. FONTAINE, *La Vie religieuse*, in *Le Monde*, Jan. 5, 1950.

26 Y. CONGAR, *Le Saint-Esprit et le Corps apostolique, réalisateurs de l'oeuvre du Christ*, in *Rev. Quest. Phil. Théol.*, 37, 1953, pp. 24-48. As signs of this liberty of the Holy Spirit, the author cites the charisms and unforseeable irruptions of grace.

[27] Cf. E. DUMOUTET *Le Christ selon la chair et la Vie liturgique au moyen âge.* Paris, 1932. There are some, however, who exaggerate, in contending that oriental piety is concerned exclusively with Christ in His divinity. For example, K. ADAM, in *Christ Our Brother*, Trans. by J. McCANN, London, 1931, p. 47 ff. Devotion to the *glorified* humanity of Christ is very strong in the East. Cf. S. SALAVILLE, *Liturgies orientales. Notions générales.* (*Bibl. Cath. Sc. Rel.*, 87), Paris 1932. p. 93 ff.

[28] See for the history of piety in the Low Countries, ST. AXTERS, *Geschiedenis van de vroomheid in de Nederlanden*, I, Anvers, 1950, p. 404. This book was summarized in a French work recently translated by D. ATTWATER, *The Spirituality of the Old Low Countries*, Blackfriars, London, 1954.

[29] Fundamental work on the history of the Beguines: A. MENS, O.F.M. Cap., *Oorsprong en Betekenis van de Nederlandse Begijnen-en Begarden-beweging*, Antwerp, 1947. Lay endeavours of the XIIth and XIIIth centuries are astonishingly similar to those of our own day.

[30] PIUS XII., Allocution of May 3, 1951. See *Docum. Cath.*, 48, 1951, col. 580.

[31] PIUS XII., Address to the World Congress for the Lay Apostolate, Actes du Congrés, I, p. 49. For historical observations, ib., p. 44f. Also, NCWC trans. n. 30, and nos. 6-10.

[32] Numerous examples in Y. CONGAR, o.c., *Réforme*, pp. 275f. On p. 286 the author shows how these peripheral attempts are incorporated into the hierarchical Church. Cf. also his article *L'Esprit Saint dans l'Eglise*, in *Lumière et Vie*, n-10, 1953, pp. 51-74. FR. P. SPIAZZI, o.c., *Missione dei Laici*, pp. 183f. gives an interesting exposition on the 'charisms' of the faithful and their connection with the ministerial functions.

[33] Y. DE MONTCHEUIL, *Rôle du Chrétien dans l'Eglise*, in *Mélanges Théologiques* (Théologie, n.9). Paris, 1946, p. 122. This article gives a very precise description of this complex phenomenon, pp. 113f. Cf. also *For Men of Action*, (Fides), Chicago, Trans. by C. E. PARNELL, containing 11 of Montcheuil's essays; regarding the matter under discussion, *The Catholic Concept of Vocation*, pp. 47-66; esp. p. 55.

[34] *Summa fratris Alexandri*, II. B, n. 396-398. In the edition of Quaracchi, vol. 3, 1930, pp. 397-401.

[35] St. John of the Cross, 13th Spiritual Saying. Vol. III, p. 294. Trans. by E. A. PEERS, 4th ed., London, 1953.

[36] See the forceful books of A. ADAM *Tugend der Freiheit*, Nurenberg, 1947, a study of the spirit of legitimate liberty. The exposition is brilliant, but at times superficial. With certain reserves, the general thesis is worthy of attention. *The Primary of Love*, Coin, 1955. As a sub title: *The place of sexual morality in the Moral Law*.

[37] M. LUTHER, *De Captivitate babylonica Ecclesiae praeludium*. Werke, XI, Weimar, 1888, p. 536.

[38] The reference here is to the book of W. NIGG, *Das Buch der Ketzer*. Zurich, 1949. (Tragedy and triumph of conscience). For the author, there is no absolute truth; there are only partial views, irreducible but equally legitimate. For him, heresy is personal conviction crushed by a majority abusing its power.

[39] Concerning this 'catholic' tendency, see note 10.

CHAPTER III

THE LAITY'S FIELD OF ACTION

COMMUNISTS have frequently tried to present Marxism as a doctrine acceptable to Christians by asserting that while the Church is free to oversee heavenly matters for believers, the earth itself belongs to men and is the domain of the organized proletariat. Nazism once made a similar distinction: if the priestly caste seeks to channel its energy toward the world beyond (the *Jenseits*), the free citizens can organize this world (the *Diesseits*) as an autonomous unit and so there will be peace. Could we not conceive a similar division in our present problem? On the one side would be religious interests, the clergy's affair; on the other, the profane order, the right of the laity. With one blow we would put an end to manifold disagreements and hopeless conflict. Pastors and monks would chant their office and care for souls; the emancipated laity would be free to build up the temporal city and assure world progress.

What a specious simplification! If the Church be not of the world, still it must live in the world and find a place whereon to stand. The sacristy is too cramped and furthermore, usually very musty. Neither priests nor faithful are pure spirits. Then too, even for the laity 'religion' means more than 'going to Church.' Religion is more than a coat which a citizen dons each Sunday morning, doffs as soon as possible and puts away for another week. To believe means to abandon oneself with reverence and confidence to the living and true God, Father and Creator, in whose hands we are held. If we arrange life and home without Faith or law, we do not merit the name 'faithful,' though we have a private oratory somewhere in the house. Land is divided, and each heir receives a share; but a living man cannot be divided into two parts, one destined for the profane, and the other for the sacred. The citizen of the State is also a citizen of the Kingdom of God even though the two communities are not on the same level. Thus, the question is infinitely more complicated than it may appear to certain politicians who make religion a private affair.

To place religion and Church in an enclosure reserved for the priests almost amounts to excluding the laity from the Church even though they may be granted occasional access within. The faithful soul is not merely a man who prays; he applies his religious values to every department of life. He is Christian by virtue not of a weekly half-hour, but of a daily twenty-four hours. In all he does he honours God and His Ten Commandments. He differs from the non-believer not only in the way he acts but in his very existence, rich in truth and joy, fruitful in vitality. Religion and Church are also his affair, at least they should be. For if this 'sense of God' is more evident today among the good, nevertheless it is so far removed from the baptized masses that Cardinal Suhard could speak of 'the atheism of Christians.'[1]

Thus in considering the laity's action, we must first speak of its religious activity. To omit this point would be to deprive the laity of the finest part of their vocation, and relegate them to an attenuated Christian existence. Not only would they be 'engaged in the life of the world,' but also they would be 'disengaged' from any other-world relation. By that very fact they would be cut off from the prime sources of inspiration and generosity needed for their temporal action.

THE LAITY ON RELIGIOUS GROUND

The layman is baptized, that is, consecrated to God. He has then what can be called an 'existential obligation' to follow this orientation and inclination toward God.[2] 'Obligation,' however, must be understood not as subjection, but rather as a means of liberation. In reality, man can only liberate himself by loosing himself from his own limitations and discovering the very reason for living in Someone superior to him and unlimited. Concretely, this discovery implies prayer and sacrifice.

Man always sacrifices, if not to God, at least to himself or to another idol. Sacrifice should be the true expression of his interior dispositions of respect and homage: external rite should correspond with a life acceptable to God. Faithful to his vocation, every baptized Christian will convert into action his response to grace, and so become a living testimony. Our generation demands sincerity; it is to modern man's credit that he detests pretence even if he sometimes allows himself to be duped by it. And so arises the appeal for an *authentic* Christianity. In regard to this precise point, the religious attitude of the layman is more eloquent than that of the priest. Nobody will suspect him of self-interested scheming. Since Christianity does not compensate him monetarily, his testimony will be all the more persuasive.

Yet we must delve below the surface of things and beyond the individual point of view. The *Communion of Saints* means much more than force of example or sway of words. Between the members of the Mystical Body which is the Church, there exists a mysterious union which unites one to another in good and in bad. The level of life of each influences the potential of the whole. Incorporated into the Church by Baptism, new members are qualified by Confirmation to enlarge and defend that community. Are all of them aware of these liturgical and supernatural realities? No one would dare to answer affirmatively especially after a consideration of the individualism and passivity of sacramental practice. United at the same table, unified by the same transforming food, they should feel the same current of life passing through all the souls about them. The mystery of Christ's redemption continues within the realm of each conscience. There it can be thwarted too. The good of the entire world is constantly at stake there. A man is neither virtuous nor sinful in himself alone. Saints are a blessing for society, the lazy and indifferent, a heavy weight that threaten to interrupt its rise.

No Catholic can pretend that the contrary is true; but when it comes to a living application of this truth, we often fall short.

The Spirit begins by giving faith to the Church and through her He addresses Himself to each man. Each member should be in his turn a light-bearer. When he hears about the light of the world or the salt of the earth, however, the layman often perceives sermon clichés and he is neither troubled nor disquieted. No doubt, he would hardly allow a poor man to starve to death on his door step, but to nourish the spiritually starved and save the morally wretched seems to him to be the priest's work. Religious modesty, no doubt; perhaps a horror of proselytizing or even respect for another's conscience! But have we forgotten the sin of omission? Communist enthusiasts are not thinking only of bread; they speak of alienation and liberation.

This point is of capital importance. Always and everywhere man is a social being with a need for others, even for the realization of his religious end. To reach God without having heard at some time the Gospel message is a difficult task. In a materialistic régime God is systematically ignored. It is forbidden to speak of religion in schools or public institutions. More recently a frontal attack on the idea of God has been discouraged in as much as it calls attention to the subject. It is infinitely better to let it die, if it is not already dead. There are some Christians who categorically state that the working world is calmly atheistic, and they are not thinking about the Soviet-dominated sphere alone.[3]

Even in Catholic countries there are many who have never heard of God in home, school, or the Church they once attended. They have even lost the notion of prayer. No longer can they discover the *answer* to the problem of life for they never learned to perceive the *question*. The first thing to do is to make them aware of the basic option.

To do so we need a more diffusive, a more stirring testimony. To some extent believers are responsible for the unbelief of the masses. The fact obliges us to reflect and measure more carefully the extent of our responsibilities. Have the laity been sufficiently taught to expend themselves? Too often they try to excuse themselves in the eyes of the world for their Christian adherence, and finish by concealing it.

There is one domain, however, where this defection has been partially overcome; namely, in the interest for the *missions*. Missionary activity enjoys great sympathy. Pontifical missionary works owe their existence to lay initiative. However, in no way do we mean to suggest that solicitude for the evangelizing of the pagans was awaiting the signal of the laity. Each time a new territory became accessible, missionaries set out. Protestants even cry 'Roman imperialism!' falsely interpreting the growth of ecclesiastical institutions.

At the present time, when 'the missions are no longer in the missions,' it is most fortunate that current Catholic ideas are having to be redefined. In the vast regions of Asia and even Africa no longer are we the bearers of 'civilization.' In the future this is to be the work of U.N.E.S.C.O. Strangely enough, that organisation will not handle the task as well as our missionaries. But their principal objective is the spread not of well-being but of Christ's message. [4] From the human standpoint the other continents are no longer an annex of Europe. In fact, the situation today is quite the reverse. If we accept this inversion in our religious views as well, then we will be more catholic —more universal—than before.

We will always have something to give, or rather Someone to announce. The Spirit of God Who radiates Charity by giving Himself forbids and hinders us from remaining inactive. This is the sense of 'the charity of Christ which impels us;' not first our love for Christ, but first of all Christ's love for all. The missionary who crosses the ocean, or in more modern terms, the airways, is not seeking to extend the influence of his order or the power of his authority over other territories; he is bringing Redemption. He is literally enlarging the domain of charity.

It is possible for non-Catholics and even for non-Christians 'to save their souls,' as we say in catechism language. Grace has already cleared a path in the wilds where the missionary has not yet penetrated. But if Christ came to die and to rise again for the salvation of all, we have no right to rest until all have received the fulness of His grace, until all give praise to the Father for the sacrifice of His Son.

Still many are the hearts in which Christ has not yet been born; it is that which should prevent us relaxing. Missionary action has its source in God and not in thirst for power, craving for adventure, or even condescending humanitarianism.

Once missionaries were compared to the *conquistadores* of Spain's golden epoch. The sole difference was that the former brought converts to Christ and to God not as conquered peoples but as saved ones. To put it more technically, the missionary concept is theocentric and Christocentric; it is not the result of human design. Its efforts are not even directed towards the more promising regions. The Holy Spirit has certain whims and fancies which drive missionaries toward dying peoples without ever revealing the 'why' of this puzzling strategy.

The most crying need in pagan countries and even in our own lands steeped in Christian tradition is the need for God. Human culture, infinitely precious as it may be, is still a by-product of evangelization. To safeguard its proper value, we must not rank it before our religious preoccupations.

It is extremely enlightening to question converted peoples on their view of the missions. Negro priests of Urundi whose parents and grand parents were still animists, have said: 'You missionaries should not think for a moment that you have taught us of God's existence. For us, poor souls that we were, this God once remained at an infinite distance. Our whole existence was dominated by terror of spirits; to appease them we had to multiply offerings. Now you have brought this far-away God close to us. For that and not for your civilisation do we thank you.'

These negro priests were probably unaware that they were quoting St. Paul (Eph., II, 13). 'But now you are in Christ Jesus, now through the Blood of Christ, you (pagans) have been brought close, you who were once so far away.' God is far away from no one, but men can drive themselves far from Him.

The Catholic community does not discharge its duty to spread the Gospel by placing the obligation on the shoulders of a few zealous souls. Totally and consciously it is a missionary *community*, a Church 'sent on a mission.' This characterizes her very essence, this is her most powerful stimulus for leaders and members alike. Missionary consciousness is the concrete translation of a Catholicity which will not be accomplished before time's end. It is a special grace for the faithful which ransoms them from narrowness and self-sufficiency. The blessings which have been bestowed on them, they must distribute to all.

In recent times we have heard about missions to the interior;

even the parish must emerge from its conservatism and initiate a reconquest. In the chapter on Catholic Action and the many-sided apostolate of the laity this will be our chief concern. First we must centre our attention on the vocation of the layman in the realm of the profane.

Do Temporal Values Exist?

Perhaps the question seems preposterous, and yet it is frequently put. The matter demands complete honesty. Too often the laity have the impression that the clergy consider them as secondary Christians involved—and necessarily so!—with this passing world.[5] In the eyes of the priests, only the Kingdom of God counts, and temporal 'values' are treated as non-existent. For them, the world is merely a means to attain 'something else.' World progress does not really interest them. Their good works and numerous charities are only sly pretexts by which they win souls. Naturally, the laity take such matters seriously; they feel themselves obliged to safeguard the human and to protect it vigorously against the inroads of clericalism. And so frequent friction arises.

The violent discussions between naturalists and supernaturalists further complicate an already thorny problem. The former emphasize the reality of natural goods created by God and entrusted to men. They warn us to be on our guard against an unconscious Manicheanism which would condemn the world as a product of the Evil Spirit. The supernaturalists, however, fear we will attribute to nature a sort of innate justice and a total autonomy, and so dim our heavenly perspective. The first group speaks acridly of mystics who disregard everything for their religious aspirations or what they regard as such. The second group condemns the seductive effects of earthly comforts in which we can easily become entangled. In prophetic tones they remind us of the passing nature of worldly things: is it really worthwhile to expend our energies on a crumbling edifice?

In short, this is the whole problem of Christian humanism.[6] Neither Catholics, Protestants, nor Orthodox have been able to overlook it. Impossible to resolve with a few syllogisms,[7] the discussion touches the heart of the Gospel and involves the very existence of the Christian layman as a layman.

In so brief a space we cannot treat the controverted question in all its fulness, but neither can we completely ignore it. Here again, silence would be sinful because hesitation only tends to complicate matters. We will have to be satisfied, however, with pointing out certain principles which, clarified by the Gospel, will help us to get a glimpse of the solution. In their broadest lines these principles are evident. Every beginner in theology knows the essential: grace does not disregard nature, but elevates it; Christ condemned sin, not creation. Neither material goods nor technical progress are bad in themselves but man can and often does abuse them. The temptation to abuse is recurring and perilous. Of this the Gospel warns us. Neither possession nor possessor is condemned but rather the greedy and hypocritical Pharisees 'who swallow up the property of widows, under cover of your long prayers.' (Mt., XXIII, 14).

In the writings of the New Testament we make no mistake about the meaning of the word *Cosmos*. The sense is twofold: it indicates either the whole of creation and man, or the horde of the enemies of God and His Christ. Taken in the first sense, the world has been created by Christ (Col., I, 16) for man, its king and priest, to raise up to the glory of its Author. (I Cor., III, 22-23). Man's sin had placed the world in bondage, but Christ the Redeemer has ransomed it to freedom and in the Church He has in principle repaired and purified it. Only in final glory will total liberation be achieved. (Rom., VIII, 20-23). In the meantime the world is still subject to the influence of the devil and sin and so in the second sense the word signifies that element which rejects the grace of Redemption. [8]

In the name of Redemption, therefore, we cannot despise creation, matter or the profane. Otherwise the supernatural would destroy the natural and would end with self-destruction. 'For the supernatural is itself carnal,' says Péguy, and mystery extends even to the dust of this earth at least by refraction. It is inserted as the leaven which will lift up humanity. It pretends neither to take away its power nor liberty, only to ennoble it. The temporal, then, enjoys an autonomy limited but nonetheless real. Although it does not incarnate the absolute supreme good it has its own laws.

According to Catholic doctrine the State is a perfect society. Independent in its proper sphere, it constitutes not only a perceptible human value, but within that sphere, the highest and most extensive value. The Church does not compete with it; she respects it. Philosophy, likewise, under the light of reason enjoys its proper principles and suitable methods; theology makes no complaint about them.

Earthly values have an objective excellence which in no way contradicts man's final end. The citizen of this world must recognize these values and develop them, not merely as trivial means to 'win merit' and 'do good,' but as ends, secondary, and yet worthy of esteem. [9] If he treats them as his last end, he has fallen into idolatry,[10] and the human personality will be the first to pay the price. The sin, however, would be in the man and not in things. If, on the other hand, man accepts these values for what they are—real, but limited goods—he will be able to fit them into a unified 'profane order,' an order which the Christian will direct heavenwards without any attendant diminution. No longer will there be scattered and diversified elements, but rather as Jacques Maritain expressed it, a 'Christian profane order.'[11]

The immediate end of human activity, both individual and social, is very worthy. Reluctant tolerance of human work is not a Christian attitude. The layman who engages in it courageously accomplishes a noble task. But if the layman is Christian, his name demands that he will not channel such activity against God or the Church. On the contrary, he will endow it with a greater dignity in the perspective of his supernatural destiny. We do not have the right to separate from man's work its inherent joy.[12]

In the Psalms, the heavens and earth sing the magnificence of the Creator. Yet what is fitting for the stars and the cedars of Lebanon, is also fitting for technical marvels. The Franciscan, Kolbe, is in complete accord with the Canticle of the sun. In hymning the triumph of an ultra-modern printing machine, he remains in the pure Gospel spirit of his Seraphic Father.[13] Some gloomy souls are forever recalling the fatal results of original sin and discovering everywhere undeniable signs of corruption. Sin has disturbed order, the spirit of evil uses this world as bait to trap pride-ridden man. It has not yet been able to strip him of his liberty or his divine vocation. The Church Councils have condemned such pessimism; it recalls the unfortunate exaggerations of Protestantism.

The values of this world are not entirely corrupt, nor are they evil to such a degree that no exorcism of ascetics or detachment can save them. For it is not with nature's destruction that grace becomes stronger and more fecund. The Christian has a task to fulfil in this world; he must make this earth habitable, not as a definitive dwelling place, or still less as an imaginary paradise, but as a field of laborious trial where sincere workers can preserve their strength for the final effort of sanctification.

Rome has never condemned human values in the name of the Kingdom of Heaven as has a certain Puritanism. In no way does she dream of founding a new theocracy similar to that of Calvin at Geneva.

The Catholic Church does not have to dominate the world—this is not the job Christ gave her. By not entering the League of Nations at Geneva, the Pope was not playing opportunist; it was a question of principle. The Church leaves national and political affairs to the powers concerned in order to devote herself to spiritual and religious interests, regardless of the outward appearances and occasional complaints. Her vocation inspires her beyond so restricted a sphere.

She must reject as a temptation the domination of kingdoms and their weapons, and choose instead, humble means. Because she is not angelic, she will always need material resources to realize her work of sanctification. But it is not her right to ride rough-shod over civil society. Ancient theologians quoted Biblical allegories in order to justify the concrete situation before their eyes; yet, as history shows, medieval Christianity was supported by other elements which the Church has no wish to see reproduced today.[14]

Her respect of temporal values is genuine. When they are accepted solely as means of religious propaganda, they lose their intrinsic stability and dignity as subordinate ends. This fact should be encouraging to defenders of the laity. Furthermore, the propagation of the faith and the advancement of culture are two different things. True, they cannot be totally disjoined and some contacts can even be beneficial. Nevertheless it is not in pursuing civilization that the Church will do the most to further it. The monks of the Middle Ages civilized barbarian Europe with their consecration to the *Opus Dei*. The Church simply by its diffusion of the Gospel, has undermined the ethical foundation that permitted slavery to continue.

These clarifications have effected an undeniable progress. Today there is less danger of confusing methods and confounding functions. We must recognize the developments of history too.[15] As long as the missionary must act as the architect and leader of agricultural development, he will be so much less available for the job of spiritual education. Human culture does not fall within the scope of the Church; nonetheless it still owes its development to her presence. If the Church would renounce her essential role to guarantee that development she would soon be unable to produce any temporal progress whatever. She would fall to the level of a philosophical system competing with other concepts of the world—she would be fatally conquered in the battle.

Just as opposites attract one another, so this truth set forth above suggests its contrary.

Temporal values must be integrated into the Christian's total concept of life and, retaining their place, be subordinated to the supreme end.

A supernatural destiny revaluates transitory interests in the light of ultimate beatitude. In the final analysis, this destiny is to be the touchstone for the use of such interests and is to govern indirectly the measure of their lawfulness. It will have the right of supervision. It can sanctify them by setting them apart as instruments for salvation or, where there is need, detaching them, for sacrifice. But above all, it must purify them, for without purification no sanctity is possible. Immature optimism alone is blind to the adhesive and enfolding qualities that matter possesses.

A sound humanism ought to recognise its limits not reluctantly but spontaneously. It should not be closed, but open to the higher call of grace. The Supernatural is not simply the prolongation of natural power. The intensification of our innate faculties will never arrive at the level of effective salvation which is a pure gift of God, or, more accurately, is God's gift of Himself to us. True humanism does not ensnare man in his pettiness nor does it enclose him in this world; rather, it opens infinite perspectives for him.[16] Strange as it may seem, it is not anthropocentric but theocentric. Considered in any other light, humanism will hypnotise man into self-admiration, and destroy him.

A genuinely human culture does not deny this superior end, but it is never free from this temptation. Relative autonomy seeks total independence especially in the headiness of initial discovery. Even a duly honoured and recognized laity can be prone to the advances of laicism. To maintain balance it needs a correspondingly profound religious sense. Should the superior ties be broken, temporal values would go astray and slip into the grasp of an unseen diabolic power beyond the exorcising powers of any man.

The use of cultural goods, both material and intellectual, is subject primarily to the *norms of morality*, of which God is the ultimate foundation. A totally amoralist concept is rather rare and, in fact, inhuman. On the other hand, there are many who object to the interferences of the moralist in particular questions.

In any objective reading of the Gospels and apostolic writings one cannot fail to be impressed by their insistence on self-denial, mortification and sacrifice. Physical culture, education and temporal well-being seem to have been by-passed by the authors of the New Testament. Numerous contemporary publications of Catholic origin fail to give this same tone. Authors—perhaps with an eye to apologetics —put the emphasis elsewhere. They fear that a religious man should appear less a man. But they forget that in Christianity no one can escape the scandal of the Cross. 'The world,' in its pejorative sense, cannot accept the message; if it did it would no longer be 'the world.' But folly or scandal, the Gospel remains the Wisdom and the Strength of God.

Christ teaches us how to use earthly goods, true gifts from His Father, and then eventually, how to renounce them whenever they may be an obstacle to our complete fidelity. When the love of the

Crucified demands it,[17] we must be prepared to cast them aside. Shall we blush then at the demands the Gospel imposes on the rich, we who live in this proletarian era?

True liberty is acquired only by the strength of detachment. Ancient philosophy already recognized that a severe training is necessary to arrive at perfect balance. The 'catharsis' was particularly imposed on all aspirants to the contemplation of supreme truth. Every farmer looking to his fields for a rich harvest knows that he must root out the weeds, that he must always prune and support his trees. Domination of the passions so led the Stoics to overweening self-sufficiency that whatever they may have gained on one side they lost on the other.

Christianity adopted the term ascetism from ancient philosophy but not before changing its content and more especially its spirit.[18] Its ideal differs from that of the philosophers by a more austere radicalism and, still more by its sublime aspirations which grace upholds. Newman made the observation that a 'Gentleman' can use all the refinements of his formation either to become a saint or to reject all religion.[19] A man's worth lies in what he is, not in what he has. A cultivated gentleman should know how to possess material and intellectual riches without letting them possess him. Otherwise, he will no longer be their master but their servant. 'Our possessions devour us,' says Gabriel Marcel,[20] and St. John of the Cross writes trenchantly about men of property—prisoners of their treasures.[21]

LAY ACTION IN THE TEMPORAL SPHERE

Every Christian, layman included, should be ready to forsake both land and home itself should the need ever arise. Should his possessions ever become an occasion of sin, he would be obliged to do so. Sometimes he abandons all in a spirit of sacrifice before a higher good. But in neither case does he depreciate these goods. Christian virginity, for example, is not a censure of the holiness of marriage.[22]

But such considerations only reveal the negative aspect of profane values. The positive side is more important. In offering his goods for a religious and moral use, the adult Christian does not diminish their worth, instead he assures them of a new consecration: the art which complements an altar loses none of its native perfection because of its surroundings. Nothing is too beautiful for the service of God. In this field the Saints showed themselves the greatest humanists.

But more is required. In imposing on us the duty to work the Creator commands a respect for work. Laziness does not honour Him. When man has received the commission to dominate the earth, he must not turn it into a museum. It must be a field of labour.

The world was not created as a static perfection but as a dynamic force. Creation is not finished; it develops and man has a role to play in the developing. For him life on earth is a work day. When he completes it, the world, especially the world of men, should have arrived at a level high enough to reflect the splendour of creation and its Creator with greater glory.

Does every temporal advancement, then, signify by its very existence an advancement for God's Kingdom? Some think so, but Biblical revelation hardly supports this opinion. In fact, the Bible maintains a certain dualism between the two orders and presents salvation as something realized freely from above and contrary to the general flow of things. Material progress can bring about a false sense of well-being in the life of the spirit just as a catastrophe can often provoke a spiritual renewal. The possibility of these accidental reversals must be recognized. A universal and upward evolution in the sciences and philosophy has yet to be proved. Evolution will always have difficulty aligning itself with theology which has solid traditional reasons for being less optimistic. The very least we can do is to be on our guard against an over eager and compromising apologetics.[23]

And yet, it is not the Church that will regret an increase of temporal well-being. She is convinced that such an advance accords with the designs of Providence. She encourages the desire for creative work and explicitly condemns selfish abstention. The less endowed have no right to bury their sole talent.

This is true above all for the diffusion of spiritual values. Each one is to promote the Kingdom of God according to his means. Noble sentiments that remain unrealized profane the truth. Thus Saint John says: 'If a man boasts of loving God, while he hates his own brother, he is a liar. He has seen his brother, and has no love for him; what love can he have for the God he has never seen?' (I Jo., IV, 20). If God is love and if He bids us share His own Life, we have the duty to follow His lead and so to propagate that Life.

There exists in this domain an attitude which is especially distressing because it is basically dishonest. Its device is to use religious pretexts to condone crying social injustices; to dismiss the poor and oppressed by overwhelming them with exhortations to virtue. Such an attitude drives the miserable to blasphemy; there will be more mercy for the rebel and the wretched than for the sanctimonious, smooth-tongued Pharisee. Here even the violent language of a Mounier and his fiery school pales before the cutting invective that Christ addressed to the whited sepulchres and merchants of the temple.

There is no sincere faith that does not manifest itself in works. In this regard the layman has an added responsibility. The expression of his testimony will be most often in the concrete language of social justice and charity inspired by faith, an irrefutable proof that Christianity does not live by cowardice and exploitation. The progress of democracy carries with it a greater possibility to share more universally this world's ever-increasing goods.[24] A growing abundance of resources paralleled by a growing number of hungry mouths—a strange coincidence! Certainly it is time for a radical revision of method.

The Christian does not look adversely on the betterment of the working classes. To resign himself to it is not enough: he must personally contribute to it so that his joy be genuine. If he fails to contribute, it is useless even to talk of a 'social sense.' All else is mere compromise and bargaining, an object of justified contempt.

The lay Catholic is the one to assume the task of constructing the temporal city attached, in its way, to the city of God. To proclaim that Catholics are the best citizens is useless; they must prove it by acts. They refuse all idolatrous worship of the State but they do not refuse to serve. This is specifically lay territory; it is theirs to be engaged here wholeheartedly and to make the Gospel spirit felt. It is a mission of capital importance: the very existence of western Christianity depends upon it. Thanks to her faithful, the Church will exercise 'not a power but a very real *action* on the temporal.'[25]

When the new and youthful spirit of the barbarians submerged the Roman civilization, Augustine wrote his masterpiece, *De Civitate Dei*. He bemoans the distressing decline of the West, but he does not throw up his hands in despair. He sees the City of God rising. Built on love, it opposes the City of the Evil One built on egoism. Yet he does not indiscriminately identify the first with the Church or the second with the State. The lines cross one another and the frontiers shift.[26] Civil institutions, too, must respect justice and charity. Judaism claims theocracy as the answer, the pagan world naturalism. We however, may treat the profane order with neither the spirituality of the first, nor the lack of spirituality of the second. With His declaration on the rights of God and Caesar, the Lord of the New Testament put an end to theocracy and likewise He firmly condemned the autocracy which ignores the rights of God.

Once in our generation did men dream of a new Middle Ages. Even today, some experience a nostalgia for the days of Christendom. To weep for past grandeurs is always futile. The Holy Roman and Germanic Empire had its drawbacks and the prince-protectors of the Church by the Grace of God, did not forego opportunities to exploit her. In our own day, we consider ourselves blessed if governments do not persecute religion. Free citizens must now aid and take charge of the office which Catholic sovereigns can no longer fulfil. Unfortunately, the framework of modern life forms more an obstacle than a support to moral progress; but that is another reason for purifying our environment through new means better adapted to our democratic views. But no citizen can use his emancipation as a pretext for renouncing his Christian vocation; the sin of omission is more serious today than ever before.[27]

In completing his new task, the mature layman should carefully avoid two pitfalls: confusion between the profane order and the sacred one, and religious excess.

Firstly, *confusion.* In professional as well as political life, the Catholic cannot disregard his responsibilities. Nor should he use his Catholicity as a shield or a means to propagate his partisan views. In problems of the economic and social order, the Church does not provide ready-made solutions. She sets out the general principles of moral and religious action and furnishes public servants with a vitalising generosity, leaving to profane science and adept statesmanship the task of elaborating particular formulas. Neither union leaders nor company officials enjoy Pontifical infallibility, and only a totalitarian régime would claim it. We must stop using encyclicals to support our private interests and to confound those of our opponents.

The second danger is *religious excess.* In the presence of a neutral state, we often think we must hallow every profane activity with religious declaration. Such an exaggeration misses the mark. Every consecration presupposes and respects the internal worth of the means used. No Church blessing can make up for technical deficiencies. Should parish school teaching be inadequate, it can never be compensated for by an increase in religious instruction. Such a procedure would be more than useless: it would be dishonest. The Catholic seal of approval on a dubious enterprise will only make Catholicism repulsive.

Likewise, if everything became sacred, soon there would be no more sanctity! The boundaries between the religious and the profane would disappear. The 'sacred' by its very nature will always be 'set apart,' though still in contact with daily life. If we wish to avoid levelling all to the lowest term then we must keep the distinction between the two. The Middle Ages closed with such a familiar attitude toward sacred things that it bordered on practical sacrilege.[28] The sense of religious respect was considerably enfeebled. The manner in which the devout of the XVth century treated their heavenly patrons and even the Blessed Virgin is not ingenuous but perfunctory; generally it is tinged with bad taste and frequently with cynicism.

The conclusion is inescapable: if the laity wishes to carry out its mission honourably, it must have a more profound religious formation. The promotion of the laity is natural and sound, but the laity must be strong enough to accept the charge. In any case, such promotion cannot be rejected on a plea of possible future blunders. The increased welfare of the workers does not insure perfectly against all waste and extravagance; but does that mean that the worker's state of misery was preferable? The laity must be given the opportunity of acquiring a greater moral formation. Conscious of its vocation, it will have a weightier responsibility; yet fidelity to the temporal city and to the Church of Christ will guarantee them an increase in generosity.

---

1 Cardinal SUHARD, *The Meaning of God*, Lenten Pastoral, 1948. Eng. Trans., New York, 1949, pp. 7-9.

2 E. SCHWARZBAUER, *Der Laie in der Kirche*, in *Theol. Prakt. Quartalschrift*, 97, 1949, pp. 28-46 and 107-133. The author of this interesting article speaks of (pp. 38ff) 'seinsmässige Verpflichtung.'

3 This is the thesis of M. J. MONTUCLARD in *Les Evénements et la Foi*, (Jeunesse de l'Eglise), Paris, 1951. The Holy Office has condemned this publication by a decree of March 16, 1953. cf. the warnings given by the French Episcopate, published previously, Doc. Cath., 1952, col. 137 and 1497. The author has in view certain industrialized and agricultural regions of France. However, we must not exaggerate the matter, and especially not erect it into a principle. In other regions or countries, vast groups, even though labelled as socialist or communist, are not composed of men who have lost all belief. What is especially lacking in the troubling pages of this book is, on the one hand, a clear view of the distinction of planes, and on the other, the realism of 'supernatural entities' which are viewed as if they were illusions. In principle, Christianity and Communism never meet as rival social systems, any more than 'man' and 'faith' are values of the same class. It is therefore very sad to see Christians of value return to pre-gospel times, to the times of John the Baptist, and busy themselves with the liberation of the working class before giving any thought to conversion. Furthermore, John the Baptist preached penance and not social betterment. The message of Christ and of God cannot, even provisionally, be withdrawn from the working class.

4 This does not mean that they are no longer to occupy themselves with works of social justice and charity, schools, etc., as we shall say explicitly further on.

5 Cf. Y. CONGAR, *Qu'est-ce qu'un laïc?*, in *Vie Spirituelle*, Suppl. n.15, 1950, pp. 389 ff. Cf. *Jalons*, pp. 30ff.

6 Cf. for example: JACQUES MARITAIN, *True Humanism*, London, 5th. edition, 1950.
  E. MASURE, *L'Humanisme Chrétien*, Paris, 1937.
  CHRISTOPHER DAWSON, *Progress and Religion. An Historical Inquiry*, London, 1945.
  CHARLES MOELLER, *Humanisme et Sainteté. Témoignage de la littérature occidentale*, Paris, Tournai, 1946.
  J. MOUROUX, *The Meaning of Man*, Sheed & Ward.
  CARDINAL SUHARD, *Growth or Decline. The Church Today*: Trans. J. A. CORBETT, Montreal, 1948.
  G. THILS, *Théologie des réalités terrestres I. Préludes II. Théologie de l'histoire*, Paris, 1946, 1949. Id., *Théologie et réalité sociale*, Paris, Tournai, 1952.
  A. CHAVASSE, *Eglise et Apostolat* (Eglise Vivante), Paris, 1953, pp. 121 ff.; pp. 162 ff.
  FR. HERMANS, *Histoire doctrinale de l'Humanisme Chrétien*, 4 vol., Paris, Tournai, 1948.
  Y. CONGAR, *Efficacité temporelle et message évangélique*, in the *Revue Nouvelle*, 17, 1953, pp. 32-49.

7 For the position of the Orthodox, read the remarkable essay by N. BERDIAJEV, *Von der Würde des Christentums und der Unwürde der Christen*, Lucerne, 1936. For neo-

protestantism see the works of Karl Barth and of Em. Brunner. Of the latter especially: *Der Mensch im Widerspruch*, Zurich, 3rd ed., 1941. L. Malevez, *L'Anthropologie chrétienne de Karl Barth*, in *Rech. Sc. Rel.*, 38, 1951, pp. 37-81.

[8] Cf. H. Sasse, art *Kosmos*, in the *Theol. Wörterbuch* of G. Kittel, 3rd. vol., Stuttgart, 1938, pp. 882-896. F. M. Braun, O.P., *Le 'monde' bon et mauvais dans l'Evangile johannique*, in *Vie Spirituelle*, 88, 1953, pp. 580-598.

[9] L. Wright, *The Apostolic Role of the University Graduate*, in *Downside Review*, 1952-1953, p. 51, gives the example of a Christian choosing the medical career in order to give good Catholic example, or to make Catholic moral principles prevail; he could also think of healing the sick and advancing medical science. This is what the scholastics mean when they speak of 'finis operis', and of 'finis operantis.' In this connection, cf. R. Spiazzi, *o.c.*, *Missione dei Laici*, pp. 352 ff.

[10] cf. J. Mouroux, *o.c.*, *The Meaning of Man*, pp. 9 ff.

[11] J. Maritain, *o.c.*, *True Humanism*, Chp. IV. Consequently it seems preferable not to oppose the temporal and the spiritual as 'the order of the creation' and 'the order of the Redemption', since this would result in two distinct categories at the best, merely juxtaposed. Creation itself is redeemed and given a superior end without losing anything of its proper consistency. It is the material object which differentiates the profane from the sacred.

[12] In this regard, reread the remarkable discourse of Pius XII. on *The Joy of Work*, of Jan. 7, 1946, *Doc. Cath.*, 43, 1946, col. 136 ff. Concerning the profound meaning of our technical civilization, see the book of X. van Hornstein and F. Dessauer, *Seele im Bannkreis der Technik*, Olten, 1949. This book is the result of the collaboration of a priest, professor of moral theology, and a lay technical engineer. Cf. P. Pavan, *Apostolato dei Laici nel mondo moderno*, Rome, 1954.

[13] Father Kolbe, a Conventual, an example of the modern saint, died a martyr in the camp of Auschwitz. In pre-war Poland he had launched a splendidly equipped printing house for the service of his Marian publications. See his blessing of *Brother Motor* in the article by M. Winowska, *Le Fou de Notre-Dame*, in *Vie Spirituelle*, 79, 1948, pp. 241 ff.

[14] Pius XII. to the Congress of the Lay Apostolate, while recognizing the merits of medieval Christianity, does not express nostalgia for it. See the *Acts*, I, pp. 44-45; also N.C.W.C. trans., nos. 4-10; esp. n. 8. Nevertheless, the Church would not be able to renounce her mandate to give imperative direction to consciences, as Henri de Lubac well shows, *o.c.*, *Méditation sur l'Eglise*, pp. 152 ff.

[15] cf. A. Dondeyne, *La Physionomie spirituelle du chrétien de demain*, in *L'Homme nouveau*, pp. 266 ff.

[16] cf. J. Mouroux, *o.c.*, *The Meaning of Man*, p. 7 ff.

[17] See for example, *Matthew*, X, 37-39 and XVI, 24-25; *Luke* XIV, 26-27, 33, etc.

[18] Concerning the forms of asceticism adapted to our epoch, see the excellent collection *L'Ascèse Chrétienne et l'homme contemporain* (Cahiers de la Vie Spirituelle), Paris, 1951.

[19] J. H. Newman, *The Idea of a University*, I, Conf. 8, n. 10 Ed. Longmans, London, 1935, pp. 208-211.

[20] G. Marcel, *Etre et avoir*, Paris, 1935.

[21] St. John of the Cross, *Ascent of Mount Carmel*. Trans. E. A. Peers, 4th ed., London, 1953. Vol. I, pp. 82-88, esp. p. 86 and 88.

[22] Cf. J. -M. Perrin, O.P., *La Virginité* (Cahiers de la Vie Spirituelle) Paris, 1952.

[23] For the 'optimist' outlook, with varying nuances, cf. L. Malevez, *La Philosophie Chrétienne du Progrès*, in the *Nouvelle Revue Theol.* 64, 1937, pp. 377-385. E. Rideau, *Consécration. Le Christianisme et l'activité humaine*, Paris, 1945. D. Dubarle, *Optimisme devant le monde*, Paris, 1949.

The extreme position is held by Father Teilhard de Chardin. His outstanding worth as a paleontologist is incontestable. But his extremely brilliant accounts of spiritualizing evolution make us ill at ease. Is it biology, philosophy, or theology? It seems to be all three at once, and we no longer succeed in distinguishing the levels. Yet the distinction of domains and of methods is of capital importance for true progress of thought.

For a serious critique, severe yet serene, refer to L. Cognet, *Le Père Teilhard de*

Chardin et la pensée contemporaine, Paris, 1952. For the general question of the influence of Christianity on the profane world, it would be useful to consult the *Documentos* of the *Conversaciones Catolicas Internacionales* of San Sebastian, 1952, n. 11-12: *La Eficacia Temporal del Cristianismo.*

24 Cf. A. DONDEYNE, *o.c.*, *Le Chrétien de demain*, p. 260.

25 Y. CONGAR, *Les Conditions théologiques d'un pluralisme*, in *Tolérance et Communauté Humaine* (Cahiers de l'Actualité Religieuse), Paris, Tournai, 1952, p. 197.

26 Cf. G. THILS, *o.c.*, *Théologie de l'Histoire*, pp. 38-39.

27 A. DONDEYNE, *Tolérance et collaboration comme données philosophiques assumées par la foi* in *Tolérance et Communauté Humaine*, p. 120.

28 J. HUIZINGA, *Le Déclin du Moyen âge*, Trad. J. Bastin (Bibl. Hist.), Paris, 1948, Chap. 14: *Emotions et phantasmes religieux*, pp. 231 ff.

CHAPTER IV

THE LAITY AND THE
POWER OF ORDERS

WHEN confronted with priestly authority, the layman who is alive to his function in the Church wonders whether or not he has sufficient liberty of action. General statements about principles help little if in practice he is completely restricted. New awakening, advancement, eminent dignity—all very fine; but besides these the layman needs the liberty to employ them.

Hierarchical authority, it is true, binds us more closely than civil authority. It commands the means of salvation which have a direct influence on the believer's conscience. The same authority, too, prescribes what revealed truths we must believe, it rules our conduct and fixes its fundamental framework once and for all so that we cannot change it. The State has less influence upon us: it is not concerned with the eternal, it does not dictate our beliefs, we can direct its progress and even modify its constitution. And so it seems that our liberty, quite at home in the civic sphere, is manifestly circumscribed in the sanctuary.

In reality, the Church is not a man-made work but rather a divine institution, a 'revelation.' We cannot change it to suit our fancy; we accept it. And still the New Testament is the era of liberation; Christ has lifted the chafing yoke of the Old Law from our shoulders.

Now we are faced with a paradox which becomes more intelligible when we realize that liberty is not synonymous with wholesale lack of direction. Liberty is not a position of indifference from which a person can turn—whenever he will—toward the good or the bad. On the contrary, it supposes a firm attachment to the end, to the good to be attained. Freedom otherwise would not be vigorous but impotent, would not constitute self-possession but dissolution, would not lay the foundations of morality but would undermine them. Liberty is not synonymous with anarchy but with a deliberate and spontaneous collaboration which seeks to realize the supreme ideal. It is the way in which man turns towards the goal of his existence, and procures its realization.[1]

The hierarchy does not want to shackle this vital potential but to develop it. The triple power of sanctifying, teaching, and governing

THE LAITY AND THE POWER OF ORDERS

constantly calls upon our free, active response and calls upon it in a measure far greater than we imagine. The hierarchy speaks to subordinates who also are living members. It must rather struggle to enlist them in its apostolic effort than to obtain their submission to its prescriptions. Furthermore, the first is a form of obedience more urgent and demanding than the second, since it involves the commitment of the whole person. The Church is not a ground school for slaves but a community of free and disciplined chevaliers.

The Church's triple power, then, constitutes a triple mode of service where leaders and members meet to bring about the work of salvation. It is a triple collaboration in the sacramental life, the life of Faith, and the moral life, in which Christ apportions the work and demands that some should obey others. In this arrangement, however, there is no place for those merely content with commanding, nor for those content with following the crowd. Those in authority are subject to the Supreme Leader, and subordinates are no less His co-operators.

The object of the following chapters will be the explanation of this thesis. We begin with the most characteristic function of the Church, its power of orders or sanctification.

THE UNIVERSAL PRIESTHOOD OF THE FAITHFUL

Under the Old Law, kings and priests were anointed to signify their consecration and dedication to God in a special way. The entire Chosen People share in that dignity. 'Listen, then, to my voice, and keep your covenant with me; and I, to whom all the earth belongs, will single you out among its peoples to be my own. You shall serve me as a Kingdom of priests, as a consecrated nation.' (Exod., XIX, 5-6).

The Church of Christ has received this heritage of the Hebrew people and the temple of Jerusalem is spiritualized in the new community.[2] It will be, says Saint Peter, 'a holy priesthood offering spiritual sacrifices' (I Pet., II, 5), and more explicitly: 'you are a chosen race, a royal priesthood, a consecrated nation, a people God has purchased.' (Ib., II, 9).

'He has proved his love for us,' says St. John, 'by washing us clean from our sins in his own blood, and made us a royal race of priests, to serve God, his Father.' (Apoc., I, 5-6). 'Blessed and holy is his lot who has a share in this first resurrection; over such the second death has no power, they will be priests of God, priests of Christ; all those thousand years they will reign with him.' (Ib., XX, 6).

This is why Saint Paul enjoins us to 'offer up your bodies as

a living sacrifice, consecrated to God and worthy of his acceptance.'
(Rom., XII, 1). In all these citations the idea of consecration is
immersed in a context of royal liberty.

Under the Old Alliance, this universal vocation did not suppress
the proper duties of the priesthood of which it was the fruit and crown.
The same is true of the New Testament; the priesthood of the faithful
subtracts nothing from the power confided to some by the imposition
of hands. Without their ministry, there would be no general
sanctification. Not every one is called on to direct the liturgy, yet
each baptised person spiritually shares in it, and so partakes of its fruits.

Within the bosom of the Church, the laity before God enjoys
a royal and priestly privilege. In the past some have sadly mis-
interpreted this truth, and more than one heretic has used it to restrict
or suppress the hierarchical priesthood. Whenever this happens,
the Church shifts her emphasis to the contested point and the doctrine
of the universal vocation is relegated to the background. And so
error causes unfortunate results in both directions. Meanwhile, the
principle remains intact, and with a renewal of ecclesiastical vitality
attention is re-directed to the rightful nobility of the community.

The Encyclical *Mediator Dei*, a remarkable document, gives a
lucid and balanced exposition of this doctrine.[3] It speaks first of all
of the functional priesthood which is possessed in its fulness by the
Saviour alone. Christ is priest, but He is priest for us. He is offering
too, but offering for us since He is our Mediator. It is not we who have
delegated Him: God has made Him our Head that He might intercede
for us. Having entered into the eternal tabernacle, He carries out
His priestly office through the intermediary of His consecrated
ministers. Only they can do at Mass what He did at the Last Supper.
By their consecrating words he makes Himself present as victim on
the altar. Power is given them not because they represent the people
but because they take the place of Christ. As ministers inferior to
Christ yet superior to the people, they are granted entry to the
innermost sanctuary.

We should not forget, writes Cardinal Suhard, that every priest
is a gift of God to the community. The community should receive
this gift with deep thanks. When, for example, the inhabitants of
the famous Ile de Sein, described by Queffelec, were abandoned by
their pastor, they were unable to confer the sacramental power—
since they did not possess it—on Thomas, the sacristan; if he is to
say Mass for them, he must be ordained by his bishop.[4]

Christ is the unique Mediator. As subordinate mediators, as
'ministers,' priests are in His service. This priesthood cannot be
imparted to the community; the community cannot be its own
mediator.

However, the community must still participate in the Eucharistic worship by 'offering' itself and by allowing itself 'to be offered.' This must be clearly understood lest we compromise the doctrine of the unique Redemption. 'In assisting at Mass,' writes Dom Capelle, 'the primary object is not to give oneself to God; it is to offer Christ and receive from Him *His* redemption.'[5] What can we add to His gift since all comes from His hands? We would do well, then, in teaching our children catechism, not to push too far the comparison of the small hosts which 'add' to the large one.

It is for us to adhere to Christ in His immolation, to submit our will and whole being in Christ to the Father. If we fail to do so we belie for our part the action of Christ. Only through Him can we, as members of His body, give to the Father the glory due to Him. Our offering consists solely and totally in this: the admission that of ourselves we have nothing to offer that does not already belong to Him.

Yet we still 'offer.' The liturgy of today puts the word in the plural: *per quem tibi offerimus*. Going further, we should immolate ourselves as victims, offering our bodies, says St. Paul, as an agreeable host (Rom., XII, 1). This we do through Christ, the one spotless Lamb, and through His priest who truly represents us and speaks for us. 'At the Sacrament of the altar,' says St. Augustine, 'we see the Church learning to offer herself in That which she offers; that is why the people answer: Amen!'[6] 'Nor should Christians forget,' says Pius XII, 'to offer themselves, their cares, their sorrows, their distress and their necessities in union with their divine Saviour upon the cross.'[7]

Here the priest is totally united to the laity. What a sorry spectacle to see the laity assisting at Mass as at a mere spectacle. Failing to grasp the significance of the sacred rites, they are ignorant of the meaning of prayer and offering, no longer are they 'royal' or 'priestly.' They do not live the universal priesthood because they do not understand the functional priesthood.

Sacrifice and Sacraments are willed and instituted by God. Taking their source from Him, they attain their end through the High Priest and His ministers. The principal motion here is a descending one, from God to men. Our response in prayers of adoration, thanks and praise—what St. Augustine calls 'the interior sacrifice of the holy society'—reascends from man to God.

Yet we should not take this description too literally. In their participation in the sacrifice and reception of Sacraments the laity are not purely passive. To submit is not the same as to accept; submission is a partial refusal. At least by his 'intention' the layman ought to enter into the faith of the mystery which has been effected by Christ and is now celebrated in the Church's worship. Without this, even sacramental validity would be wanting. But, for a fruitful reception, much more is needed. And so the importance of what theologians call 'dispositions': an active faith, contrition, and love, which open the soul to the divine gift. According to St. Thomas the baptismal character renders the Christian a partaker in the priesthood of Christ and assures him genuine power, the power of entering into the Church's worship to receive the Sacraments and, in Marriage, to administer the Sacrament.

Inversely, in praying, the believer is not purely active. Prayer is, first of all, a grace, the faithful response to the goodness received from God. To pray is itself to receive, and the hope of receiving more. The Sacrament of Faith and the prayer of Faith are the arms of God by which He draws the creature to Him to achieve inseparable union.

Is this mystery inaccessible to the laity? No, it is no more inaccessible to them than to priests. Duties and function vary, but the mystery is one. Thank God, lay people today are showing a greater desire to partake in that priesthood and are manifesting a deeper 'understanding' of it. No longer do they stop at the Court of the Gentiles. The veil hiding the sanctuary has been removed, and the laity too claim their share in the liturgy.

THE LITURGICAL MOVEMENT

The name of St. Pius X is invariably linked to this movement. Thanks especially to his Eucharistic decrees, his religious influence will astonish future historians. The movement has brought about a return to the sources, a fact of the utmost importance. It does not, however, represent the past, as might an antique collector, but seeks to restore the ancient in all its vigorous youth. To mould an amorphous mass into a community of persons, to rescue piety from a certain unhealthy self-centredness by launching it into full ecclesiastical life: such are the movement's goals.

Pointless retreats to outmoded practices have driven some zealous advocates to the absurd, to the excess of ritualism, a complete and gross betrayal of the liturgical spirit. It is not enough to give every layman a missal or to put a new emphasis on Gregorian chant in order to revive dead parishes. The spiritual revival is not obtained as soon as a pastor celebrates Mass facing his people or administers Baptism in the vernacular. The problem is infinitely more serious.

In the Orient the participation of the faithful in the mysteries of worship has always remained more alive. Modern Anglicanism and even continental Protestantism is showing liturgical aspirations, to such an extent that firmly entrenched die-hards are decrying the development of neo-papism. The liturgy glorifies God through Christ in a totally disinterested and public service: it touches the summit of religious life. Msgr. Romano Guardini has written some extremely valuable pages about 'the game' of the sacred rites. [8]

Of heavenly origin the liturgy introduces its participants to supra-terrestrial realities. A Benedictine High Mass or the psalms sung by a monastic choir with all the restrained majesty of the Roman rite is, at least for us, of a far greater intensity than the Byzantine splendour. The *Opus Dei* of the monks is not so much a task performed in praise of the Lord as it is the very work of God for the salvation of the world at a privileged moment in time.

The community sense is expressed by the liturgical plural. The *Confiteor* is, of course, in the singular: I cannot burden others with my sins; but the absolution before Communion is given in the plural. The *Credo* is a profession of faith which commits me personally. But to receive blessings, we extend our hands together in supplication. We pray, not next to each other, but together, an entirely different thing. The piety of my neighbour is not merely edifying for me; we form one, sole body of prayer and not a sum total of individual needs. Christ, our Intercessor, celebrant and leader, presents to the Father one harmonious voice of adoration, one throng of supplications, one offering of praise and thanks. And because of His devoted regard for all our poor requests He is heard. The one Spirit unites us in one organism of pardoned love.

Without the doctrine of the Mystical Body the prayer of public worship is incomprehensible. This great mystery strikes the balance between personal desire and community aspiration. The unity of the ecclesiastical conscience purifies my mediocre and petty preoccupations. As a member of the holy nation I forget my own narrowness. When the people of God are struggling to save immortal souls, I blush to think of my selfish little schemes. In common we ask for our daily bread and the remission of our collective debt, but only after we have asked for the coming of the Kingdom. For the lay person there is no school of formation stronger and surer than the liturgy.

The ritual of worship transcends the fleetingness of time; it holds the reflection of the divine majesty and the perpetuity of the work of Christ. Yet it is not rigid to the point of immobility; it adapts itself to history's situations and to the new forms of expression produced by the world's evolution. It would be difficult to define precisely the boundary between official liturgy and the popular devotions that gravitate about it. What today is popular and not strictly liturgical may tomorrow receive official approbation. Thus it is that the new Paschal Vigil has incorporated the renewing of Baptismal vows, and has done so in the people's own language.

This, of course, brings us to the keen dispute concerning the Church's use of Latin. How can lay people be interested in the unfolding of a worship celebrated in a dead language, inaccessible to most of them?

Before passing judgment, we ought to examine calmly the various elements of the problem. We must bear in mind the structure which has been built up over the centuries, especially, the meaning of the Mass and its ceremonies. [9]

In Protestantism where the entire ritual centres on the faith-producing Word, it is absolutely necessary that this Word be understood by its listeners. If it were not understood, instead of serving as an intermediary, it would become an obstacle. Thus we find in the reformed worship, a determined effort to grasp word and syllable. For the same reason the Protestant worship objects to the language of gestures, a language necessarily less clear. Objects and sacred signs suggest to them rather the presence of magical powers. One wonders whether the reformed programme of worship retains a pure enough notion of the transcendence of the divine and of the ineffability of grace. The majesty of God can be approached only in a cloud. No one denies that God is Light, but, as St. Paul says, a light inaccessible to mortal eyes. Human words will never be capable of expressing the mystery. At best, they can suggest an analogy and indicate a path. There will always be a time when silence is more eloquent than long discourse. The mind must bow down humbly before a Subject which it can never master.

In the Mass the Catholic sees something more than an instruction. Assuredly it is a practical instruction, but it is more an almost silent adoration of the Most High. Worship is commanded by God, not man. Likewise, it is from on high that it should be first explained; it starts from God. Not before a human public does the celebrant advance, but before the face of the Almighty. Moreover, he can celebrate with only a server present.

The mysterious *aura* surrounding the climactic moment of consecration is instinct with the transcendence of the holy action wrought by Christ over the offering, His own Body.

Through the ministry of the Church, He renews His immolation sacramentally. More than a remembrance, the Mass is a true 'action,' liturgical celebration, a real and efficacious presence of the Body and Blood of Christ, surrendered and sacrificed in high adoration to the Father in order to reconcile men with Him.

Such an action is far more important than the doctrinal explanations and pious exhortations that may surround it. When the High Priest (Heb., IX, 14), enters through the Spirit into God's presence, offering His blood in atonement, man can only kneel in silence.

Obviously in the liturgy there is a preparatory part called 'the Mass of the catechumens;' it includes the lessons and homilies. Throughout this part of the Mass the priest turns toward the people to teach them, and he must, or should, speak in the language of the people. The sermon has nearly always conformed to this need. The epistle and Gospel, too, should be placed within the grasp of the congregation, either through the solemn chant, or, at least, through a reading. This adaptation, not only desirable but also necessary, is the first we expect from any true liturgical renewal.

In France and Germany and in some other countries, this has already been realised in the Sacramental rites, though usually with the exception of the Sacramental 'form' properly so-called. The prayers and rites of Baptism and Matrimony are extremely rich and singularly effective in preparing the faithful to receive more ardently the grace of the Sacrament. For those present, this will frequently prove a radiant discovery. In some regions occasions to bring to the sick and their loved ones the consoling beauty of the Church's words in Extreme Unction and her spiritual help for those in agony are all too rare. The blessing of mothers and their new-born infants at the time of their Churching, all the other ceremonies that mark the great moments of life and death, when rendered in measured and clear language, will impress everyone, even the simplest, whom we should serve first of all.

So, too, there is a growing desire to put an authorized translation of the breviary into the hands of nuns.

It is obvious that progressives are impatient and discontented with these meagre concessions won from the traditionalists. Without any kind of authorization, some have gone even to the point of celebrating Mass in French or German, sometimes with a disconcerting coolness. Their utilitarianism, like their psychology of the common man, is short-sighted. In concentration camps and barracks for eastern refugees, the Mass, stripped of all ceremony, loses nothing of its intensity or spiritual depth. Rather, the converse is true. Can the same be said when, under the pretext of bourgeois culture, all external ceremony and 'distinction' (in the etymological and in the modern sense of the word) is violently rejected? Do we realise the dignity of our actions, and do we pass it on to those who scarcely know the meaning of Faith? A lesson in fundamentals is more urgent than a show of solidarity. Respect is a value that our age takes all too lightly and as a result working-classes themselves suffer.

The sacrificial sections of the Mass are not destined for our instruction. This does not, however, mean that the faithful may renounce all effort to understand; quite the contrary. But even so, they need not necessarily catch every word pronounced by the priest. If they are aware of the central event taking place, they can unite themselves both to the visible action of the celebrant and to that of the invisible High Priest. Following the Host and the Chalice with their eyes, their hearts will silently adore and unite them to the immolated Christ.

Thus the two aspects, 'oneness' with the community and the 'distance' of the mystery, are reconciled. The Eastern liturgy reaches the same reconciliation by another way. There the consecration takes place behind the closed iconostasis; the sacred words, however, are chanted aloud so that the community can unite themselves to the sacrifice. In the West we see without hearing. Thus the nearness and the separation are connected and act upon one another. The sacrificial act is not in fact simply the act of the people; it is the supreme act of adoration of the Saviour Himself.

As long as the present system remains in force, translations and commentaries (especially dialogue Masses and group singing) will greatly help to prevent any disunion between the priest and faithful. The supplications of the *Kyrie*, the praises of the *Gloria*, the pride of the just and faithful shining through the *Credo*, though in Latin, are not incomprehensible to our parishioners, however little their instruction. The *Sanctus*, too, will be for them the solemn entry into the sanctuary, and the *Agnus Dei* will bring them together, purified, to the common table. From the *Preface* to the *Pater*, the peaceful meditation of the people should not be disturbed by the noise of ushers making the collection; together with candle lighters they are often more disturbing than the sombre Latin.

Nor is the low Mass a nonsense. The faithful's missals now assure a contact. Are we conscious of the fact that never before in history has the richness of the liturgical prayers been so open to everybody? Converts from Protestantism have said more than once that they live the non-sung Mass with a particular intensity. The liturgical movement has shortened the distance between the nave and apse both in architecture and in religious psychology.

THE FAMILY SANCTUARY

It is significant that in the Western liturgy the vernacular has always been used for the marriage ceremony. This is the only Sacrament whose ordinary ministers are lay people. Only in case of necessity do they administer Baptism. The spouses in the presence of the priest, the Church's authorized witness, posit by their mutual consent the sign that confers the Sacramental grace.

The priest's blessing only ratifies and consecrates their reciprocal gift which symbolizes the union of Christ and His Church. Like this greater union, it too finds its most profound sense in the fecundity of personal and creative love.[10] Saint Augustine says Christian parents have a mission toward their children which is ecclesiastic or, as he says, 'episcopal.'[11] The Father, says St. Thomas, is the principle of generation, being and education;[12] he continues the work of creation. As principle of sanctity and continuer of the Redemption His role is irreplaceable. No school, no youth organization can ever completely replace the family surroundings as *the* means for the development of a religious sense.

In Catholic Action circles and elsewhere the *mystique* of marriage has evoked an extremely abundant literature. Theologians have examined it closely and undoubtedly they can shed some light on the subject.[13] Only lay people, however, can give direct witness of a high conjugal spirituality.[14] Nor should they hesitate, at the appropriate time, to speak of conjugal *asceticism*, an extremely rare title in Catholic book shops. For, without a generous and enlightened asceticism, any mystical life is bound to be only transitory.

It has been said that Marriage is the vocation of those who have no vocation.[15] But, in Christianity, can we speak of the vocation of Marriage? This word vocation has assumed a distinctive religious meaning. We hardly ever speak of a cobbler's vocation or of the vocation of a government clerk. Yet the vocation of an educator or doctor never fails to arouse enthusiasm in idealistic youth. These careers demand devoted service to living people, and so they have a semi-sacred character about them, a sort of quasi-religious appeal. A vocation is a treasure to be carefully cultivated. If this idea can be maintained with regard to Marriage, it will help to preserve the union from the chilling blasts of a hedonistic world.

In the Bible a vocation comes from God. It separates the elect, such as Abraham the patriarch, from a corrupt environment sealed with the sign of wickedness. For St. Paul Christians especially are 'the chosen saints.' The basic and common vocation is entrance into Christianity. Christ calls His own, even from among the Gentiles. Once within the sphere of sanctity they must shrink from all impurity but not by cutting themselves off from their fellows. For, in the Christian assembly they will participate in intimate communion with their Head and with all the members.[16]

If we want, therefore, to keep the original Biblical significance of the word 'vocation' we must speak of a 'vocation to *Christian* marriage,' thus transcending the viewpoint of merely natural law to enter into the perspective of Saint Paul. For him marriage between baptized spouses pertains fully to the mystery of salvation by which God became man to communicate His Life to us in Jesus Christ, the Saviour, Head, and Spouse of the Church. The conjugal union is invigorated by the reflected light of the sublime mystery that unites Christ to His Church. From that union proceeds the sanctity of marriage. 'For it is necessary,' says Péguy, 'that Christianity continue,' and that the Mystical Body attain its perfect stature with the passing of the centuries.

The moral applications the Apostle deduces from this doctrine are well known. He insists not only on the hierarchical arrangement which subjects wife to husband, but far more on the communicative and redemptive charity which assures their interior life of union. The 'vocation' is crystallized precisely in the love of one partner for the other, in the complete and selfless devotion necessary to ensure the partner's happiness. Such a love radiates the diffusive charity of God. Charity does not seek self-gain (I Cor., XIII, 5), it is not turned in upon itself. Charity in marriage does not breed that dual egoism which makes of each partner a degrading instrument of pleasure. It desires the grandeur, the happiness and the joyous fecundity of each.

Christian marriage unquestionably forms a smaller community, distinct but in no way hermetically sealed or totally cut off from the whole society of the Church. The family will not shut itself off from this Holy Nation's beneficent influence and it will certainly not refuse to play its part. Only under such conditions can it be something great. Wherever the apostolic ideal of a rejuvenated Catholicism has passed, we see family groups forming and seeking mutual aid towards spiritual growth, a growth more easily nurtured in common.[17] It has been said that these homes are reanimating the parishes and, even more, are inaugurating a revival among the clergy and among all specialized vocations.

If, indeed, all men are called to join the people of God, if there is *a vocation to the Church*, there are also particular choices (*vocations within the Church*) which should assure the continuation of the highest spiritual functions and values, sources of the Mystical Body's vital functions. There is not one, but two Sacraments whose social purpose is particularly essential: Marriage and Holy Orders.[18] To the latter, not because of the Sacramental functions connected with it, but because of its office of prayer and its total gift to God, we can join the different forms of the religious life.

Still these higher vocations must be nurtured in the bosom of the family. Priests and monks should never forget that they are the sons of lay people. Too often, when they preach on chastity, their approach suggests a belief that direst seduction is incarnate in the feminine sex. The peril is all the greater since it finds so much corroboration and support within men's hearts. These bombastic preachers, projecting their interior troubles onto an outward enemy, would become more tender if they would only allow themselves to dwell from time to time on the remembrance of their own mother.

The spiritual life does not flourish in cloisters alone. Without Christian families constantly replenishing them, convents would soon empty and the ranks of our clergy would vanish. No one will deny that, as Saint Paul says, married people are 'divided' between two loves; it is equally certain that virginity for the Kingdom of God is superior to marriage. The perfect holocaust, virginity, according to some Fathers of the Church, is equal to martyrdom. Nevertheless the living forces which engender saints are ordinarily nourished in the traditions of generosity of which Christian families are the select guardians.

High sanctity in the conjugal union will be rare, more rare than in continence. Yet spouses are not condemned to mediocrity, not at least while they are conscious of their state and refuse to deny the mystery of self-denial and devotion, a mystery which extends to the very hill of Calvary. Sanctity is also for the laity.

---

[1] Cf. J. GUITTON, in L'Eglise et la Liberté (Semaine des intellectuels catholiques), Paris, 1952, p. 50: 'Independence and submission are sometimes opposed. In reality, they are one: independence without submission is licence, submission without independence is slavery.'

[2] L. CERFAUX, Regale sacerdotium in the Revue Sc. Phil. Théol., 28, 1939, pp. 5-39. M. FRAEYMAN, La spiritualisation de l'idée du temple dans les épîtres pauliniennes in Eph. Theol. Lov., 23, 1947, pp. 378-412, J. BLINZERL, Ierateuma in Episcopus, a collection of articles presented to Cardinal von Faulhaber, Ratisbon, 1949, pp. 48-65.

[3] PIUS XII, Enc. Mediator Dei, Nov. 20, 1947, esp. n. 79-103 on the participation of the faithful in the Eucharistic sacrifice, Act. Apl. Sedis, 39, 1947, pp. 552-560. Eng. Trans., On the Sacred Liturgy, New York, 1948 ed., nos. 80-104. For the theological explanation, consult B. BOTTE, A. CHARLIER, A. ROBEYNS, B. CAPELLE, Le sacerdoce des fidèles, in Cours et Conférences des Semaines Liturgiques, X. Louvain, 1934. B. CAPELLE, Problèmes du 'Sacerdoce royal' des fidèles, in Quest. Lit. et Par., 1940, pp. 81-93 and 141-150. Id., Pour une meilleure intelligence de la Messe, Louvain, 1946, esp. pp. 23-31. G. THILS, Le Pouvoir Cultuel du baptisé, in Eph. Theol. Lov., 15, 1938, pp. 683-689. H. M. KOESTER, Die Magd des Herrn, Limburg-Lahn, 1947, pp. 415 ff. on the priesthood of the laity. P. F. PALMER, The Laical Priesthood: Real or Metaphorical? in Theol. Studies, 8, 1947, pp. 574-613. L. LECUYER, Essai sur le sacerdoce des fidèles chez les Pères, in Maison-Dieu, 27, 1951, pp. 7-50. G. RAMBALDI, Sacerdozio gerarchico e sacerdozio non gerarchico, in Civiltà Catt., 1951, vol. 2, pp. 345-357 Id., Ministri di Gesù Cristo e membra del suo Corpo mistico. Ib., vol. 3, pp. 59-69. L. PELLAND, Le Sacerdoce des fidèles, in Sc. Eccl. Montréal, 2, 1949; pp. 5-26. J. M. GRANERO, Sacerdocio y Laicado, in Razón y Fe, 148, 1953, pp. 325-350. Y. CONGAR, o.c., Jalons, p. 173 ff. A. PIOLANTI, Il sacerdozio

dei fedeli, in *Euntes Docete,* 6, 1953, pp. 166-187. P. CELIER, *Réflexion philosophique sur le sacerdoce,* in *Documentos,* n. 13-14, 1953, pp. 16-30. For the priest, we use the term 'functional' or hierarchical priesthood, since the priesthood of the laity is also in its own way 'liturgical' and 'sacramental.'

4 CARD. SUHARD, *Le prêtre dans la cité,* Paris, 1949, p. 88. Eng. Trans., *Priests Among Men,* Chicago, 1949, p. 88. A propos of the film *Dieu a besoin des hommes,* cf. J. GUITTON, *Le Laïc peut-il être prophète dans sa communauté?* in the *Vie Spir.* Suppl. t. 5, 1952, pp. 66-73, esp. p. 69.

5 B. CAPELLE, o.c., *Pour une meilleure intelligence . . . ,* p. 25.

6 S. AUGUSTINE, *De Civitate Dei,* X. 6. Cf. H. DE LUBAC, o.c., *Méditation sur l'Eglise,* pp. 117 ff.

7 PIUS XII., Enc. *Mediator Dei, Acta. Apl. Sedis,* 39, 1947, p. 560. Eng. trans., o.c. On the Sacred Liturgy, n. 104. Cf. Y. CONGAR, *La participation des fidèles à l'offrande de l'eucharistie,* in *Lumière et Vie,* n. 7, 1952, pp. 54-72, esp. p. 65.

8 R. GUARDINI, *The Spirit of the Liturgy,* chap. 5. This is found along with another of Guardini's works, *The Church and the Catholic,* in a single volume entitled *Integral Catholicism,* N.Y. and London, 1953. The German original, *Vom Geist der Liturgie,* is in its 17th edition, Fribourg, 1951.

9 H. A. P. SCHMIDT, *Liturgie et langue vulgaire. Le problème de la langue liturgique chez les premiers Réformateurs et au Concile de Trente (Analecta Gregoriana.* vol. 53), Rome, 1950. By the same author, a well documented bibliographical study under the title *Liturgica,* in *Katholiek Archief,* 6, 1951, col. 297-334. B. CAPELLE, *Plaidoyer pour le latin,* in *Quest. Lit. Paroiss.,* 31, 1950, pp. 65-71. The work of P. H. SCHMIDT demonstrates concisely that the discussion about the liturgical language was dominated by the controversy between Catholics and Protestants about the existence of the Mass as a true sacrifice. This influence is still felt today. The Reformation completely rejected the idea of sacrifice and proposed a worship by words, in opposition to every type of worship by actions. In this context, it is not difficult to grasp the importance of the decision of the Council of Trent, Sess, XXII, can. 9, Denzinger, n. 956: It is licit to recite the Canon in a low voice and it is not true that the Mass must be celebrated solely in the vernacular. In other words, the heart of the problem was of a doctrinal and not a disciplinary nature. The Council likewise omitted all the proposed declarations on the excellence and merits of Latin as a sacred language. Furthermore, it prescribed in chap. 8, Denzinger, 946, that during the Mass the faithful be frequently given explanations of the prayers and of the mystery of the Sacrifice. The Council also took into account the fact that the Eastern churches used the vernacular in the liturgy. Thus, it cannot be claimed that the unity of the Church must necessarily be expressed by a single liturgical language. See also: H. CH. CHÉRY, *Le Francais langue liturgique?* Paris, 1951, and the report *Langues Liturgiques* in the *Quest. Lit. Paroiss.,* 34, 1953, pp. 98 ff.

10 Recall the discussions raised by the publication of H. Doms, *Vom Sinn und Zweck der Ehe,* Breslau, 1935. French translation: *Du sens et de la fin du mariage,* Paris, 1937. A decree of the Holy Office, dated April 1, 1944, *Acta Apl. Sedis,* 36, 1944, p. 103, states that the primary end of marriage lies in the procreation and education of children; the secondary end, namely, the personal perfection of the husband and wife by their mutual giving, is subordinated to the primary end and depends on it. Indeed, it is evident that this giving does not terminate in itself but is of its essence directed toward the finality which assures its fundamental, ontological signification. The two ends do not succeed each other in the chronological order. They imply each other and give each other their specific character.

11 ST. AUGUSTINE, *In Joan. Tract.,* 51, n. 13.

12 ST. THOMAS, *Summa,* Ia IIae, q. 100, a.5, ad 4; ib., IIa IIae, q. 102, a. 1 et 3; etc.

13 See, among others, A. M. CARRÉ, *Compagnons d'éternité. Le sacrement de mariage,* (Coll. *Chrétienté,* 1), Paris, 1938. Eng. Trans. *Companions For Eternity,* Blackfriars, London (pamphlet). J. DERMINE, *La doctrine du mariage chrétien. Commentaire de l'encyclique 'Casti Connubii',* 7th ed., Louvain, 1945. J. LECLERCQ, *Marriage a Great Sacrament,* Dublin, 1951.

14 Cf., for example, the *Journal* of ALICE OLLÉ-LAPRUNE, published under the title *Liens*

immortels, Paris, 1940. A. CRISTIAN, *Ce sacrement est grand. Témoignage d'un foyer chrétien*, Paris, 1938. R. MAISTRIAUX, *Mariage, route de sainteté* (Action Familiale), Tournai, 1945. P. DE LOCHT, *Essai de bilan de la littérature conjugale*, in the *Revue Nouvelle*, 17, 1953, pp. 113-132. See also *L'Anneau d'or*, a review of family spirituality, directed by FR. H. CAFFAREL, Ed. du Feu nouveau, Paris.

15 See the significant remarks of J. FOLLIET on the *Sainteté d'aujourd'hui*, in *Les Chrétiens au carrefour* (I), Lyon, 1947, p. 179.

16 Cf. L. CERFAUX, o.c., *Théologie de l'Eglise*, esp. pp. 143-151. K. L. SCHMIDT, art. Kaleo, ekklesia, in *Theol.Wörterbuch*, III, pp. 488 ff. The Church is precisely the 'convocation', the assembly of those who are called.

17 FR. WEYERGANS, *Richesses et périls des groupes de foyers*, in the *Revue Nouvelle*, 17, 1953, pp. 141-148.

18 FR. JUERGENSMEIER, *Der mystische Leib Christi als Grundprinzip der Aszese*, 5th ed., Paderborn, 1936, pp. 274 ff.

CHAPTER V

THE LAITY AND THE MAGISTERIUM

IF THERE IS a domain where the laity seems condemned to inactivity, certainly it is the field of doctrine. In virtue of their authority it is the bishops who prescribe what the laity must accept as the word of Christ. The Protestant confronts the creed of his church and the preaching of his pastor, armed with his Bible, to determine what he himself will believe. And so he acquires a heightened sense of personal responsibility, a sense which in this particular form is unknown to the Catholic. The latter, however, experiences a happy confidence born of the conviction that the Word of God is safe within the bosom of the Church. His bishop and pastor transmit this word to him; he 'believes' not in them but in God, the supreme truth.

THE SERMON FROM THE HEARER'S POINT OF VIEW[1]

It seems quite natural to the Catholic to find himself sitting before the pulpit, silent and attentive. He accepts the doctrine without criticising, passing judgment only on the preacher's eloquence or lack of it.

But in this matter he is not afraid to speak his mind. More than one preacher has been approached with friendly suggestions.[2] The layman demands a certain self-effacement in the preacher in order to let the Gospel shine through in all its purity. Above all else he has come to hear the voice of Christ. He is quite aware that what is said on the pulpit does not always transmit the message in the same way or with the same certitude; applications are added to the essential. He learns to distinguish between definitions that are infallible and those that are not, between the doctrine of the Church and opinions that, however worthy of respect, are nonetheless less certain and not imposed absolutely.

Often his notion of infallibility is not very profound, sometimes it is inexact. He does not confuse it with impeccability, as do many Protestants, nor does he equate it with a species of papal omniscience. Sent from on High the Church obtains 'truth and grace' for him, or better, the Word does this through and in His Church. The privilege of doctrinal inerrancy, though exercised by weak, hesitant, and even sinful men, is guaranteed by the assistance of the Holy Spirit. He sends them neither new revelations, nor visions, nor heavenly voices. Brought by Christ, the fulness of revelation has been confided to the Apostles. In the course of the centuries the thought of the Church penetrates more deeply into the heart of the message left by the Saviour, but the deposit is no longer increased. The magisterium or teaching authority jealously guards it; it will 'interpret' these truths in the sense intended by God and 'propose' them in an accessible manner to succeeding generations. In the exercise of its mission —and it is in no way transformed into an oracle—the hierarchy must faithfully obey both the word of the Bible and the tradition of the Apostles. This presumes on her part conscientious study, for heavenly aid in no way subsidizes laziness.

The Church, therefore, does not claim to be superior to the Word so that she might treat it as she wills. Yet she is convinced that Christ will keep His promises and that the Holy Spirit will not neglect His office as Doctor of the Truth. Like us, the Orthodox churches recognize the infallibility of the Church as a whole, but they reject indignantly any personal privilege for the Pope in this matter. It is this fundamental point that separates us. Generally the Orientals are well aware that, according to Catholic teaching, Papal declarations must satisfy certain requirements before having absolute value. The Bishop of Rome must speak *ex cathedra*, that is, as Shepherd and Teacher of all the faithful, as one using his full power to decide definitively a question of faith or morals. Under such conditions is his 'definition' truthful and irrevocable, *ex sese*, by itself, and not through the approval of the Church.[3]

It is this *ex sese* which violently offends the Orthodox. In it they see the consecration of individual whim. Because they are irritated, they neglect to analyse the extent of the formula. For the Council adds that Papal infallibility is exactly that which Our Lord gave *to His Church* . The Pope is not above the Church so as to command it from the outside. In the solemn moment of defining he is expressing the faith of the whole community, but not as their agent. Not from the community but from Christ alone does he hold his power, to benefit the community and not to subjugate it. He 'represents' it, then, but only as its leader designated by God. The flock does not lead the shepherd but follows him. The people are not handed over to him as property, but confided to his vigilant love. They remain the *flock of Christ*. The purpose of the privilege is to guarantee to all the possession of the truth; in no way is it to confide to one man, as a satisfaction for his personal pride, an overwhelming dominance over all others.

Moreover, the agreement of the entire Church is usually acquired beforehand. The solemn definition, then, is only a removal of final hesitations. This disturbing *ex sese* is aimed at Gallicanism which claimed for the French episcopacy the right to approve proposed Papal decrees. Historically, this tendency arose as the result of the Western schism during which several Pontiffs vied for the tiara. In no way, however, can these accidental difficulties modify the fundamental structure of the Church.

The resentment aroused in the East by the definition of the Vatican Council has had an unexpected consequence: some theologians have begun to doubt the infallibility of the episcopal college despite the unanimous conviction of tradition in the East concerning this matter. Out of the purpose of this privilege, these theologians make a kind of preliminary condition.[4] According to them, the bishops should be swayed by the views of their faithful as if the latter were not the flock but their constituents. Apostolic tradition, however, hands down the episcopal power received at the bishop's consecration in a descending line through the imposition of hands. The letters of St. Ignatius, for one, teach that the people are subject to the bishop. 'Surely, all those that belong to God and Jesus Christ are the very ones that side with the bishop.' And again: 'Surely, Jesus Christ, our inseparable life, for His part is the mind of the Father, just as the bishops, though appointed throughout the vast, wide earth, represent for their part the mind of Jesus Christ.'[5] The testimony of St. Clement of Rome on the obedience due to the 'episcopes' instituted by the Apostles is even more explicit.[6]

Christian antiquity grants that one diocesan leader or even several can turn away from the faith: never does it ask that the community be the judge of their orthodoxy. That is a form of democracy which would have been inconceivable in such an age. The compromised bishop is tried by his patriarch, by a Council, or by the Pope. How many appeals, even from the East, were laid before the Apostolic See! Only declared heretics revolted against the established order.

Still we must keep in mind that bishops remain organically united to the body of their churches. Doctrine is not an inert object; it is the living thought of believing men. Instructors and instructed alike receive it from the mouth of Christ and His Apostles. It is never a personal good that shepherds can dispose of as they wish.

Surely, they must guard this treasure jealously. Any conservatism, however, will connote a rigidity which will halt any evolution of dogma. Inertia would supplant homogeneous growth, and instead of security suspicion and revolt would ensue, of which the bishops would be the first victims rather than the laymen.

Evidently infallible definitions are few and far between. Certain rigorists, it is said, would be happy to find a Roman decree in the morning mail every day. For them intellectual laziness has displaced the real spirit of faith. Dogmatic definitions are almost always provoked by heresy. Since they are defending against error, this accounts for their negative form. They close one path, but they leave open many others. Even a positive teaching, such as the Assumption, leaves the field free for theological research on subsidiary questions and, in fact, encourages such investigation.

The faithful generally receive official proclamations with respect and with enthusiasm. Resistance and agitation condemn themselves. Secret meetings of recalcitrants provoke only trouble and error. The Apostles and bishops of the early Church were not men to tolerate such abuse. Above all, their wish is that the mass of the simple faithful be not deprived of the integrity of Catholic truth.

Heresies have a sad history. Although they are officially condemned, they still manage to do great harm. The suspicions they arouse create in the midst of orthodoxy the 'integrist'—rigid conservative of the worst type. For him, it is fear rather than a robust faith that dominates. Afraid of himself and afraid of liberty,[7] he sets up for his comfort a neutral zone between truth and error, a sort of no man's land where all are forbidden to enter. Ever since the Reformation distorted the hierarchical priesthood, such temperaments have always thought it rash and inopportune to speak of the universal priesthood of the laity. Any effort to preach such a doctrine is tantamount to heresy. Thus, a precious Catholic truth runs the risk, not of being lost, but of being relegated to obscurity.

In regard to this, a remark of Fr. E. Mersch is very pertinent: 'Truth and error are not separated by a no man's land which is neither the one nor the other and which prudence would urge us to shun. On the contrary, truth and error touch along their whole course. Truth advances up to error all the way, but no farther; to stop short of that limit, if only to remain at a safe distance, would be to fall into error and to stamp as false what is still true. Everywhere, but especially when in dangerous territory, truth must suppress any tendency to excessively anxious precautions that would make systems swerve to keep from skirting a possible abyss.'[8]

Truth and virtue are not exactly the same. The latter must hold the middle way and keep its distance from both excess and defect; it must pass between the two. Yet truth's enemy lies only on one side, and in this sense it is extreme. It can yield none of its ground, central or peripheral. Truth must be lived in its entirety.

The Testimony of the Catholic Sense

In safeguarding the deposit of revelation the community has its role to play. Unfortunately the faithful are not always sufficiently instructed in that role. It is not enough to possess the truth; they must be so absorbed by it that they will be able to radiate it.

By doing so they will bear witness by their Catholic lives. This testimony is not the exclusive task of the hierarchy; only the hierarchy renders this testimony by way of authority. Yet, the entire community is a sign raised up before the nations. No member is excused from this mission, and should he excuse himself, he would to that extent lessen the demonstrative value of the sign. Jesus Himself said: 'The mark by which all men will know you for my disciples will be the love you bear one another.' (Jn. XIII, 35). Seeing this unity, the world should conclude that the Father has sent Christ (ib. XVII, 23). Now this unity is not a mere feeling of harmony; it is more profound than that, for its roots are in doctrine. Revelation fuses truth and life.

The best and least suspect type of preaching is always sanctity of life. It is the definitive argument, *par excellence*. St. Peter cites the case of stubborn men who were won to the Gospel 'not by word, but by the example of their wives,' (I Pet., III, 1), and he specifies: 'by their modesty and reverence.' (ib., v. 2).

The teaching apostolate implies an interior illumination by the Spirit of Christ. As is the case with sanctity, so here the illumination is not reserved to the clergy alone. To be sent as a witness—for that is the apostolate—supposes that one has 'seen' the mystery manifested. In the Biblical sense, that means that one has embraced the message by one's entire life. Hence, it is for the laity an immense possibility of activity, a possibility from which, unfortunately, we have too little profited. The layman's active influence shall not be the object of toleration on the part of a grumbling, fretful hierarchy, for the radiating faith of the laity is the richest fruit of the hierarchy's harvesting. Likewise, the hierarchy know that all narrowness on their part, far from preserving doctrinal integrity, would even favour the development of sects. They do not propose to smother but rather to awaken the Spirit among the simple. To prevent every contamination from without they do not stifle prophecy but rather supervise it. Rigorism is a poor approach. That is evident even in the liturgy where severe prescriptions arouse, by reaction, individualistic practices, and thus cause more loss than gain. [9]

Before defining the Assumption, Pius XII consulted the body of the bishops. He asked them to inform him about the faith of their people. This procedure would be quite irrelevant if the opinion of the flock were only the carbon copy of the official and approved teaching. Each bishop would simply be voting twice. Evidently, the Pope also wanted to hear the voice of the people, and that supposes that the people 'have something to say.' They are, in fact, asked to give testimony to this doctrine.

Obviously, the unlettered are not going to be summoned to resolve complicated theological problems. But faith is not principally a question of erudition, brilliant deductions, and subtle distinctions. More than once, the simple but upright faithful have judged with more good sense and supernatural wisdom than many of their masters, and that even in questions concerning major dogmas. The day when the world, in the words of St. Jerome, awoke astonished to find itself Arian, it was the doctors more than the masses who had been led astray. On the strength of Byzantine quibblings concerning the insertion or removal of one Greek letter, many clerics decided to deny the divinity of Christ. At the first heretical onset Christian commonsense concluded simply that if the Son is not God like the Father, then Christianity is dead. Even by the third century a lack of harmony between popular faith and more intellectual theology was noticeable.[10] In spite of the fact that Clement of Alexandria and Origen were great Christian thinkers, and notwithstanding the latter's genius, they did not arrive at an exact expression of Christian dogma. This only proves that theology is hard work. For even the best run the risk of being mistaken especially when they make the first hazardous attempt at systematization. After all, how many heretics came from the ranks of the clergy? The enthusiasts were usually from the anonymous mass, but the leaders were almost always cultured people who enhanced one aspect of the truth at the expense of its complementary aspects, and who obstinately persisted in restraining themselves to this narrow outlook. Chesterton said: Heresies are detached truths run wild. Heretics do not lack intelligence, yet they have no aptitude for nuances, and usually feel themselves superior to the sheeplike mob.

Some thoughtful men fear lest in leaning upon the community, theology may let itself be led by popular devotion and so become enmeshed in a jumble of foolishness. Is this not frequently the case in Mariology, they ask? It is a curious thing, but here Protestants show themselves more conservative—I was going to say more clerical— than Catholics: for in the eyes of the Reformers, marial piety is only superstition and pagan syncretism. And are we to recognize such intuitions among the ignorant as authentic?

The history of Ephesus in 431 might suggest such an hypothesis, but the explanation is much more simple. The patriarch, Nestorius of

Constantinople, a dynamic thinker, fired with a cartesian brilliance, questioned the Virgin's title as Mother of God. According to him, Christ was a person other than the Word. The scandal was enormous and popular sentiment was violently disturbed. Was Arianism again coming to life under a new form? If the Son of Mary was not the Son of God, but another person, what would now become of Christianity? So reasoned the Pope and the erudite Cyril of Alexandria. When at the end of a harassing day, the Council condemned the adamant Nestorius, the enthusiastic crowd improvised a procession with torchlight and incense to honour the Fathers of the Council. One of the first Catholic processions that history records, its character was Marian.

The Fathers of the Council were careful not to deify Mary. Protestants agree to this, however much they disapprove of the procession. If the Virgin was not a pure creature, the Son whom she bore would not be true man and Christianity would be at another impasse.

The hesitations on the subject of the Immaculate Conception were more pronounced. The discussion had been continuing for centuries, and even the great scholastics pronounced a negative verdict. Redemption is universal, they reasoned, and hence Mary, too, enjoyed the grace of salvation and could not have been without sin. Duns Scotus found the flaw in this adroit logic with some keen counter-reasoning. There can be no doubt that the Mother of God was redeemed in a perfect way; in fact, so perfectly was she redeemed that she was preserved from every stain of sin and so had no need to be delivered from it. Catholic thought has unanimously supported the latter opinion. On the eve of the definition by Pius IX, there remained only a few classroom theorists who clung to their doubts about the Marian privilege.

Obviously, continual preaching, under the benevolent eyes of the bishops, is most responsible for this popular agreement. In Catholicism more than anywhere else the opinion of the faithful is under the influence of the ordinary magisterium. This is not said by way of criticism. The activity of the professional theologian consists in examining in the light of revelation the religious ideas propagated among the people. Their method must be severe, rigorous, and unprejudiced. They must make it their duty to encourage certain propositions, to weed out others, and to purify almost all of them. Thank God, they will not always have to curtail and, in no case, are they to disregard the Christian sense in which the Spirit Himself works.

In last analysis, it is the living faith of the whole Church that will indicate the general direction that should be taken to reach the decisive stage. Expressed in doctrinal affirmations, this faith is found too in forms of worship and piety. The institution established by Christ was grounded on an authoritative principle, but was not to ignore any common—not to say democratic—contribution. In point of fact, since all must be saved, revelation is destined for all. If no one escapes the obligation of believing, so too no one is totally deprived of the light of common faith. The fervent believer is attached with all his heart to those essential views of the Church which are positive. As for recurring theological objections, he quietly leaves them to the care of the professionals; they are the ones who must resolve them. In the meantime, he wisely realizes along with Newman that ten thousand difficulties do not make a doubt.

It is quite childish to reduce the sure touch of this Christian sense to a caricature of illuminism. One could easily make of it a sort of scarecrow too, should he ever take a fancy to dissociate it from theological reflexion and historical investigation. So exposed, it would be nothing more than the height of irrationality. Critical analysis is extremely demanding whenever an appeal is made to that 'knowledge by connaturality' St. Thomas so highly praised.[11]

P. Rousselot describes this apprehension of the truth by real contact as a contact at once vital, intellectual and affective. 'Imagine to yourself a woman who before the definition of Pius IX believes in the Immaculate Conception. It seems to me there is no way of rigorously deducing this dogma from that of the divine maternity, and, whatever is thought of the demonstrative value of traditional documents, we can suppose them unknown to our simple believer. But that in no way forbids her from feeling herself in a state (of real certitude and) of unshakable adherence to the Immaculate Conception. No, she says, I could never believe that Our Lord would leave His Mother, even for an instant, under the power of the devil! Nor can she be shaken in this conviction. She sees, then, by a kind of illumination the synthesis of these terms: divine maternity and Immaculate Conception. There is no question here of conscious error for the will cannot impose assent upon the intellect by a command extrinsic to it. Unless the intellect, aided by some intelligible principle (*lumen sub quo*), sees one of the terms related to the other and *in* the other, such an imposition is in vain. So, I say, that in the case of our devout woman, there can be not only an unshaken conviction in fact, but also a legitimate conviction by right.'[12]

There is nothing in all that which contradicts the laws of the spirit. Even in a perfectly constructed piece of reasoning, there is a synthesis of view that can never be adequately explained merely by dissecting all its constituent elements. In one sole glance the truth in all its complexity is seized.

We need to have that spirit of sensitivity which Pascal opposes to the crudeness of geometry.[13] Unfortunately, theologians are not always distinguished by this quality. Their praiseworthy fidelity to the demands of criticism can blunt their intuitions—these they especially distrust. Unconscious though it may be, they do become impoverished. To accuse them of a lack of piety, however, would be unjust and defaming. They, too, can learn something from the school of the humble, who are often laymen. Theologians should not stand off from these faithful souls in order to form a 'separated' theology. The Church scholar rather bases himself upon the decisions of the magisterium. 'The theologian, like any good Catholic, gives his assent, but does so only on extrinsic grounds, namely that the Church has defined the proposition. . . . He needs the mediation of the authoritative Church inserting the verb *est* and offering her testimony to satisfy him, for he himself does not have the keenly developed sense necessary to seize the truth directly and by itself. He is in harmony with the truth, but in its more diluted and less personal state.'[14]

The evolution of dogma does not depend exclusively on classroom logic. By reason of this very fact, even the non-initiated can influence it. Some certainties are based rather on an ensemble of converging indications. Individually viewed, they would be insufficient. But bound together, or rather, all tending to a particular point, they constitute certainty. And should one last hesitation remain, it is cut away by the infallible declaration that culminates the slow maturing process. Never was the unity of faith between the faithful and the supreme Pontiff so strikingly exemplified as in the definition of 1854, the Immaculate Conception, unless perhaps it was on the occasion of the declaration of Mary's Assumption, which was the joy of our generation.

THE DOCTRINAL MISSION OF THE LAITY

In the evolutionary process just described, the influence of the community was in the foreground while the contribution of the individual layman remained in the background. Yet each of them has his own doctrinal mission to accomplish. The spread of religious convictions in a private milieu, such as his own family or social circle, depends in large measure on the layman. They are not asked to preach. In their personal contacts alone they can transmit from person to person the truths that they live. If up to the present they have scarcely worked at this, it is time to think about it. Protestants and Communists use a considerably larger amount of enthusiasm in propagating their systems. The Catholic voice is scarcely heard. They don't shock; in fact, they act so negatively that they often pass unnoticed. We are not complaining because they do not advertise themselves as evangelizers. But they could transmit the faith, if only they would become living witnesses of it, as the people of St. Paul's time were. In those days it spread, from neighbour to neighbour, from city to city. The many striking discourses on the prophetic role of laymen must be actually realised in the concrete circumstances of daily life.

On the profane level, whenever a Christian value is at stake, laymen are vitally concerned. Chesterton, Belloc, de Reynold, Maritain, and Mounier; historians, journalists, and Catholic thinkers play a role which the fathers of the Church in their day did not neglect. Yet there are more philosophers and sociologists than lay theologians.

Admittedly, theology is a branch of knowledge unreservedly clerical; yet that does not mean it should hibernate in an ivory tower, far from reality. Men who are striving to lead a Christian existence and not simply to perform a Christian act from time to time, cannot disregard doctrinal culture.

Catholic intellectuals more than once have claimed to have the faith of a Breton peasant. If this sentiment expresses respect and a holy reserve in the face of mystery, it can only be commended. Generally, however, it is used to describe men who have carried their professional development and humanist education to an enviable degree while in religious matters, they hardly know any more than their childhood catechism. Poorly equipped, they fear that any probing examination would only cause inextricable difficulties. Much better, then, to leave things as they are; rough handling would probably reduce to powder the venerable relics. Still, anyone who would have a virile and victorious faith must pay the required price of effort and study.

No sincere intellectual will be content with a grammar school acquaintance of the vital questions; nor will anyone expect encyclopedic knowledge from him. The intelligence of a truly adult Christian is all that is required.

It is impossible for him to solve problems of the moral order without the dogmatic premises on which they depend. To suppose otherwise is blind pragmatism. Moral problems are met in every field of activity: medicine, law, sociology, economics, and even the technical sciences in so far as they remain human. Is the priest, then, expected to be a moral specialist in all these branches of knowledge? No, yet the layman will render invaluable service in making his special difficulties known to the priest. They have been asked to present the Church to the world; they must also present the world to the Church, a concrete and dejected world in search of order and love.

If there is a gap between morality and reality, let us not, however, be too quick to throw the blame only on the moralists. How is it possible to draw up an effective moral code of medicine or social and political economy without a 'mixed' team, a close collaboration between cleric and layman? Now, less than ever before, will improvised solutions (or collections of truisms) be sufficient to assure success with such difficult questions. Not without reason, therefore, does the present Pope insist that all specialists carefully reconsider the ultimate meaning and religious implications of their respective fields.[15]

These laymen have a right to speak frankly and so a right, too, to demand favourable conditions that will not paralyze their efforts. In no way do Pontifical documents want to abrogate their rights even if they do warn them against certain dangerous errors. (*Humani Generis* should not be interpreted any differently). To proceed in this matter with a narrow rigidity or with resentment is indicative of a weak faith. Suspicion would take the place of mutual confidence and charity. It is only at the price of immense sacrifice that the Church maintains its universities and superior institutes; she herself will not undermine their vigorous life. At the line where faith and science meet, there are bound to be obscure points; that is why both must search more diligently to bring about a clearer understanding.

A believer who is well-instructed and well-disposed will have more opportunity than is commonly supposed to spread serenity and joy. His zone of influence frequently extends further than one would ever imagine. There are Catholics, moreover, who are officially commissioned to teach.[16] Sometimes they receive a 'canonical mission.' This does not imply strict power, but rather signifies the authorization and guarantee of the Church.

Catechists in mission lands are so commissioned. Ten times more numerous than the missionaries, they exercise a more direct influence. Natives themselves, they have easier access to the souls of the people they are helping christianize. Young communities do not hesitate to accord to their lay instructors, the greater part recent converts from paganism, a position of the highest importance. Out of necessity? No doubt, but also out of the freer power of adaptation of which our older communities now hardly seem capable. Have these latter become too clericalized? The danger is not an imaginary one and, as the native clergy increases, so will the mission lands, in their turn, feel that danger. But, what remains important is that the Church, here and elsewhere, should so maintain her youthful vigour that every day the Gospel message may unfold to them more and more the overwhelming discovery of God.

Pagans, however, are not found only in Asia and Africa. They live in our midst, so numerous that in our big cities, the work of catechists has become indispensable. Happily, there are volunteers, both men and women, willing to consecrate their hard-earned leisure, first to their own formation and then to the arduous work of educating those lost sheep whom grace is seeking.

Modern religious teaching method has made undeniable progress. Famous educators have put their talents, their experience, and their Christian hearts at the service of our schools and religious courses. We have laboured too long with outmoded methods, abstract devices of pure memorization that only ensure boredom, methods lacking body and soul, cut off from all vital considerations, as if the burning sense of God could be communicated by multiplying formulae and cold notional entities.

To redact a 'course' in religion is a gamble. Sometimes the result is religious disgust or at least disgust for what is presented as religion. It is a trial by fire. Every 'professor,' then, who chances it without deep-seated humility, a fundamental spirit of self-denial, and a completely disinterested charity, is doomed to lamentable failure. The children will suffer most of all. An instructor who himself hardly believes can teach them to recite their catechism perfectly, word for word. But the faith is much more delicate; bathed in the living light of grace, it is transmitted from soul to soul. Sometimes our teachers, religious and lay, give us a glimpse of a priestly soul, one entirely aware of his responsibilities, his gaze ever fixed upon the living God.

As indispensable as technique and adaptation is, (they will never be perfected enough), still personal fidelity to a higher call remains the essential. According to St. Paul, it is the divine Word Himself, not the human echo, who is the saving force. The preacher or instructor is not a carrier of the Word; rather, he is carried by Him. The layman, called to such a mission, will accomplish it with infinite respect and will be the first to be blessed: for, above all, he will be instructed by God.

---

1 The title of an article written under the pen name SILENS as it appeared in the French original. It has been translated as the main article entitled Preaching in Preaching, A Symposium, Cork, 1953, pp. 1-31.
2 Ibid., p. 15.
3 Council of the Vatican, Constitution De Ecclesia Christi. chp. IV., DENZINGER, En-

chiridion Symbolorum. n. 1839. Cf. A. CHAVASSE. *La véritable Conception de l'infaillibilité pontificale d'après le Concile du Vatican,* in *Eglise et Unité,* Lille, 1948, p. 57-91.

[4] Metrop. SERAPHIM. *Die Ostkirche,* Stuttgart, 1950, p. 73.

[5] ST. IGNATIUS, M. *Ad Philad.,* 3; *Ad Ephes.,* 3. Ed. F. X. FUNK, *Patres Apostolici,* Tubingen 1901, I., pp. 266 and 216. Eng. Trans. *o.c., Epistles of St. Clement and St. Ignatius* (ACW), Westminster, Md. and London, 1949, p. 86 and 61.

[6] ST. CLEMENT OF ROME, *Epistle to the Corinthians.* As Christ was sent by God, the Apostles are the ambassadors of Christ. They appointed bishops and deacons: chap. 42. Foreseeing discord, they even determined the succession in the ministry: chap. 44. Ed. cit., Patres Apost., pp. 152-156. Eng. trans., ed. cit., pp. 34-36.

[7] M. ORAISON. *La peur en psychologie religieuse,* in the *Vie Spir.* Suppl. n. 22, Sept. 15, 1952, pp. 277-301. This article, following depth psychology, gives a very penetrating analysis of the progressive and integrist types. See also in regard to integrism, Y. CONGAR, o.c., *Réforme,* pp. 246-247 and 604 ff.

[8] E. MERSCH, S.J., *The Theology of the Mystical Body.* Trans. by C. VOLLERT, S.J., London and St. Louis, 1951, pp. 75-76.

[9] Y. CONGAR, o.c., *Réforme,* pp. 301 ff. Also, cf. *Downside Review,* Summer, 1953 or *Cross Currents,* Summer, 1953, p. 363-364.

[10] This is the title of a remarkable article by P. J. LEBRETON: *Le Désaccord de la foi populaire et de la Théologie savante dans l'Eglise Chrétienne du troisième siècle,* in the *Revue d'Histoire Eccl.* 19, 1923, pp. 481-506 and 20, 1924, 5-37.

[11] Of this knowledge by vital adaptation under the direction of the gift of wisdom, ST. THOMAS gives a very instructive account, III. *Sent.* Dist. 35, q.2. He takes up the matter again in the celebrated passage of the *Summa Theologica,* IIa IIae, q. 45 a.2.

[12] P. ROUSSELOT, S.J. *Note sur le développement du dogme,* in *Recherches Sc. Rel.,* 37, 1950, p. 118.

[13] BL. PASCAL, *Pensées.* Ed. Paleogr, Tourneur, Paris, 1942, p. 64. Eng. Trans., W. F. TROTTER, London, last ed., 1954, pp. 1-2. See also E. NEUBERT. *De la découverte progressive des grandeurs de Marie. Application à son Assomption corporelle.* Paris, 1951.

[14] P. ROUSSELOT, o.c., p. 120.

[15] Cf. F. M. BRAUN, etc. *Morale chrétienne et requêtes contemporaines* (Cahiers de l'Actualité religieuse). Paris, 1954. J. ZARAGUETA. *Le Laïcat apporte au clergé son sens des réalités humaines.* In *Documentos,* n. 13-14, 1953, p. 94-100. J. DELFOSSE. *Pour une opinion publique à l'intérieur de l'Eglise. Ib.* p. 172-181.

[16] Codex Juris Can. 1333. cf. O. VON NELL-BREUNING, o.c., *Das Recht der Laien,* pp. 70 ff. Professors of religion and catechists do not, therefore, exercise a sort of diminished teaching authority; nor would they be able to impose their personal opinions. But they are approved and qualified without 'preaching' in the strict sense. An instructive account of the obligation of parents in the religious training of their children can be found in *o.c. Missione dei Laici* by R. M. SPIAZZI. p. 241. The author also gives some historical indications on the 'lay preachers' of whom the first Franciscans provide a very interesting example. The Osservatore Romano, in two articles of Sept. 15 and 16, 1954, criticised a certain form of 'Lay Theology' which would no longer be submissive to the Magisterium of the Church. There is only one theology in the Church, not two; but laymen can make a great contribution to the work of scientific theology.

CHAPTER VI

THE LAITY AND
CHURCH GOVERNMENT

DOCTRINAL AUTHORITY in the Church is intended to preserve the integrity of revelation. This does not mean that bishops are to hoard the deposit like a heap of golden coins in a coffer; they are also its dispensers. The faithful, in their turn, are to receive and especially to live the proposed truth. Their life is their witness to the vitality of dogma.

The magisterium and the ecclesiastical jurisdiction meet on more than one level. This double power serves one mission given the Church by Christ, to lead men to their final end, God. 'You, therefore, must go out making disciples of all nations . . . teaching them to observe all the commandments which I have given you.' (Mt., XVIII, 19-20). The leaders, then, must be able to bank on the obedience of all the members. 'For,' says the *Epistle to the Hebrews*, 'they are keeping unwearied watch over your souls, because they know they will have an account to give.' And by way of admonition it adds: 'Make it a grateful task for them: it is your own loss if they find it a laborious effort.' (Heb., XIII, 17). This is the sole and authentic way of realizing Christ's command together with the grace that it brings. The filial love of God's children removes servile fear but it does not remove the commandments: for those who love, Christ's orders are not a burden. (I Jn., IV, 18 and V, 3).

THE STRUCTURE AND LIFE OF THE CHURCH

The Church is a living organism, not a skeleton. Yet, without a framework she would have no solidity. Her fundamental structure has been forever fixed by Christ; no one can change it. In such a sense, the Church is *not* democratic; we have no right to elect a group of men to draw up a new constitution.

Upon this fundamental plan rest all the prescriptions of the hierarchy. It is, in fact, the source of their binding power. Heaven, says the Gospel, ratifies what they bind or loose. These directives come from on high and none can rightfully ignore them. This is the *via juris*, the way of law. Still, the Church's Code of Canon Law admits another way, the *via facti*, the path which usage or custom has marked out. By this second path the community can influence and vivify legislation.

This phenomenon must be accurately interpreted. The right of custom is only valid in so far as authority gives consent. In the Church people are not qualified to create laws; they can at most prepare the way for them. For the approval of a custom the consent of the legislator, as demanded by Canon 25, need not be given explicitly. Often it is given tacitly or affirmed in general terms.

In the course of history the applications of this principle have been numerous and often of far-reaching consequences. Occasionally it has created entirely new situations. The clerical obligation of saying the Office was introduced by custom and only later codified. The Jubilee Year indulgence was provoked in 1300 by a popular pilgrimage to Rome where crowds (even before the publication of any Pontifical Bull) had come in great numbers to St. Peter's in quest of spiritual favours. Unwilling to disappoint the pilgrims, Pope Boniface VIII sanctioned their desires.[1]

Inversely, in view of profound changes in circumstances a positive ruling supplanted by different custom becomes outmoded without the intervention of any revolutionary action. Before the monumental achievement of the present Code of Canon Law, the history of ecclesiastical legislation was woven in large measure by the constant interplay between decrees and customs. Nor is the present Code immutable; changes in laws are foreseen and regulated (Canon 22).

Though the hierarchy is always superior to the laity, both bishops and subordinates form but one living community. As such the Church is a definitive institution and will not be replaced. But if she is wary of 'fashion,' her historical dress is nonetheless capable of adaptation. She prefers to change it slowly, as does every respectable institution. As in the details of liturgy and rituals, respect for the past forbids sudden and violent changes. Church Reforms are the result of a long maturation.

Meanwhile, Church government is linked by innumerable ties to the network of human society. Obliged to live in the world, the Church cannot be completely free from the changing social situations conditioning the life of the people. To give one example, in the first centuries of Christianity Roman centralization was unthinkable simply because continual relations between distant regions and the centre were impossible, owing to the difficulties of communication. As civilization evolves, ecclesiastical legislation must evolve with it. It could not treat global-minded citizens of the twentieth century in the same way that it directed Christians of the Middle Ages.

Modern labour-management relations cannot be established on the same social level as those between the Lords and serfs of the Middle Ages. Furthermore, laws must be reorientated in the light of the changing concepts of moral problems. The right to private property remains basically the same, but its application depends in great measure on the cultural level of the society. Today a principle must be applied in light of the ever growing interdependence linking men of all parts of the world. The common good demands an increase in personal contribution. Some obligations, formerly under the domain of charity, now seem quite certainly to be within the realm of justice.

The rapidity of evolution becomes all the more noticeable as we enter the field of government. The community is ever expanding. The narrow limits of the city-state and the multiple divisions of the feudal system are unknown to the modern nation. And as this in its turn becomes gradually integrated into a world government there will remain but the memory of national sovereignty, once so vigorously defended. Humanity is influenced profoundly by the change of social institutions. For men carried along by the flow of events, extra-temporal decrees cease to exist. Only that which is eternal in man can be ruled by immutable norms.

Concrete Christianity, rooted in history and set in society, will not always nor everywhere have the same appearance. It is equally impossible to govern her at all times in the same way. With increasing insistence circumstances will demand an adaptation of legal structures. Lay people, more directly in contact with the profane world, will be particularly sensible to new exigences and will demand with greater insistence the necessary precisions. In this regard their growing anxiety and impatience is apparent. Never before has humanity advanced at so rapid a pace.

By contrast, picture to yourself the solemn dignity of an ecclesiastical procession. Even if you do not condone modern man's recklessness, you can at least sympathize with his grievance: 'All that is medieval! The Church is always late!' Too late? That remains to be seen. It is with a certain reluctance that the Church sets aside her time-consecrated ways. Nor is this surprising since they were inspired by a mentality preoccupied with the eternal. Her attachment to these customs, therefore, is not simply a form of idolatry for the past.

Whether we like it or not, an intelligent adaptation will always hold the middle road between leisureliness and opportunism. Wistful reflection on 'the good old days' is useless since the present situation is radically different. To seize upon the latest novelty when vital points hang in the balance is puerile and betrays a faulty sense of responsibility.

Meanwhile, ecclesiastical authority must grant the layman's right 'to be heard,' if it wishes to keep up with present-day needs. Authority will not always succeed with equal brilliance because this type of manoeuvring falls under the virtue of prudence, a domain in which the Church is not guaranteed infallibility. Even indolence and despotic action are not excluded. It would be equally useless to solicit the apologetic support of history.

And so we are led to the section concerning reforms.

REFORM IN THE CHURCH

We use the words 'reform *in* the Church' deliberately, to avoid all confusion with the Protestant reform quitting the community; that reform founded a new Church opposed to the old. Naturally, it looked upon itself as a return to antiquity and claimed to have re-discovered gospel formulas long since betrayed by Rome. That there was a break both sides agree; when the break occurred matters little. Catholics see its consummation in Luther's burning of the Pontifical bull at Wittenberg; Protestants maintain that the deviation dates immediately from post-Apostolic times, through the fault of those who put themselves in authority.

In the light of Christ's promise of eternity to His Church, Catholics will always reject this hypothesis. They will admit, however, that the leaders of the Church are in constant need of serious self-examination. Authority must not refuse to confront its activities with the will of Christ so as to follow that will as closely as possible and in the purest manner possible. Completely aware of human weakness, the Church readily recognises such weakness, even among her leaders.

In his remarkable book, *Vraie et fausse Réforme dans l'Eglise*, Father Congar insists on the necessity of periodic revision. His *Introduction* shows us the spirit in which he means these words. Our times, he says, hunger for sincerity and courage. Christ's authentic message, in all its purity and without compromise must be presented to the world—to the world as it really is and not as we like to imagine it. It must use a language which is intelligible, and an organisation which can be integrated into modern life. Why entangle it in a mass of out-dated, useless trappings that either hide or disfigure the essential features? To keep silent, however, when frankness is demanded is still a sin against truth. Should we try to disguise obvious abuses with subtle pretexts the result would be disastrous, the rude awakening inevitable. It would be unwise to forget the lessons of the sixteenth century.

On the other hand, he continues, to compare the modern Catholic trend of returning to the sources and of self-criticism with the Protestant revolt is unthinkable. 'This self-critcism is bold, some-times brutal, but it is definitely not springing from a lack of confidence or love for the Church; on the contrary, its source is a profound attachment, a willing confidence which transcends disappointments. . .'[2] To prove their unfailing fidelity to the hierarchy, our Catholic lay people are ready to sacrifice everything.

Nor is our present position comparable with that of the Modernists who want to remain within the fold of the Church and yet are completely hostile to any positive faith. They too speak of 'reform'; but for them it means to abandon all revealed religion, retaining only the exterior formulae in order to hide their rationalist ideology and sentimentally subjective experience. The exact opposite of sincerity, it betrays a duplicity which today's Christians justly hold in contempt. To stifle their protests under the pretext that they might sometimes say disagreeable things or show a lack of politeness would be supremely unjust.

The study of reforms demands an especially serene atmosphere where candour will detract nothing from the objectivity of thorough examination and will respect the unconditional desire for truly apostolic and fruitful renewal. A storm-filled sky and an atmosphere troubled by bitterness between clerics and laymen is hardly conducive to work as delicate as it is urgent. In spite of all their good will, some are treading a dangerous path. To win the ear of the laity or to give evidence of a would-be broadmindedness, certain priests, quite unjustly, do not even hesitate to impugn the hierarchy or the preceding Catholic generation. And so come the mass attacks, especially in the realm of social controversies, against yesterday's leaders who were incapable of interpreting the signs of the time and are thereby responsible for the dechristianization of the proletariat.[3]

This apostasy of the masses is only too real. Yet we must be careful not to seek an oversimplified explanation. Would it not be Pharisaical of us, in our self-complacency, to lay the full responsibility for this loss on our predecessors? Whenever a country has been defeated in war, the 'innocent' will always arise to hunt down the 'traitors' and to blame them for the humiliation. Despite all this, it is generally true that everybody was somehow responsible for the causes, proximate or remote, that provoked the downfall. If the working masses have lost their religious practice or even their faith, one of the causes is certainly a universal materialism that is undermining every class of society without distinction.

In industrial technology a profound revolution has been effected. The life of the worker has been completely transformed. One need not be a specialist in sociology to recognize the fact. Add to that disturbance the gradual laicising of human thought through a liberalist philosophy and you can understand how, in every field of social activity, concepts of life have been born that are at least un-Christian, if not strongly anti-Christian. The baptized have certainly not escaped the influence of such ideas. To this disintegration the State, whether neutral or hostile to religion, has added the finishing touches.

A certain number of employers listed as Catholic have neglected the warnings of *Rerum Novarum*. There are some today who outrageously ignore the directives of *Quadragesimo Anno* as well as those of other more recent Pontifical messages. We must not excuse them, but to content ourselves with stigmatizing them will not further our cause. The future is more important than the past; the most urgent task is to begin to work here and now: to conceive, to prepare and to construct a more humane work organization and to animate it with the purest Gospel spirit. The City of God will undoubtedly always suffer more from the apathy of its sympathizers than the fury of its adversaries. We need not urge others to strike their breasts because we are all sinners.

Raising our voices in protest is hardly a sign of energy, still less of virtue. The doubtful laurels of Léon Bloy make some people uncomfortable, but similar invective hurled at the bourgeois sounds even more hollow when the literary talents of that ungrateful mendicant are absent. Such thrusts only succeed in exasperating the mentality of the desperate whose first victims are these very authors. If the situation is so aggravated, then any effort at recovery is stifled even before it begins. No vigorous and liberating action can find life in an atmosphere of surrender.

To hope does not mean to shut oneself up in inertia. Manly patience is enterprising and tenacious, and devotedness renders it fruitful. That applies first of all to the study of the problems. If pioneers are needed, they must be courageous, but not foolhardy, fighters ready to brave the fire of the front lines. Emmanuel Mounier was such a man, but he was very careful not to put the Church at stake in any of his tactical moves. He did not shirk his responsibilities; ever ready to obey the injunctions of superiors, he would repudiate harshly those mimicking fools who, lacking either his intellectual vigour or —his most prized gift—his unalterable faith, wanted to cry out still louder. [4]

It can happen that the will to reform or to adapt, although it proceeds from authority, can remain in great part a dead letter. At the time of Protestantism, Pope Adrian VI experienced this tragedy. His unparalleled good will and matchless sincerity were thwarted by the obtuseness and indifference of his large circle of advisers and attendants. His cunning adversaries did not hesitate to misuse his declarations. And so there is great need of a large and powerful spiritual current to grasp the idea of reform and assure its practical execution. More than one nobly aspiring Council has obtained but meagre results because its efforts remained confined in a too narrow sphere. [5]

Too often theologians and even bishops are theoreticians somewhat removed from concrete realities. Luther could draw crowds; he knew how to gather together whatever tormented the unstable spirits of his contemporaries into a dynamic synthesis, which carried everything before it. Authoritative reforms, to be effective, need to be backed and consolidated by a religious rebirth which extends to every class of the community. Only with Trent did this come into being. In those countries that remained Catholic the great saints of the sixteenth century dominated the course of thought and were in fact the true promoters of this renovation.

Thanks to a similar influence in the thirteenth century, Francis of Assisi and the gospel-centered movement of the mendicant orders shaped the Christianity of the Middle Ages. All of society, the laity included, was caught up in it. This movement of reform did not fall into heresy. Francis refused to play the demagogue; his strength rested precisely in his scorn for violence. Without forcing it, he brought about a rebirth in the interior of souls.

The revitalisation of Christianity, moreover, should be given consistence in social institutions. A pious temperament is inclined to believe that all will be well if only moral values will be honoured. As long as the reawakening of conscience is not followed by a vigorous application to concrete situations such a view will remain too narrow. To preach piety and moral integrity exclusively becomes odious since a sense of reality demands as well the rebuilding of social structures. [6]

Uprightness alone will never suffice to solve structural problems of unemployment. If, for example, tomorrow all workers were transformed into exemplary Christians, completely faithful to the moral law and fathers of large families, that would not in itself increase employment. The problem's solution depends on redistribution of population and economic resources, on raw materials and their transportation, on the possibilities of export, and on similar factors. Nevertheless, we may hope that convinced believers, seized by a more generous and active devotion, will study the situation more carefully and work out suitable remedies. More profoundly aware of their responsibilities, they have more chance to set in motion throughout all of society forces capable of producing a favourable change. Catholics too often allow themselves to be surpassed in inventive power by non-believers. It is not enough to organize novenas of prayer to save the situation, we must get to work! If we do not, we are giving substance to the Soviet caricature of the praying peasant whose field is covered with brambles and weeds. Any such image is clearly a most false form of supernaturalism. Religion is not a magic carpet that lifts us to a terrestrial social paradise at the crucial moment.

INCARNATION OR DISINCARNATION

Today, similar situations are to be found in one degree or another over almost the whole globe. Let us not, however, neglect regional and historical differences. By generalizing we lose contact with reality. The need is one of adaptation to the different countries and people. In Rome where all is centralised the fact is well known. The danger is not that we return to the partitioning of the Middle Ages, but that in excessive uniformity, we risk the extinction of viable elements—and we are not rich enough to allow ourselves that luxury. Whether Russian or American, generalised planning is no remedy.

Contemporary France and Spain, for example, are not alike. Though materially existing side by side, they live in entirely different epochs. In France, the funeral speech *Feu la Chrétienté*, ('The late Christianity') is an already outmoded refrain; while in Spain, the ancient régime lives on. All are agreed that the Christianity of the Middle Ages, at least in most countries, has seen its splendour and should henceforth, be left to rest in peace. It has run its course and will not return, at least not in its original form. History does not know such revivals, it is not the cycle the ancients imagined. Its progression is in one direction, sometimes climbing, sometimes falling, but always directed towards its final end. No matter what anyone says, we are not awaiting a new Middle Ages.

In France, the causes that ended the ancient Christian order were of so violent a nature that its evolution was the more rapid there. And with varying speeds, she has swept along the rest of Catholic Europe, and continues to do so. If some centres like Paris give signs of evident Christian vitality, its communistic suburbs still believe nothing but the ideal of Marx and Stalin. Ancient paganism was not without a certain sense of religion, a vague intuition of an Absolute Being, superior to the world. But the modern age, the age of technology, has mastered the only things it considers as real, the world and matter. That is the only liberation it is proud of, the only one it is eager to perfect. It is often so far removed from Christianity that it does not even trouble to fight us. It is not aware of our existence.

Some apostolic, ardent Catholics have tried to bring to the heart of the proletariat the Gospel message in one form or another. They have consecrated vast amounts of energy in forming social works and youth organisations. Between the two World Wars, this approach was called the principle or method of incarnation. [7]

This term implied that, to attain its end of sanctification, the Church had to fulfil here on earth a task of raising the people. She must not remain indifferent to any human value, but must openly engage herself in all of them. By preaching social justice and fraternal charity she would help procure for the masses a higher standard of living.

It has been said and will be said again that by her action the Church is taking men such as they are and where they are without disguising her intention to remake a healthy environment for them. This is the reason for the great Catholic youth, family, and worker organizations. The religious climate of these groups allows Christians to breathe a fresher air and removes them from the suffocating influence of materialism. [8]

The 'incarnate' Church should not hesitate in entering into contact with the flesh and blood of temporal society. She must engage her enemies on their own ground, she must fight them using every legitimate human means. She cannot sit with folded arms when the opportunity of further influencing the masses presents itself. In the fields of education, the press, recreation and social organization she must assume leadership. To this end, many 'social' Catholics have consecrated and will continue to consecrate the best part of their energies.

The danger for these defenders of Church rights is that the influences and contaminations of the world they are trying to conquer will conquer them. The danger is insidious; we are victims before we realize it. With an almost imperceptible movement our focal point shifts from interest in the end to interest in the means, and they in turn assume prime importance in our feelings. Moreover, the fight is not evenly waged, since the Christian conscience is more demanding and more sensitive than the world's. To rival others in cleverness, and if necessary in cunning, is a difficult task for the children of light.

They must also be careful not to implicate the Church in all sorts of temporal conflicts, by confusing religious interests with group or party advantages. When Catholicism represents only the leisure class or, worse yet, when it allows itself to be reared as a rampart to protect the bourgeoisie and capitalism, it is simply driving away the working man. And should others as a reaction build Churches for workers alone, they likewise would destroy universalism and catholicity. For some, social relief is the specific end of the Church; the Kingdom of Heaven thus takes on a rather worldly character. It is a return to the clerical imperialism that has been tormenting so many souls and troubling even those sympathetic to religion. For many an intellectual, the figure of the chaplain-director of social groups proves disquieting and even provoking.

That is the ugly side of the highly esteemed method of 'incarnation.' Its advocates must beware of such traps; and yet perhaps the worst thing is that until now they have not succeeded in making their influence felt extensively enough. Dechristianization has gained not only the industrial suburbs but also the vast agricultural regions. In France, Christian social action has never become the redoubtable force capable of repulsing the enemy and affecting the inner life of the city. In some cases its zealous devotion has been able to establish Catholic groups at the cost of very great sacrifice. Unable, however, to use them as shock troops, it has been forced to mobilize all its reserve strength to keep them from disbanding. Undoubtedly the massive block of irreligion was here and there chipped, but it has yet to be seriously marred. Because it could not possibly penetrate the enemy lines, the ardour of combat disastrously cooled.

Little by little people began to wonder if they had set about the problem in the right way. Following the setback, doubt and hesitation infiltrated into loyal hearts. More than one layman, more than one priest threw up his arms in despair before 'the failure of the Y.C.W. apostolate,'[9] asking, what good is it to wear ourselves out? We are not facing reality.

With disillusions such as these they cannot make progress against the current. They do not simply resign themselves; they refuse to drift, but with this the best of their remaining force is consumed. Looking at the situation, they ask themselves if a change is still possible, and, on second thoughts, if it is even desirable: thus appear the typical symptoms of a defeatist crisis, a mental attitude that oddly enough seeks refuge in totalitarian methods.

Every form of Catholic organization, including the parish, doubt experiences because its contact with the masses is so superficial. Certainly, we say, urgency demands that all these decayed tissues be cut away and something else tried in their place; nobody knows exactly what. Often we are ready to seek the most radical remedies at the risk of amputating still living organs. Some, after a fruitless trial of the 'immanence' method, turn to Transcendence with its 'completely other' note about God and religion. Far from being an earthly power, they say, the Church must establish its quarters in heaven.

The mirage of a purely interior Church that operates under the inspiration of the Spirit alone and thereby is freed from heavy obligations, abuses and scandals, astonishingly resembles the more or less ethereal Orthodox type.[10] In the Eastern Church the bishops willingly abandon every temporal concern to the State. Except for certain controlled services, they scrupulously avoid all intrusion upon the social scene. Active religious congregations that carry a large part of the apostolate in the West are unknown in the Christian East. There the Church is principally the liturgy and the sacraments. To avoid commitments here on earth, it concerns itself with eschatalogical perspectives only. And so a complete absence of conflicts with civil authorities results. Anticlericalism is practically unknown in the East, since there is nothing in the pretensions of the clergy to nourish it.

The famous 'incarnation' programme then has to give way to disincarnation. The proponents of the new programme think that they have somehow refined or purified the Church; what they fail to realize is that they have at the same time made her unreal.

Some positive thinkers reason thus: 'To wish to chain the Church to any one phase of her development is ever to deny her growth under the pretext of favouring her present established position. . . . The Christian spirit betters institutions by inspiring them, not by monopolizing them.'[11] Such a view is quite exact, but note that it remains on this side of total spiritualization.

The term 'incarnation,' furthermore, is frequently misunderstood by its attackers. When someone charges that it pursues moral and legislative paths to the exclusion of religious and theological virtues,[12] he simply confuses the reality with its outward appearance, and so identifies it with organisations already dead or dying. Where there is no incarnate *spirit*, there is no real *incarnation*. When a structure has been emptied of all animation resulting from an ardent living faith, a person acts rightly in battering that hollow structure to bits; but then the destruction would be wrought on a caricature. The Reformers used a similar process: instead of revivifying the ecclesiastical institutions, they suppressed them.

Even disincarnation sometimes adopts attitudes that dangerously reflect the despicable manoeuvres of a justly hated clericalism. 'Good tactics!' some would shout about any infiltration into neutral and communist organizations for the purpose of exerting a hidden religious influence. The Marxist school assiduously practises this cell infiltration for an anti-religious end. To enter the enemy camp in disguise is a commendable deceit in modern warfare but not in evangelizing. To proceed by indirect ways, to hide one's convictions temporarily to catch another off his guard, exceeds the limits of genuine prudence. Later on, when the intruder is discovered, he should expect an indignant reaction. If he somehow escapes the reaction, he will no longer give any witness at all. Many a one, inspired and zealous in the beginning, has allowed himself finally to be assimilated by the dechristianised milieu.

The method that circumstances impose does not matter. Whether one enters the masses in an 'off-hand' manner or establishes a distinct group in their midst is of little consequence. Everything depends on the spirit that animates such an apostolic worker. It must be thoroughly sincere, without any provocation, it should give unequivocal witness, a witness that fears no opposition.

This same frankness is necessary before public authorities. If the Orthodox Church has never had similar conflicts with the State, we must never forget the price it pays. We in the West are hardly prepared to pay so much for tranquillity; we refuse to yield the smallest part of the Church's liberty to the rulers of the moment. We reject all servility, even at the risk of inevitable conflict, and even of systematic persecution. The life of the Church is not confined to the sacral; she has more to do than to direct worship. Her mission is to promote the practice of Christian law even in the most profane surroundings. In refusing all temporal jurisdiction, writes Father De Lubac, she does not abdicate her mandate to direct the consciences of her faithful followers with authority.[13] Her task is not only to suffer, heart and mind lifted to heaven; she must also fight that her members may have the greatest possibility of winning the eternal prize.

She must, then, preach Christ as the Gospel demands. Even if thereby she arouses suspicion or provokes division, she cannot limit herself to exercising a charity that shames the name of her Founder. In doing so she would certainly offend no one; she would, however, end by relegating herself to the silence of the sanctuary, abandoning to the devil the world she should be transforming.

That witnesses of the Faith will be dragged before tribunals is foretold in the Gospel. Those who take Christ's part will be denounced even by their own kin. The world will persecute the disciples as it has persecuted the Master. The preached word is a stumbling block, scandal for the Jews, folly for the pagans—a folly which in their opinion should not be tolerated. To this end they coalesce the power of the State with every social force that can be mustered to smother the voice of the message. Such is our lot as Christians, and we must not deplore it; we have to overcome these obstacles, or, rather, our Faith in Christ has already conquered them.

So it is the sword, and not peace. Until the end of time, the Church will remain the little flock which, notwithstanding its size, proposes by the power of the Spirit to convert this immense world. It is wrong to imagine that the Church will become contaminated by extending her hand to man's miseries when Christ touched all the wretched, even the outcast lepers. Only the possessed never felt the soothing touch of His hand, and it is yet to be proved that the social domain is suffering from diabolical possession.

Perhaps the reader will think that in order to repudiate total disincarnation, we are invoking great principles which, theoretically at least, are unquestioned. Now it is time to push on to the heart of the question. In every country and in every age, the message should take hold of men as they are and make of them the seed of salvation. Fundamentally, the proponents of transcendence have no other thought in mind. At the price of extraordinary sacrifices (for which they must be given great credit), they too try to make the disinherited, the religious wanderers, and their present enemies worthy of God's Kingdom.

But we would wish them still another resource: that they have a still greater confidence in the power of grace and a more active and victorious faith. St. Paul did not cry out: 'Woe is me if I cut myself off from the people or if I do not share in their demands!' but he did say: 'Woe is me if I fail to preach Christ!' And there is no Christ save the Crucified One, the Saviour of the people because He allowed Himself to be crucified by them.

His message must flow into every branch and activity of human society. The Word is not to be chained: It is free as the soaring eagle, and in Its name the Church demands the right to put herself at the service of all.

Depending on place and time, she will translate the demands of liberty, in diverse ways. If she chooses to do so by organizing Christian schools, Catholic Boy Scout troops, or even Catholic labour unions, nobody has the right to accuse her of abuse of power or of medieval obscurantism. That this kind of realization may increase the danger of secularization is true. Often groups have exceeded what is beneficial or even licit. Yet why should fear of exaggeration be the norm of dynamism?

If, then, the Church expresses and guarantees her spiritual independence through certain organizations, we have no right to condemn her pretensions as exceeding their proper limits. Her interventions should be measured with prudence, her methods carefully sifted, her intentions and actions repeatedly purified: the call to transcendence exists to keep her on her guard. We fully appreciate the services of this tendency; it is not to be reproved unless it makes exclusive claims. On the other hand, an extreme incarnationism over-balancing one side of the scale is equally fatal. To urge passage between the two dangers is wearisome yet practical advice. When official Catholic institutions, such as primary schools or universities, mutualities or day-nurseries take their place in the profane world, they retain their special purposes and should not be attached too closely to the hierarchy. The bishops are not to be immediately responsible for every action of a Young Christian Worker. Directors of social works are not in the pay of prelates, and should not take refuge behind a bulwark of episcopal mandates. As adult Christians they have to assume their full responsibility, and avoid even the shadow of a 'clericalism of the laity.'

Such a sin exists. The guilty are those who present their solution to disputed questions as 'infallible' and unhesitatingly condemn their adversaries as 'heretical.' No one has the right to bind the Church to his personal ideas, no matter how reasonable and honest they may appear, for that could only end in an intolerable moral pressure.

On the other hand, identification with an openly Catholic group obliges lay leaders to a more prudent reserve and so restrains somewhat their freedom of action. The prestige of the hierarchy at least to some extent accrues to this sort of organization and gives it a privilege of great value in the eyes of believers, a certain assurance, for example, by the presence of a chaplain. To abuse such a confidence is to deceive the simple. Under these conditions every suspect method or demogogic procedure is doubly condemnable, for in addition to its own malice, it compromises the Church which appears to condone these dubious procedures.

We must not show ourselves more Catholic than the Pope, nor must we think we have invariably grasped the spirit of the times better than he has. For example, we are free to judge that the English political régime is a preferable type. Now in Great Britain there is no party that includes in its programme the defence of the Church's rights. But to conclude from that to the suppression of similar parties in other countries is questionable logic. In fact, such an idea is unthinkable until opposed groups renounce their 'laicist' or anti-religious action. To prepare for such an armistice and facilitate psychologically a change of heart on both sides of the barricade is certainly highly commendable. To open the doors, however, to an enemy who will not disarm is rather naive pacifism.

Vigilance remains the keynote. Unconditional State seizure of a nation's life is not a temptation reserved to totalitarian countries alone. When statism wishes to favour us with a single school system, we thank them gratefully but refuse; liberty of education is closer to our heart. But if we refuse strict uniformity, we must settle for a reasonable pluralism based on mutual respect—respect that does not exclude but rather encourages collaboration of all honest forces.

Because of his individual limitation, every man needs aid from the social organization. Helping man without oppressing him, the community should not frustrate his liberty, but rather enable him to use it and so develop his personality. The social pressure of the masses withers the spiritual aspirations of the poor man. It is impossible for scattered forces to resist effectively this crushing weight. Religious-minded workers must co-operate. If at the outset it appears impracticable to purify a society composed of so many non-believers, there is nonetheless, an urgent need to consolidate a part, at least, of the terrain where the faithful might live according to the demands of their faith.

Let us not cry too quickly 'a state within a state!' We are not proposing that the faithful wall themselves within a ghetto. The windows and doors of the Catholic edifice everywhere should remain fully open—and especially its doors. Inflexibility and timidity provoke an isolationist psychosis. The fever of the besieged is equally disastrous for attackers and defenders. Catholics can separate themselves from society only at the price of being bad citizens, but society cannot force them to be bad Catholics.

We must beware of simplist solutions: in reality they are often deceiving. If we want to be realistic, we must take account of the complexity of problems and of the internal divisions of the human city. The clergy alone, or even together with lay auxiliary troops, cannot force the issue. The relief of the proletariat is not the principal work of the priest; his proper mission is the salvation of souls. Society looks to him for the inspiration necessary to accomplish truly constructive social work. This supposes lay directors capable of receiving that inspiration and translating it into actions. Without that, any claim about the assumption of human values will be fraudulent. To forbid priests to give lay people a special religious and moral formation is to condemn these people to mediocrity. Technical capacity alone will never be enough to solve the very human problems of labour-management boards or pressing questions of state.

It is not the Church's part to dictate techniques. In his social declarations, the Pope determines principles in view of their end, dispels doctrinal errors, and especially outlines the spirit that is to animate and guide generous souls. An inalienable mission exists for the layman. The hierarchy has no intention of tearing it from their hands: too often an ecclesiastical assistant has played the little dictator.

To play such a role is to falsify his vocation. Still it would be unjust to deny the possibility of extenuating circumstances; some urgent necessities must be met without delay. In the Middle Ages, the Church found herself practically alone to create schools, hospitals and asylums. In the modern epoch, she no longer claims this monopoly. Still she has no intention of recognizing a State monopoly. Adamantly, she claims her undeniable right to practise both intellectual and material charity against intolerance and abuse of power wherever they appear, even within her own organizations.[14]

LAY STATE OR CLERICAL STATE?

When outlined against the most important and largest domain of public life, the State, this problem becomes of burning interest. Unfortunately, a confused vocabulary complicates the issue: the words *thesis* and *hypothesis*, *laicity* and *tolerance* are used with widely divergent meanings. Moreover, we must be careful not to consecrate absolutely any particular moment of history or to consider our preferences as universal norms. Because we are so intimately involved in all these controversies, it is only with great difficulty that we maintain the serenity and 'distance' desirable for an objective judgment perfectly capable of fine distinctions and the different aspects of a singularly complex reality.[15]

As a human social unity, the State is obliged to recognize the worship of God favourably—not a vague religiosity, but the true religion that honours God in the manner fixed by revelation. No one can extol religious indifference: to do so is to deny the divine transcendence. Truth and error are not two values that can compete with equal rights. If that were the case, 'truth' would be nothing more than a Utopia.

On the other hand, the act of faith is the most personal and free act there is. The Church holds that nobody is to be forced to believe. *Nemo credit nisi volens*, writes Saint Augustine. Moreover, the idea is contradictory; you can plunge someone by force into the baptismal waters, but if his consent is absent, he will come out as he entered—a pagan. Conversions obtained at sword's point are, to say the least, suspect.[16]

These two principles, equally stable, seem to conflict on more than one occasion. Yet one never resolves a problem simply by denying one of the two factors. Both must be kept to maintain the balance. And to do this we must proceed cautiously.[17]

First, let us examine the word liberty. In no way does it imply the absence of all obligation. Talk about *liberty of conscience* can lead one to suppose that all attitudes, even the most fundamental, are left to individual whim. Such a supposition would end in the destruction of the human order. Still we can, according to a phrase of Pius XI, claim *liberty of conscience*, that is, as the inalienable dignity of the human personality. The question, then, is not one of absolute independence, 'which is absurd in a soul created and redeemed by God';[18] rather it is a bold response to all totalitarian oppression.

Next let us peruse the famous question of the *rights of the truth*. We should never forget that we cannot treat human beings as philosophical principles, nor can we treat these principles as persons. In cold terms, truth and error belong to the conceptual order: they are not juridic persons. Living men, however, are true subjects of rights and of duties.[19] Examining the 'rights' of the erroneous conscience more closely, we learn that under the circumstances there is no question of a true moral claim, but only of an excuse to preserve from sin the man who acts in good faith. In no way then, is the Church's function as supreme norm of conscience challenged.[20]

There is, too, the famous distinction between *the thesis and the hypothesis*.* In one form or another, a distinction of this kind appears indispensable. Stated in its traditional terms it can be criticised as too facile and, even too pragmatic in its invention for the case at hand. Furthermore, authors are not agreed on the precise sense that should be attributed to it. By the word *thesis* some understand not only the principles but also the situation corresponding to the principles.[21] In this way, an officially Catholic State would be found on the side of the thesis. Then the *hypothesis* would be a way of acting, not perfectly in harmony with principles, yet nonetheless, imposed by force of circumstances.

Within this interpretation there is danger of arriving at a system seriously tinged with opportunism. It would lead one to believe that the Church claims liberty for herself when in the minority, but that when sufficiently strong she is resolutely determined to employ every means of force to impose her will on the majority. This objection against Catholicism is fairly frequent.

Perhaps it would be better to reserve the title of 'thesis' merely to a consideration of abstract principles. The *hypothesis* would then be found in the concrete circumstances that make up the lives of men and societies. And thus, we would live never in the thesis but always in the hypothesis. The thesis would then be no more than a part artificially separated from the whole. As a true directive it would always have genuine value but it would not have to be exclusive.

There are many other factors, doubtlessly less important, yet so undeniable that any solution desirous of being more than an illusion must take them into account. Moreover, the thesis is not limited to State support of the Church; it implies also respect for Church independence and the dignity of the human person. We might even add—the precaution is not unnecessary—that it pre-supposes the distinction of the two powers: the power of the temporal society and the hierarchical power of the Church.

Thesis and hypothesis are then opposed not unlike the abstract and the concrete, or rather like the dominant though complex idea and the empirical, living institution.

In medieval times when public life was centered in the princes, it was easier to speak of the duty of the State. Then, one spoke of the king and his subjects and determined their respective duties. When the State is no longer incarnate in one man but emanates from a nation that establishes its own directive organs the matter is more difficult to express. In a democratic society the State too quickly becomes an intangible, anonymous entity exempt from all divine and human law. And yet, it owes its life to the free decisions of its responsible leaders and members.

The prince of the Middle Ages was the privileged if not unique subject of all society's duties with regard to the Church. Today, people have replaced the king; governments are nothing more than the embodiment of the people and the expounder of their collective will. Hence obligations which formerly fell to the prince now are incumbent on free citizens responsible for the organization and life of the State.

We can readily understand, then, why it is possible to speak of a State Christian no longer by virtue merely of authority, but by its very life. The influence of its living members is felt more strongly now than it was under the ancient régime.[22]

Still another evolution exists whose importance should not be underestimated. Today, we are more keenly aware of the distinction between the civil and religious domains[23]—this is certainly not something to be regretted. In considering this we return to the very animated discussion regarding laicity of the State. To face this problem with frankness and without useless regret seems to be highly advisable if we are to arrive at a practical arrangement acceptable to both sides.

In making a synthesis of philosophy and theology, St. Thomas began by distinguishing the two planes of thought with a greater accuracy than his predecessors. When particular spheres become visible, thought advances, for the special properties of the different orders, are then more distinctly defined.

We are witnessing the new advance with which the specific value of the natural and technical sciences is being more clearly defined. The very transcendence of revelation demands this autonòmy. The result of it is a truly human enrichment in which every open mind must rejoice. Yet we must not close our eyes to the materializing tendencies of the scientific school and *technocratic* civilization.

In the political order the same reasoning prevails. The 'laicity' of the temporal order, that is, its distinction from the sacred, is stated by the Gospel.[24] Why, then, should it not be acceptable, as long as it does not aspire to an absolute and closed autonomy that could degenerate into 'laicism'?

In the course of centuries, this laicity has expressed itself in various ways. As we have noted, the history of different nations is not synchronized. In rereading the Syllabus of Pius IX, the declarations of Leo XIII on liberty, and the messages of Pius XII on the democratic constitutions of peoples, one cannot fail to sense the profound change, not of principles but of historic situations that have introduced a decided shift in accent.[25]

It is not surprising that the hierarchy experienced at first a feeling of uneasiness and opposition in the face of the so-called modern freedoms, for these were in fact announced with rationalist pretensions and anti-christian challenges. The nineteenth century thought it had effected the triumph of reason and the total independence of the collective will with regard to morals and God. Equally encumbered with the same anti-religious mortgages, the first theories of biological evolution put the Church on her guard too. If they have lost some of their virulence, laicising tendencies are still far from being inoffensive.

In a theoretical discussion, it is comparatively easy to remain calm; when one speaks of Spain and France, however, disputes flare up. Let us try to look at things impartially. The Iberian peninsula did not know the French revolution; it had been sheltered from two world wars. On the other hand, it has been torn by bloody civil wars whose memory alone pales the faces of the survivors. For centuries Spain fought in the breach to defend her Catholic Faith against the Moors, against the Reformation and finally against Marxism. Her proud, self-willed temperament, inclined toward undisguised absolutism, has almost led her to identify 'Spanishness' with Catholicism. At the very least, her ardent, knightly character does not seem fashioned for a democracy of the Anglo-Saxon type.

An objective observer will fear the return of extreme violence and the first victim would undoubtedly be the Church. As things stand now, most Spanish believers beseech heaven for the salvation of the Caudillo and his army. They are hardly disposed to heed the counsels of their foreign co-religionists who prefer to see a larger, more sensitive outlook, fewer police, and more capable and determined social workers. That alone can prevent the resentment of the poor— *los mas bajos* as the Spaniards say—from one day exploding into new disaster.

Spaniards claim that their nation is wholly Catholic. If we consult the baptismal registers, the claim appears accurate. Still an elementary prudence demands that we distinguish between personal conviction and mere conformity, between fervent Christians and the indifferent and opposed temporarily reduced to silence. We must not place too much hope in the last two categories. Those who from temperament or fear are today resigned will not hesitate to follow the revolutionaries of tomorrow. Present measures of constraint will provoke a serious reaction. The education of the mind is an arduous task that must begin among Churchmen and responsible lay people. Until now they have been too inclined toward a wholesale condemnation of every representative of democracy, (whether it be Stalin, Eisenhower or Jacques Maritain) instinctively preferring security by force to confidence in humanity and the means of religious persuasion and transformation. Their attention and their efforts should be directed toward building a city sociologically Christian and not merely one juridically Catholic.

For, as one of them has written, 'the State is not built with rational truths or with truths of faith, but above all with collective truths.'[26] M. Jacques Leclercq develops this idea in the following manner: 'The State's duty to promote truth should be interpreted as formation of socially favourable conditions which enable citizens to find truth.'[27]

In the famous articles of the revue, *Esprit*, MM. Vialatoux and Latreille have similarly distinguished between the State and the popular community: the first should be lay, the second, Christian.[28]

The separation, however, has obviously been pushed too far. We freely accept a lay State in the sense determined by the French Bishops.[29] But to pretend, for example, that Belgium could be lay while Flanders and Wallonia could be Christian would only cause smiles. Keeping in mind the nuances made above, the State itself should recognize God; otherwise it will lack a logical objective basis for its authority. The popular community should on the other hand renounce religious coercion which though not juridically organized, can be just as oppressive and nauseating as that of the law and of the police. The intolerance of Madrid students propagates more bitterness than all the severity of the Spanish Constitution.

Even in the eyes of the most progressive French Catholics, the lay State is not an ideal one if it lacks the corrective of a personalist Christian society so cherished by the authors of *Esprit*. Let us not equate them with the progressives following in the wake of Communism. When the former reject the clerical State as a renewal of the Jewish theocracy replaced by the Gospel, or of the Caesaropapism which restricted the Church so gravely throughout the ages, we must not immediately brand them heretics or denounce them as short-sighted.[30] Like us, they abhor a form of government that proclaims neutrality but soon drifts from indifference to religious hostility. Without being niggardly, however, we could wish that more of them were realistic and consistent in constructive activity.

Permit us to add a theological comparison. Incarnation and disincarnation, theocracy and laicity are themselves theological terms dealing with relations between the divine and the human. Could we not apply to the problem under discussion the lessons which have come from the battle between Nestorianism and Monophysism?

In forbidding to the Church any action in the human sphere, one tends towards a separatism of the Nestorian type. The duality of persons in Christ, conjured up by the patriarch of Constantinople, resulted in the break-up of the vital tie that makes the Man-God a unique subject, and left instead only two mutually impenetrable elements and consequently, there is no more Redemption.

Likewise, if the temporal society breaks away from the Church completely, it will arise a pagan idol. Then, the most remote contact with the final end of man is broken. At most we would have two superimposed plans with no bond between them. The Germans call this *Zweistocktheologie*: in the upper storey is religion, sequestered and imprisoned; and the ground floor, windows barred and doors bolted, is nothing more than a sombre dungeon for man retired within himself.

At the opposite extreme there exists a sociological Monophysism, which fixes the temporal and the religious in inextricable confusion. As in the Christological heresy, the divine element would absorb the human element instead of penetrating and ennobling it. Strictly speaking, Christ would then be neither man nor God, only a pious mixture. In the same way, the fusion of the Church and City tends toward a chaos wherein the sacred is very literally profaned and the profane loses its very destination, dignity and redemption. Such disorder is profitable neither to Church nor to State, but rather impedes the life of both.

While avoiding any illegitimate intrusion on the part of the clergy, well-understood laicity will make the civil community an open society benefiting from the wider perspectives of social progress and efficacious sanctification. It is true that saints and mystics will sometimes be the greatest benefactors of their homelands. To organize the temporal as if it were destined to be our definitive home is to condemn humanity to everlasting hard labour in the prison of this world.

The Laity in Charge of Their Lay Work

This sub-title contains nothing revolutionary; it simply enunciates the concrete application of the doctrine already exposed.

To see in this a programme of autonomist claims would not only falsify and strain the position but would also vitiate it by creating a 'layistic' atmosphere. We are seeking to preserve religious interests in the social realm. If our purpose is to build and not to destroy, we must see this profane world in the light of an idea of life openly Catholic but still far removed from all subjection to any kind of clericalism, old or new.

After all, specifically lay work receives its real consecration from the fact that the worker as a member of the ecclesiastical community takes his inspiration from a higher principle and envisages a superior end for his work which in no way detracts from its intrinsic value.

Consequently, in public life he maintains a broadness large enough to effect a loyal collaboration with representatives of other 'philosophies,' provided they observe the same tolerance and are not set to undermine the Christian conviction of their fellow citizens. It is worthless to recognize the contribution of Christianity to civilization verbally if in the meantime one *does* everything possible to cause this Christian spirit to disappear as soon as possible. Such an attitude makes understanding inaccessible and enmeshes its defenders in self-contradiction. If it is true that Catholicism enriches Western culture, then it is equally true that it cannot be eliminated without impoverishing that culture. And so even from the humanist point of view it must be granted the right to live.

We have in common with socialism, it has been said, an interest in 'man.' But unless they are merely playing on words, socialists should not treat man as a being essentially and totally imprisoned in this world. Let them leave the question open. Catholics, for their part, cannot deprive human work of its proper orientation, the common temporal good. Under these conditions the two groups can walk a good part of the way together even though their basically differing concepts of life must necessarily come to the fore now and then and cause friction. The difficulty is inevitable. While losing none of our courage all of us must bear these inconveniences. If we do not, believers should, as Saint Paul says, retire from this world.

A German theologian, H. M. Koester, gives an interesting description of the spirit of the lay Catholic.[31] The mission of the layman, he says, amounts to this: he is to organize the realm of the profane in such a way that it is in accord with the gratuitous bestowal that the Word makes of Himself. And so it will be his job to combat the remnants of fallen nature that exist in the communal life of society. As far as his influence extends, his prime concern will be to order the field of human energy so that its sane and harmonious proportions adapt humanity more and more to the Body of Christ. The layman is to rescue the world from its hostile indifference to God, from the self-efficiency of its laicism. He is to place nature in the milieu of Advent; that is, in a situation of expectancy. Such a mission he will accomplish by conquering and ordering all institutions —public, social, economic and cultural, according to nature's laws, as they were determined by God and orientated toward Him.

We are in complete agreement with the author; only the word 'conquering' displeases us. It smacks of imperialism. Catholics need not master temporal institutions in order to exert stronger influence. On the other hand, they would do wrong to leave the world make itself without them,[32] and in many circumstances it will be clear that, to give an impulse to the whole, they ought to have their own organizations.

Father Koester continues: That part of the world which falls to the layman ought to be assumed by him as an extension and prolongation of his own redeemed humanity; he is to judge it by the norms that direct the behaviour of his own nature. His person and his corner of the world are to be orientated beyond himself toward God. Thanks to this, a world which is becoming purified will be incorporated in the universal restoration under a new Head, Jesus Christ, who wishes to take unto Himself all the domains of life just as He has taken up all of our human nature. The priest's role, then, shall consist in elevating this world renovated by the laity to the supernatural and to that end he shall dispense the sacraments, especially the Eucharist. In the fertile union of nature and grace with their offspring, salvation, the layman represents nature and the priest, grace, with this reservation: the layman cannot by-pass the sanctifying help of the clergy.

Fr. Koester's twofold division gives us an over-simplified image; it unfortunately leaves us with the impression that the layman first prepares nature in a movement beginning from the bottom and envisioning at the top the further addition of the priest's sanctifying power. The layman, however, first needs grace and priestly help to cleanse his own nature. The author, too, concedes this at the end of his remarks. In reality, the whole movement comes from on high; it seizes nature, especially in the layman's activity, in order to sanctify it all at once and not in a process of two steps, to orient it toward the celestial reality, that is, its final end. If from the start laymen are unaware of this, the 'two-storey' theology which they—and we—want to avoid will be the inevitable result.

Continuing his exposition, the author rightly emphasizes that through the priest's hands the layman receives grace from on high so as to pass it on to his fellow creatures. He is on the same level as they are and so he can influence them more directly than the priest, who, isolated more or less by his office, will not attempt to take the place of the layman in effecting this mission of diffusion.

Such is the foundation upon which rests the autonomy of the layman's responsibility for the laity's work. They are not seeking a spiritual independence that will put them outside the Church community. They merely wish to accomplish their specific task by devoting themselves wholly to it. In no way are they aiming at a separation from the Church, but rather at an emphasis of the distinction of spheres so that bishops may be spared the odious accusation of 'playing politics.' Refusal of overweening protectionism is a sure sign of maturity.

A wholesome pedagogy condemns parents who refuse to realize that their children have come of age and can now decide for themselves. Yet this independence is the very purpose of education. The Church knows this—even if all her priests do not seem to realise that lay people are not perpetually children—and she develops among her faithful prudence and Christian strength so that the exercise of their just liberty may lead them to salvation and not to ruin.

To emphasize this point, Cardinal Verdier once addressed the following words to his clergy: There was a time when pastors reigned as princes by the grace of God; in our time, they are no more than constitutional kings.[33] If the eminent prelate could pursue his thought today, he would undoubtedly say they are no longer princes at all. Other than the inalienable dignity of their ordination, they have nothing but their apostolic zeal with which to influence the crowds. The sacred power which the bishop renders them assures them of neither competence nor prestige in cultural works. The studies preparatory to the priesthood envision only pastoral service. It would be deplorable, however, if with regard to general culture they appeared to be on a primitive level. They cannot boast of a universal knowledge, and the simple recognition of this fact would create the best impression. Only a real primitive could disagree. Parishioners do not demand that their pastor be an intellectual, but they earnestly ask that he be kind, humble, detached, and if possible, a saint.

If it is legitimate to speak of certain priestly superiority, that superiority lies exclusively in the spiritual order. Occasionally, there will be some scientific celebrities. The Church rejoices with men like these: for the myth of the obscurantist clergy is all the more easily dissipated. Catholic universities and pontifical academies have an apologetic value that should never be disregarded.

The parish priest as a rule does not seek the company of intellectuals; rather, he dreads it. Because of a lack of comprehension or tact, he sometimes finds himself embarrassed, and this is unfortunate. The simpler people demand less. Without any particular pretension, they are often more open to the message. In this sense, the words of the Gospel are always true: *pauperes evangelizantur*. They show themselves more grateful, too, for the zeal that the priest consecrates to them.

Certainly the soul of a distinguished scholar is no more valuable than that of a worker or a farmer. But the social and therefore religious influence of the intellectual is indeed far-reaching. And so for him there is more responsibility, and consequently, a more urgent duty for the priest of preparing him spiritually for his future mission. Even if the working class were to comprise 95% of tomorrow's population, no one would dare say that the remaining 5% accounted for only one twentieth of the fortunes and misfortunes of society. Actually, these 5% will often give the tone to the rest as long as the desire to advance remains society's most powerful stimulus.

The twentieth century has truly become the century of the masses: it is high time that we became interested in their leaders. The elite will gain in importance from day to day, provided, of course, that they do not isolate themselves.

Among the ranks of the clergy one not infrequently hears this statement: 'It is most important to impress upon the laity that they themselves have to direct their own work.' The counsel is one of pure gold so long as it does not end half-way. The 'impression' must carry over to reality; otherwise, it is mere sham, illusion rather than conviction. To be on the board of directors is not enough for laymen; they must also be conscious of leadership and must feel its responsibility.[34]

With regard to the priest a question of equity is involved. In this larger apostolate, he will be in charge as a priest and the layman will be in charge as a layman. Far from excluding each other, the two missions imply one another. While this may appear to be a truism, nevertheless the maxim is not without meaning, even if it does not yield concrete solutions as if by magic. From the first it is exceedingly important to take an exact position regarding principles. The one cannot do the job of the other. Each must organize his work according to his respective mission. On the part of the layman that will demand a greater broadening of spirit and a sincere docility before the hierarchical power he is to accept as a gift of God. On the part of the priest it demands such a respect for the Christian personality that he will not attempt to reduce it to the level of an unintelligent instrument. All autonomism is destructive of personality. In the order of Redemption God gives man the dignity of a second cause in his own salvation and the role of collaborator in the salvation of others.

The clergy and laity each work in their own way. If they oppose one another as rival factions, then one will overturn the other and dissension will be the result. On the contrary, both parties should feel themselves integral parts of a vast organism that can only grow through cordial collaboration. Instead of each contesting the influence of the other, they should both seek rather to respect and evaluate the various tasks and dignities of each; on it depends the harmonious building of the Body of Christ. The priest alone is the custodian of the sacred gift and the rightful teacher of doctrine. To receive these treasures, the layman must go to the priest and bring others to him. But the priest must never forget the lesson of humility and charity which Christ gave His disciples by washing their feet at the Last Supper. Like the Master, the priest should draw all to himself, that is to say, the whole world; but not all its affairs. Otherwise, his abuse of power will provoke resistance. Christ exercised this universal attraction in the sacrifice of the Cross. The wish to dominate all, even for a most praiseworthy end, is a human device in no way inspired by faith. A disinterested service will rather be the well-spring for true recognition. Only then will the priest be aiding laymen to be truly 'lay' in the Christian sense of the word, and laymen will in turn be aiding the priest to be truly a priest by manifesting their eagerness to receive his priestly gift and power, doctrine, sacraments, Gospel law—all that charged with grace. By the witness of his Christian life in the world the layman will radiate in all directions the descending movement coming from God, so that at every moment the horizontal diffusion will remain in vertical dependence upon God and His Church.

In this way, every part, as Saint Paul says,[35] will fulfil its function in the measure given to each of the members for the realisation of the Body. The hierarchy cannot suppress the role of the living faithful, free and responsible collaborators, without harming and destroying the Body. If the members think they have to shake off a yoke and claim total independence, they will in the process impede the flow of supernatural force. Once this is done, the Body can only become emaciated and perish, and the layman will no longer be a layman but an infidel. If even while making acts of faith, he refused to dedicate himself actively to the Church, he would also squander his vocation. If he only would not try to hide his laziness under the specious pretext that the activity of the clergy is too usurping! Perfect equilibrium will never come in a day. None the less, it remains the only ideal norm commanding all the Body's vital actions until that Body of Christ attains its full measure.

* According to the *thesis*, the State is bound to promote the true religion of God; the *hypothesis* refers to particular cases where, because of another greater good, this duty of the State is either modified or totally suspended. (Tr.).

1 For the analysis of this phenomenon and for other historical examples see Y. CONGAR, *o.c.*, *Réforme*, pp. 319 ff.

2 Y. CONGAR, *o.c.*, *Réforme*, p. 39. Selections from the *Introduction* of this work, trans. by L. C. SHEPPARD can be read in the *Downside Review*, Summer, 1953. Reprinted in *Cross Currents*, Summer, 1953, pp. 358-365.

3 Examples of this superficial mentality are to be found in certain violent pages of the collective work entitled: *La déchristianisation des masses prolétariennes*. (Centre d'Etudes sociales Godefroid Kurth, Session 1946-1947). Tournai, 1948.

4 Among others, see E. MOUNIER, *Feu la Chrétienté* (Carnets de route), Paris, 1950, passim.

5 It does not suffice, says FATHER CONGAR, *o.c.*, *Réforme*, p. 280, to mobilize prelates and theologians; the clergy and the people must enter into the movement.

6 To the 'moralism' of the simple conversion of the heart by prayer and example, it is highly imperative to add the extirpation of abuses and the constructive measures of a new Christian and human order. For the Gregorian Reform and that of the mendicant orders, see CONGAR, *o.c.*, *Réforme*, pp. 192 ff.

7 Concerning the question of principles, cf. G. THILS, *Transcendance ou Incarnation?* Louvain, 1950.

8 'Such an action does not end the Christian's relations with others; to the contrary, it is a way of developing greater efficiency and a more powerful solidarity.' A. DON-DEYNE, *o.c.*, *Tolérance et Communauté humaine*, p. 121.

9 *O.c.*, *Les Evénements et la Foi*, p. 126. Cf. *ib.*, p. 98: 'That we might become conscious of this drama, we needed to see the overthrow of our supposed conquests, the crushing of our apologetical systems, the scandal of clericalism, Vichy and resistance . . . .'

10 Concerning this temptation to pure interiorism, see H. DE LUBAC, *o.c.*, *Méditation sur l'Eglise*, pp. 140, 173, 180. This tendency is particularly outstanding in *Les Evénements et la Foi* with its pressing insistence on the sin *of* the Church, a prisoner of out-moded structures which affords a spectacle of deviations and betrayals. Whence re-course to the invisible Church. See v.g., pp. 108, 131, etc.

11 H. DUMÉRY, *Les trois Tentations de l'apostolat moderne* (Rencontres, 28), Paris, 1948, p. 126. Fr. M. D. CHENU is another opposed to clerical 'organizations': *Corps de l'Eglise et Structures sociales*. In *Jeunesse de l'Eglise*, 8, 1948, pp. 145-153., Cf. also H. C. DES-ROCHES, *Laïcisme athée et structures religieuses*. Ib., pp. 117-145.

12 *Les Evénements et la Foi*, p. 162. This text is taken from No. 5 of *Jeunesse de l'Eglise*.

13 H. DE LUBAC, *o.c.*, *Méditation sur l'Eglise*, pp. 152 ff. Pius XII. underlined this duty of the hierarchy in his address to the Cardinals and Bishops, Nov. 2, 1954. See the *Osservatore Romano* for Nov. 4, 1954.

14 In a discourse to the Christian Workers of Belgium given September 11, 1949, Pius XII. warned Catholic organizations against the temptation of not using but abusing their power. Cf. *Docum. Cath.*, 46, 1949, col. 1285. Likewise, in a radio message to the International Jocist Congress of September 3, 1950, he dispels all narrowminded 'workerism', Cf. *Docum. Cath.*, 47, 1950, col. 1549 ff.

15 The recent literature on this problem is abundant. As an attempt at classification of the various opinions, you will find useful the work of C. MELZI, *Laicità e confessionalità dello Stato*, in *Scuola Cattolica*, 80, 1952, pp. 194-222. The author has a very complete bibliography. Cf. also: *Dieu et César. Le problème de la conscience religieuse devant l'Etat*, in *Docum. Cath.*, 49. 1952, col. 718-750.

BISHOP FELTIN, *L'Eglise et la liberté* (Semaine des Intellectuels Catholiques), Paris, 1952. We especially call to your attention the conference given by P. ROUQUETTE, S.J., *Le problème du pluralisme religieux*, pp. 211-224, and that of M. A. DANSETTE, *L'Eglise et la Liberté dans l'Histoire du XIX. siecle*, pp. 198-211.

Concerning relations with dissident Christians, consult: Pasteur J. CADIER, BISHOP CHEVROT, etc., *Unité chrétienne et Tolérance religieuse* (*Dialogues*, 3), Paris, 1950.

From the point of view of principles, one of the best joint works is the collection already cited of R. AUBERT, L. BOUYER, etc., *Tolérance et communauté humaine* (*Cahiers de l'Actualité religieuse*), Paris, Tournai, 1952. Note especially the contributions of R. AUBERT, *L'enseignement du Magistère ecclésiastique au XIXe siècle sur le Libéralisme*, pp. 75-103. A. LÉONARD, O.P., *Liberté de foi et tolérance civile*, pp. 123-160. B. OLIVIER, O.P., *Les 'Droits' de la conscience. Le problème de la conscience errante.*, pp. 163-190.

In favour of 'laicity', read the very remarkable articles of J. VIALATOUX and A. LATREILLE, *Christianisme et Laïcité*, in the review *Esprit*, 17 B, 1949, pp. 520 ff. and 18 B, 1950, 387 ff. For the opposite view, E. GUERRERO, *El Estado laico como ideal de régimen politico cristiano*, in *Razón y Fe*, 142, 1950. pp. 341-354; 143, 1951, pp. 29-44 and 140-157. *Mas sobre la libertad religiosa en Espana*; *ib.*, 149, 1954, p. 327-342. Also L. PALACIOS, *El Mito de la nueva cristianidad*, 2nd ed., Madrid, 1952.

With finer distinctions, the various articles of P. A. MESSINEO in *Civiltà Cattolica*; among others: *Libertà religiosa et libertà di coscienza*, a. 101, 1950, III, p. 237-247. *La Stato e la Religione*, a. 102, 1951, I, p. 293-304. *Democrazia e laicismo di Stato*, a. 102, 1951, II, p. 585-596. *Stato laico e Stato laicizzante*, a. 103, 1952, I. p. 129-140. *Laicismo politico e dottrina cattolica*, a. 103, 1952, II. p. 18-28, etc. The last two articles are reprinted in *Doc. Cath.*, o.c.

The works of J. MARITAIN are always worthwhile. See esp. *True Humanism*, London, 1950; *Religion and Culture*, (Essays in Order, 1). Trans., J. F. SCANLON, London, 1931; *Christianity and Democracy*, Trans., D. C. ANSON, New York, 1944. *Man and the State* (Ch. R. Walgreen Foundation Lectures), Chicago, Ill., 1951.

From a more theological point of view: CH. JOURNET, *L'Eglise du Verbe incarné*, I, Paris, 1941, pp. 217 ff.; F. M. STRATMANN, O.P., *Jésus-Christ et l'Etat*. Translated by P. LORSON, Paris, Tournai, 1952.

16 J. MOUROUX, *Je crois en toi. Structure personnelle de l'acte de foi*, Paris, 1949. G. PHILIPS, *Le mystère de la Foi*, Louvain, 1952. A. LÉONARD, *Liberté de la foi, Tolérance et communauté humaine*, pp. 133 and 146 ff.

17 Cf. B. OLIVIER, o.c., *Les 'Droits' de la conscience*, p. 184.

18 PIUS XI., *Enc. 'Non abbiamo'*. Eng. Trans., *Concerning Catholic Action*, N.C.W.C., Washington, p. 21.

19 The very pertinent observation of P. ROUQUETTE, *a.c.*, *Le Problème du pluralisme religieux*, p. 220.

20 Cf. B. OLIVIER, *a.c.*, *Les 'Droits' de la conscience*, p. 180. In an outstanding address to Italian Catholic jurists, Dec. 6, 1953, Pius XII. set forth two principles: 1. Whatever does not correspond to truth and to the moral law has *objectively* no right to exist, to be propagated or to act. 2. The State's failure to restrain such movements or institutions by laws and coercive measures can nevertheless be justified if the State is acting in the interest of a higher or more extensive good. God Himself shows this *tolerance* since He allows to exist the evil that He condemns. Hence, such action cannot be immoral. The affirmation that religious error must always be suppressed is not of absolute and unconditional value. There exists no precept with this sense—neither from God, nor from the human and Christian conscience, nor from the Church. On the contrary, one must recall the parable of the tares which must be allowed to grow amongst the wheat (*Mt.* XIII, 24-30). In the concrete case, the Catholic State should base its decision on the comparison of the distressing results of tolerance with the disastrous consequences which intolerance threatens to provoke in the bosom of the Community of Nations, and, indirectly, even within its own territory. Cf. *Acta*

Apl. Sedis, 1953, pp. 794-802, esp. under n. V. Cf. G. Di Meglio, in *Amer. Eccl. Rev.,* 130, 1954, pp. 384-387.

[21] Cf. J. Leclercq, *Etat chrétien et liberté de l'Eglise* in the *Vie Intell.,* February, 1949, p. 99. With a slightly different distinction: A. Léonard, *a.c., Liberté de la foi,* p. 156.

[22] Cf. B. Olivier, *Les 'Droits' de la conscience,* pp. 189 ff.

[23] A. Dondeyne, *o.c., Le Chrétien de demain,* p. 265 ff.

[24] 'It is Christ who has promulgated the laicity of the State.' Sub-title for the *Docum. Cath.,* 49, 1952, col. 717, in the translation of the article of P. Messineo, *Stato laico e Stato laicizzante.*

[25] R. Aubert has an excellent exposé on this point: *a.c., Le Magistère ecclésiastique et le libéralisme,* esp. p. 97. See also: A. Dansette, *a.c., L'Eglise et la liberté,* pp. 198 ff. A, Léonard, *a.c., Liberté de la foi,* p. 148. *Ib.,* p. 152: 'Laicity is one of the juridic expressions of the faith; we do not believe that it is the only one.'

[26] C. Santamaria, *Autour de l'Etat idéal,* in *Docum. Cath.,* 49, 1952, col. 748. (Taken from *Documentos,* 1952, n. 10.)

[27] J. Leclercq, *a.c., Etat chrétien,* p. 110.

[28] J. Vialatoux and A. Latreille, *a.c., Christianisme et Laïcité.*

[29] Cf. *Supra,* Chap. I. note 11.

[30] E. Guerrero, *a.c., Estado laico,* p. 156, rather strongly criticises the opinion of J. Maritain on 'Christianity'. Notwithstanding this, in his review of *Man and the State* published in *Razón y Fe,* 149, 1954, p. 90 ff. he states that he is substantially in agreement with Maritain concerning principles, except in regard to the prohibition of heterodox propaganda, prohibition which Fr. Guerrero wants to maintain especially in the name of national unity,.

[31] H. M. Koester, *Die Magd des Herrn,* Limburg-Lahn, 1947, pp. 424 ff. We are translating according to the sense and not according to the letter, but as exactly as possible.

[32] Cf. the excellent remarks of Card. Suhard, *Growth or Decline? The Church Today.* Trans. by J. A. Corbett, Chicago, 3rd. ed., 1950, pp. 74 ff, Esp. p. 76. *The Meaning of God, ed. cit.,* N.Y., 1949, pp. 35 ff.

[33] Card. Verdier, *Discours* of February 20, 1931. Cf. *Docum. Cath.,* t. 25, col. 588.

[34] F. Varillon, *Sacerdoce et laïcat,* in *Masses ouvrières,* March 1947, pp. 40 ff. Reappeared in Y. Congar and F. Varillon, *Sacerdoce et Laïcat dans l'Eglise (Problèmes du clergé diocésain,* 2) Paris, 1946.

[35] Cf. *supra,* Chap. II., pp. 19 ff.

CHAPTER VII

THE LAITY AND CATHOLIC ACTION

IN OUR TIME, the Church has addressed an explicit call to the laity to obtain their collaboration in her work, particularly in Catholic Action. In its present usage, the term is recent. Apart from in Italy, where it was originally introduced to designate the social activity of the laity, it acquired its technical meaning only under the pontificate of Pius XI, who made the success of Catholic Action his personal responsibility and one of the dominating objectives of his pontificate. Here as in everything that touches the profound life of the Church, the riches are so abundant and varied that theology experiences great difficulty in its attempt to synthesize them. It can only succeed in doing so by prolonged study and by attempting various successive approaches. Let us try to describe these stages.

Note first the parallelism with the dogmatic treatise on 'the Church.' The first systematic work in this matter dates back to the time of the Reformation; still no genius of the stature of Saint Thomas Aquinas has been found to give these expositions their definitive structure. Yet the study of the problem is in full progress and even now is undergoing all the phenomena proper to growth. In the history of theology three centuries is a short time. What, then, must be said of the thirty years of official Catholic Action?

The very mention of this name immediately evokes all the thorny problems surrounding the hierarchy and the laity and often involve heated arguments. Difficulties arrive in flocks whenever anyone attempts a commentary, no matter how general it may be. The officially commissioned organization of the lay apostolate is a fairly recent undertaking; one or two generations hardly suffice for its assimilation by the general body of Christians. It interferes with all the lines of forces in the Church and puts to the question all the relations between clergy, religious, and laity; such delicate interplay is not resolved in a moment's time. The flowering of monastic life once knew similar anxieties. The activity of the mendicant orders and later that of religious congregations was not accepted everywhere without controversy; history keeps alive the memory of often virulent conflicts.

But these tensions do not arrest life. Any authentically evangelical force eventually breaks through and is accepted, though sometimes only at the price of an adaptation of its original form.

There is talk today of a 'crisis' in Catholic Action. This is no reason for discouragement. If a young man does not enter a crisis, he is lost; if he does, every hope is permitted. The Chinese ideogram 'crisis' has two meanings: It can mean both a grave danger and an exceptional opportunity. What is more the two often touch each other. In the light of revelation and theology, we must first make a detailed and rational study to establish what Catholic Action is not and then to determine progressively what it is.

NEGATIVE APPROACHES

Are we in the presence of a *supremely desperate attempt at clericalisation* in which a group of well-disposed servants let themselves be dragged along by priests, who are only spiritual politicians?

We find an echo to this accusation in the small book of H. U. von Balthasar cited above, which visibly roused the theological world.[1] According to him, Catholic Action was created by an arbitrary decision from above. The failure of this artificial institution is evident where it should have been most successful, among adults. The only hope comes from the Lay Institutes recently recognized by the Roman Constitution, *Provida Mater*. The lay members of these new groups belong to the juridical state of perfection. In binding themselves to the evangelical counsels, they enjoy the freedom necessary to consecrate themselves to apostolic labour, an ideal forbidden to married people because of their state in life. For Fr. von Balthasar, the Lay Institute constitutes a type of habit-less religious community; for the moment, however, only his evaluation of the layman's apostolic action interests us. If he is right, Catholic Action is impossible to effect and, perhaps, even unthinkable.

Is it exact to say that it owes its origin to one authoritarian act?[2] Such an absolute assertion has no basis. The movement started by Pius XI was not simply an answer to a need of the moment; it also incorporated aspirations and organizations that were far from new at that time. What was new was this official character consecrating and authenticating lay activity. Basically, the apostolic zeal of the simple faithful is as old as the Church. Pius XI taught this repeatedly and his successor is no less explicit.[3]

But what about the *artificial* character of the undertaking? E. Michel formulates this reproach in strong terms: 'lay groupings of Catholic Action, hybrid creations of a modern clericalism attempting by these intermediaries to escape from its ghetto, but only succeeding in pulling the laity in with it.'[4] Hence among thinking Catholics an unconcealed resentment against this politic of constraint and an unambiguous refusal to enter in this regimentation.

The picture is obviously too pessimistic. Proof of this lies in the existence of similar apostolic movements among the laity of the dissident churches. Protestants and Orthodox are not accustomed to seek inspiration from Rome and can never be accused of clericalism. It could well be, however, that with his appeal to the laity Pius XI was ahead of his time as was Saint Pius X with Eucharistic devotion. Neither measure has always been perfectly understood; both have met resistance, especially from the German speaking countries. In addition, Pius XI had to reckon with the hostility of the Nazi régime.

A show of hesitancy on the part of the community is not necessarily a reproach to the hierarchical initiative. The Pope's call to the layman was not imprudent even if his clear-sightedness seemed premature. Far-sweeping views of faith will always be too much for the eyes of the timid. In fact, one wonders whether Rome has been too fast or Catholics too slow. We need only recall the coolness with which many well-disposed circles received the social encyclicals.

Nevertheless, this apathy on the part of adults toward Catholic Action needs an explanation. Sometimes churchmen, priests or not, confuse the spread of religion with the strategic positions and influential posts the clergy happen to occupy in the world. Yet the strongest organizations—and they have to be strong!—can cause us disillusionment. The precautions of certain Church-leaders are guided by a narrowness of spirit rather than by any insidious intention. They cling to the tiller to avoid the uncertain steering of novices. Such an apprehension, however, is at the base of every totalitarian régime. Fear of the abuse of liberty becomes the leader's sole motivating principle. Always somewhat incomplete, wisdom of this sort sterilizes education. The most radical way to keep infants from falling is to tie them to a chair; but if you keep this up long, there is a good chance that they will never walk.

Gone are the days that saw the parish priest as the embodiment of the law and prophets for his parishioners; no longer will the mayor and schoolmaster come to the rectory to receive their orders. However, there are still ways of softening characters and gilding chains so well that the spiritless will wear them without disgust and even with a certain pride. Should such a system be practised under the guise of religion, we would be in the presence of a blatant violation of conscience. But the revolutions of history have undertaken to remove all actuality from the legend of the Grand Inquisitor. At the moment, we are not

considering those laypeople, men as well as women, the right arm of
their pastor in all parish activities, those who show a zeal of the
highest value. Current German Catholicism, among others, is graced
with a great number of such people. Irreplaceable as they may be,
however, they do not represent the specific ideal of Catholic Action.
The latter do not approve of 'those plain-clothes priests who can be
distinguished from the clergy only by the fact that they do not
say Mass.' On the contrary, Catholic Action calls the laity to the task
of the laity in the religious and profane worlds. It is based—and this
must be emphasized—not on the separation but rather on the distinction
of spheres and of duties.

There are always certain kinds of people who show their need to
lean on a more vigorous temperament, especially when the latter
offers the guarantees of the cassock. Such timid souls shudder before
every responsibility. Some leaders instinctively surround themselves
with second class workers, easily manoeuvrable and 100% followers,
who will clearly never afford themselves the luxury of a personal idea.
In a recent declaration, Pius XII deplored this lack of responsible
initiative. And he is not speaking of clericalism here, because the clergy
certainly are not the only ones who have committed this error.
'The True Concept of Catholic Action is not in harmony with the
mentality of those members who consider themselves inert wheels of
a gigantic machine, incapable of self-movement as long as the central
force does not set them in motion. It is inadmissible to picture Catholic
Action leaders as operators standing before the instrument panel of
a power plant, eager only to throw or to break, to limit or to direct
the current in the vast circuit.'

'Above all, they must exercise a personal moral influence, the
normal consequence of the esteem and sympathy they know how
to win, which will lend weight to their suggestions and counsels, and
authority to their experience.' [5]

Let us not judge an entire movement by the defects that occasionally
show in one particular realisation. To make a fair judgment, a larger
and fundamentally sympathetic view is indispensable.

Can it be said that Catholic Action has suffered a total loss?

There were certainly many disappointed hopes among those who
considered Catholic Action a magic recipe. It showed itself ineffective:
the proletariat masses are not re-entering the Church, dechristianization
continues, the influence of Christianity on public and social life
remains weak or non-existent.

There is no advance . . . we are marking time . . . the island of
Christianity in the midst of the pagan sea is more heavily populated
yet remains an island . . . even the feast of Christ the King is quickly

waning . . . we waste our words on methods that no longer work
. . . nobody believes in the formula any more. . . . And so the list
of grievances multiplies. [6]

Let us first look at the essential.

The idea, and even more, the realization of Catholic Action is a
matter so complex and delicate that many work a long time before
discovering its secret. One could apply here the maxim of Chesterton
that Christianity was never applied to find out if it was ineffective:
it was discovered that it was difficult to apply and so men excused
themselves from ever putting it into practice. Such a line of action
hardly justifies a condemnation of Catholic Action.

The initial enthusiasm could hardly be expected to last. In the
wake of the great discovery, most did not fathom the inherent
difficulties of the undertaking. Men had already been labouring
many years to reconquer little by little a world fast becoming pagan.
For the priests the burden was heavy and sometimes literally overwhelming. Amidst such difficulty, the Papal call to the laity resounded
like a clarion of liberation. Had someone at last found the magic
solution which would bring back the masses in one sweep and assure
a superabundant harvest? Unfortunately, after the first fruits had
been won, the crops dwindled more and more.

Revelation does not unfold such glorious perspectives. This new
method likewise appears slow to crack the hard shell of materialism.
Not an universal and infallible remedy, it is rather an immense
programme of work. The preparation of leaders alone requires years
of effort and often, once formed, they too become engrossed in other
pre-occupations and a new beginning with new candidates is needed.
You cannot conjure up by magic a team of zealous and capable laymen.
A stubborn and crafty propagandist trained in all the techniques is
still not a man of faith and even less an apostle. And furthermore the
inertia of those who are Christian in name only is disarming for a
leader's enthusiasm. Ready-made solutions falter before complex
problems. Worst of all, truly dedicated men must bear the criticism
of those expert captains who have never been to sea.

Only a tried faith can resist deceptions. We have many promises
of eternity, but let us beware of the mirage of easy victory. No
one has told us that the Church intends to establish her domain here
on earth; the Gospel forewarns us about obstinate resistance and even
persecution. What awaits the disciples is not necessarily success, but
a life of witness to the Master. And this result is always obtained,
even in the face of contradiction. From this viewpoint, sincere effort
is always a victory; effective in itself, the word of God surpasses human
weakness. There is no doubt that a false supernaturalism would be

the most dangerous substitute imaginable in the matter. But a lack of supernatural faith would dry up every source. Moreover, without such faith we could not witness the undeniable renewals being effected in the very heart of the masses.

Unlike fatalism, faith does not maintain that environment must always exercise a depraving effect and that social influences destroy religious life. On the contrary, it encourages them to aid this life although it in no way envisages a new nature free from original sin and concupiscence. Faith calls out to the disinherited and to those farthest astray. The path is steep and the crowds of the spiritual proletariat prefer to descend the slope rather than to climb its craggy heights. And still in the midst of roaring factories and in the heart of filthy slums you will find the elect who aspire to the very peaks of sanctity. It is worth the trouble to help them in their climb.

If Catholic Action is a work of faith it needs saints. Now these will always be the exception, but they must be there to lead the way. They march at the head of the parade followed by the miserable crowd of sinners. We must not scatter them, says Péguy, but lead them; that is how one obtains long processions for God. If mystery is incarnate in weak men and floundering social institutions, we should not be scandalized but must rather work to perfect and heal them.

For example, here is the testimony of a former Jocist who worked in a factory:

What struck me most in the Y.C.W. is that the soul of a young girl worker is worth the sacrifice of a life. And this too: every young worker, no matter how poor, how abandoned or how low she has fallen, has a divine vocation; she has the right to a noble and dignified life and it is possible to make her understand it . . .'

They do not all reach this level. But, as another said, there are many who continue to feel the apostolate of their youth 'like a character printed on their souls as in certain sacraments.'

Among adults, Catholic Action has not experienced the rapid penetration that it has among the naturally more receptive young. Burdened by family cares and generally weighed down with trouble and worry, adults are less inclined to 'enroll in the ranks of the apostolate.' Group reunions are less exciting to them; they prefer to work on a smaller but deeper scale. They do not march in parades behind the flag except in a totalitarian régime, and even here it would be ridiculous. They, too, have their study groups, times of recollection and supernatural contacts.

Moreover, Catholic Action far from exhausts the notion of the lay apostolate; it has no monopoly. Alongside it, there is room for many activities, less regimented and oft-times more effective. Perhaps in the beginning, the rather tempestuous enthusiasm of youthful groups considered the old parochial societies and venerable brotherhoods with some contempt. They classed them among the 'auxiliary' works designed exclusively to favour the rise of the new combat teams.

Societies with a strictly religious programme have taken offence at this, and sometimes not without reason. Traditionally, their aim was the sanctification of their members. Now everything seemed to give way to the conquest of others as if the apostolate no longer needed personal virtue and was no longer to be directed toward an increase of personal sanctity. Was not that a false pragmatism?

Yet the misunderstanding is not difficult to account for. Too many pious congregations seem to fall back on an individualistic and narrow spirituality so often pitifully sterile. The words of the Pope, moreover, granted enviable privileges and a rousing priority to Catholic Action. This caused some vanity among the young workers, excusable in view of their inexperience.

The non-organized Christian, too, can be an apostle. Pius XII did not hesitate to enlarge, if not the framework, at least the notion of the apostolate to include the activity of the Christian mother who is the perfect teacher, or the doctor, defender of Catholic morality, or even the statesman championing a generous social policy. He recognized 'the powerful and irreplaceable value, for the good of souls, of this ordinary performance of the duties of one's state by so many millions of conscientious and exemplary faithful.' [7]

But the most serious reproach directed against Catholic Action is of a theological nature: *it presumes to organize the Holy Spirit Himself*!

Protestants make a similar objection against what they call Roman sacramentalism. But why could not the Spirit of God, for the diffusion of grace, institute ritual signs and, similarly, for the transmission of the Message, raise up volunteer groups? In doing this He is dependent on neither the one nor the other but, on the contrary, retains His full sovereignty. His influence is not limited either to rites or to works. Rather, *it is He Who organizes us*.

He creates the organism of the Church, the Body of Christ. Sacred Scripture not only uses this biological allegory but also the political images of the Kingdom, the people and City of God. Under the direction of the Spirit, the College of Apostles organized the local churches. If the Spirit can organize the very prayers used in liturgical worship, how can He be forbidden to organize action as well? Is it for us to restrict Him with our individualist prohibitions? Could anyone think of claiming such a prerogative? In the battle for the Kingdom, it is *He* Who recruits the troops.

Organization will never be an end in itself; it will always remain a means. But it is an indispensable means because men are not pure spirits and cannot overlook mutual social aid. Again, we must be careful: it is the soul that establishes and develops the body; but the corporal burden must not be so great that the soul finds itself unable to direct the ensemble. Pius XI once invoked this principle to justify the smallness of the Vatican City territory: it had to be large enough to guarantee the spiritual liberty of the Holy See without another extra inch.

The vital driving force is inventive. Young and vigorous, it produces new organs and constantly regenerates already existing ones while at the same time it weeds out and rejects artificial superfluities.

The danger of rank overgrowth is not illusory. To maintain the primacy of the spiritual over the mechanical aspects of organization, we need a constant and vigorous asceticism and a daily check on our methods to insure their suppleness and adaptive power. Otherwise, too soon we will become entrenched in traditionalism and administrative depersonalization. When the hierarchy approves and encourages a group or a work, it does not brand all others as incapable nor does it condemn the more liberal forms of apostolic activity. Every institution of recent origin is tempted to label its predecessors as outmoded. The Church asks for nothing more than the chance to greet a new Francis or a new Ignatius in each succeeding generation.

Organization does not dispense with the Spirit Who inspired its foundation and assures its continual vigour. It is quite like the state of grace: not a tranquil self-sufficient possession, but the vibrant life of God completely dependent on the urgings of the Spirit Who, under form of actual graces, keeps it alert and working.

PARTICIPATION OR COLLABORATION?

This sub-title is likely to conjure up images of a scholastic dispute of the late Middle Ages; basically, however, the question is one of theological exactitude and psychological efficacity. A significant fact is that Pius XI spoke of the 'participation' in his celebrated definition of Catholic Action and used this term regularly in his innumerable letters and discourses on the subject. His successor, however, often substitutes for the term 'participation' the apparently more neutral expression of 'collaboration.'[8] Are we to see in this a strategic retreat or a devaluation of the earlier concept?

We must examine the question more closely.

To participate in the Mystical Body means to be a member of it and enjoy its benefits. To participate in the hierarchy means to share in it in becoming part of the directing body that represents Christ and communicates grace by means of authority and in the sacraments. Thus, to a certain degree, priests participate in the hierarchical institution, in the episcopal powers. They are mediators, preachers, judges, ministers of sacrifice and sacraments, distributors of supernatural gifts. Rightly are they considered messengers of God and lieutenants of Christ. [9]

If the simple faithful 'participate' in the royal priesthood, it is only in so far as they are receptive subjects of the High Priest's grace and are associated in His Redemptive act as willing and generous beneficiaries by spiritual oblation of themselves. Evidently, in the mystery of the Communion of Saints, they will spread about them the beneficent effect of grace not by ritual but by a Christian life which communicates itself. This does not confer on them any authority in the technical sense. No baptized person can pass on his own sacramental gift to his neighbour. He can lead him to the confessional or the communion rail; he can lavish on him words of counsel or comfort, but he has no precept to give, nor has he any power to absolve or consecrate.[10]

This power is reserved to the validly ordained clergy commissioned by the bishop. By his office the priest continues the grace-giving work of Christ and applies it to succeeding generations. He links himself to the chain of efficient instrumental causes constituted by the Saviour's humanity, His saving mysteries and their ritual celebration.

To state it more simply, there will always be activities rightfully belonging to the priests, activities that the laity can never assume. And inversely, there are lay activities which the clergy will never be able to carry out; here, at least, every attempt at clericalism is excluded from the start.

Under such conditions, what remains of the heralded participation of the laity in the hierarchical activity? Nothing or almost nothing *if* the whole life of the Church were reduced to the conferring of sacraments. At most, one could still think of Baptism administered by a layman in case of necessity, and of the mutual consent by which Christian spouses administer the Sacrament of Matrimony to one another.

But outside Her ritual acts the Church lives the interior life of faith, charity and the apostolate; and this life lets in and even solicits the activity of its most simple members. Whether their work be individual or collective, it will always contribute to the interior life of that same Body, ruled by the same Head, under the movement of the same Spirit. Consider the sacraments for an example. Separated from faith, they are ineffectual. They do not work automatically, for, as a gift of God, they imply a trusting abandonment on the part of man. To lead men to the sacraments the Spirit uses two means: the hierarchical priesthood, and the apostolic activity of the laity dependent on it.

The laity can claim a 'participation' provided we understand that word in the broad sense intended by Pius XI: he spoke not of a participation in 'the hierarchy' but in 'the apostolate of the hierarchy.' He was not a man to grant to the first comer the least particle of sacred authority. Elsewhere he himself uses within the same phrase 'participation' and 'collaboration' interchangeably.[11] His celebrated definition was, he said, inspired by a text of St. Paul to the valiant Christians '*quae mecum laboraverunt* in evangelio,' (who have worked for the Gospel at my side. . . . Phil. IV, 3).[12] Nor is this the only place where the Apostle greets his co-workers; he enumerates them in the final chapter of Romans (XVI, 1-13). The term 'collaboration' agrees better with the Pauline concept of directed activity. In the context of Catholic Action, moreover, it better emphasizes that the specific character of the laity's work is not mere instrumentality.

The Scholastics affirm that the instrument can 'participate' in the action of the principal agent without 'collaborating' with it. Collaboration, even hierarchical, supposes then a certain autonomy, a personal and free engagement of which the instrument is incapable. How can a mere instrument take any initiative? You 'use' an instrument but you 'call' a fellow worker. Without the slightest doubt, laymen prefer to think themselves 'called' rather than 'used' or 'manipulated' and this by reason of the very dignity of their free obedience.

Once more we free ourselves from every sort of clericalism and collectivism that uses and mis-uses its dehumanized citizens. Catholic Action is not placed in the hands of the clergy as an instrument for domination; one cannot handle men as a blacksmith does a hammer or a writer a pen. They are invited to voluntary and gratuitous service: if the call urges them to answer with words and acts, the duty of giving this 'response' will impart to them the virile awareness of their 'responsibility.'

As visible signs producing grace the sacraments can be called supernatural 'means'. The priest is bound by the sacramental rites and he administers them, St. Thomas says, as an instrument.[13] The treasure he bestows is not his own but God's, and that is why the holiness of the priest has no direct influence on the effect of the sacrament. If the case were otherwise, a more virtuous pastor would confer 'better' sacraments even though every Communion would be the same Body of Christ and every Baptism the same divine life given to all.

Notwithstanding its special relation with Confirmation, Catholic Action is not a sacrament. Its influence is obviously and understandably not of the same intensity everywhere, for it depends on the degree of generosity, zeal, disinterestedness, and even technical ability of its members. If they are lacking this motivation, the undertaking will be only an empty sham and a sorry spectacle. To call upon an efficacy inherent in the sign instituted by Christ is impossible in the present instance; everything depends upon the potential of grace put to work by the authors of the undertaking.[14]

Pius XII's use of the word 'co-operation' does not diminish the perspectives of Catholic Action; rather it helps to personalize it more strongly.[15]

THE COMPLEMENTARY THEORY INSUFFICIENT

When Pius XI first initiated his work, there were many regions suffering from a lack of priests; furthermore it was impossible for them to carry the Christian message to some particularly isolated sectors of society. Thus it appeared urgent to extend the influence of the parish priest by the addition of a devout laity. These part-time auxiliaries had to supply in some measure for a lack of vocations.

In many supposedly Catholic countries, the number of ordinations is strongly declining and an aging clergy is finding itself totally incapable of carrying out normal pastoral duties. In Latin America what can a parish priest do with the care of some twenty thousand baptized souls?[16] If absolutely necessary, the laity could take on a part of the priestly activities: obviously they could neither offer the Sacrifice nor hear confessions; but they could be assigned to give religious instruction and even to baptise. This was the case in Mexico in the time of Calles' persecution. Today behind the Iron Curtain they are practising the same self-sacrifice in order to compensate for imprisoned, fugitive and executed priests. For the Church, it is a question of life or death: outside a school system under the sway of paganism and churchs converted to secular use, the growing generation must be catechized.

Among the laity of these Soviet-dominated lands are many judicious promoters of the Gospel message and great confessors of the faith bolstering up the faith and courage of others or secretly bringing them Communion. However, it was not this disastrous situation that suggested Catholic Action to Pius XI. In his age, Russia had not yet pushed her frontiers to the very heart of Europe, had not yet enclosed sixty million Catholics within the sphere of her direct influence. When he spoke of areas forbidden to the clergy, the

Pontiff had in mind factories and workers' quarters, the great commercial and political institutions then practically inaccessible to the priest. It is there he uncovered the privileged domain of lay action, and with this vision in mind made his revolutionary proclamation: 'The first apostles of the workers will be the workers.'

The occasion that gave place to the foundation of Catholic Action is not to be confused with its formal principle. The scarcity of priests was the starting point and the psychological event that opened the way for Catholic Action. Yet it is immediately evident that here, too, the spirit is greater than the letter. It is for the layman to observe and spread the law of Christianity in the heart of the family as in the factory. The lack of priestly vocations has concentrated attention on the possibilities of the faithful and given them a sharper awareness of their duty.

How many times has the Pope drawn his encouragement for them from the sacramental doctrine, from Baptism and Confirmation especially, from Eucharistic solidarity and the demands of Christian social charity! In order to save those members of the Mystical Body most prone to danger, he uses the same exhortations of St. Paul to his many and varied helpers, men and women, who 'true in charity' spread the message from house to house, from city to city.

Now in principle all this work is independent of the number of priests. Were there only one priest, the baptismal character would keep its dynamism and the Eucharistic bread its power of unifying the entire Body. Of its very nature Christian existence demands the apostolate.

Without the priestly ministry, the community could not last nor could Catholic Action. The latter's vigour will necessitate many more priests and zealous ones. Wherever they are lacking, as in South America or the Philippines, Catholic Action is experiencing extraordinary difficulties in getting under way. Still it remains a work of the laity. The principal reason for its existence is the need for living as a Christian and for propagating Christianity not within the walls of the sanctuary but to every nook and corner of the world.

In tracing the exact boundaries between the natural sciences, philosophy and theology mark an undeniable progress in the organization of our human life. Likewise, the clear distinction between the sacred and profane constitutes a very appreciable advance, provided the final aim is kept in view. Mixing incompatible elements only causes trouble and finishes by impoverishing the whole. If separation is regrettable, equalization of planes is equally so: order demands distinction in unity.[17]

Besides the parish, the Christian's interest extends to family life, working environment, the social and economic organisations, urban life and the sphere of international relationships. All these elements are stamped with the profane and there the priest is not 'at home'. The ordinary citizen, in this society, must live as a Christian with ultra-terrestrial aspirations. He must be sure to put the crucifix in the place of honour in his home, in the factory, in the council chambers; and for all that, these places will be no more transformed into churches any more than family, economic and political sciences will be changed into theology.

Perhaps at certain times Catholic Action is concerned much too exclusively with adding a certain religious decor to profane life, not unlike those pious souls who weave ejaculatory prayers into their work. It is more important to sanctify the work itself, to produce a work of quality and genuine craftmanship, a work of scrupulous honesty. To educate a family, to regulate production, to govern a country, in view of temporal well-being, these are not a priest's duties; they are the work of fathers of families, industrialists and civil servants. Both God and Caesar have their place and legitimate demands. Not that Caesar has nothing to do with God or that in the end God will not judge Caesar, rather that in the meantime all must recognize Caesar's rights and obey him.

Christian couples are to build a Christian home; Christian workers to lead a life of Christian work; Christian politicians to pursue a Christian-inspired policy. All these acts can have an eternal meaning and value without any loss of their specifically temporal character. If they were to be emptied of their natural substance, they would no longer be worthy of supernatural destiny. If Catholic Action collaborates unhesitatingly in this profane-Christian order, it will make the world less unfit for the Kingdom of God and more endurable as a temporary dwelling for God's children. In the political world, it will not raise up a prelate-prime minister like Msgr. Seipel in Austria, or Tiso in Slovakia. It will render such types unnecessary by preparing lay elements of prime value for a lay mission of prime importance.

Still, we must not overemphasize nor forbid Catholic Action any direct apostolate in religious matters. By affirming that 'the laity remains without initiative in the sacred domain,' there is a great risk that even the best-intentioned of them will lose what is most precious in their Christian vocation. To establish a 'total disproportion between the temporal and the spiritual' is to admit that the two realms are merely superimposed and have absolutely no vital relation with one another.[18]

The Question of the Mandate

To indicate the difference between Catholic Action and looser forms of the lay apostolate, it is often stated that only the former is organized.

Ever increasing organization is a sign of the times. In nature and in society, said Pius XI, everything is systematized.[19] Effectiveness depends on the discipline that governs people and institutions. Is it only the forces of evil that should increase their influence by deliberate, concerted action?

Pius XI did everything in his power to combat that idea. His impetus promoted the great youth movements, somewhat abused in the process of their development by military terminology.[20] If the liturgy did not so insist on 'the reign of truth and life, of holiness and grace, the reign of justice, charity and peace,' one could almost give an imperialistic meaning to the feast of Christ the King. But who would want to keep youth from translating its enthusiasm in terms of battle when Saint Paul himself was so obviously fascinated by the figure of the Roman legionary? All is well so long as this war-like zeal attacks the real enemy lying in wait in the soul's interior.

But the element of 'organization' is not enough to distinguish Catholic Action; pious societies are organized too. Only that is Catholic Action which enjoys a special mission, a 'mandate' recognized by the hierarchy.

The word has occasioned much writing and aroused sharp discussion. In the opinion of some it has created a false emancipation that has been expressed by the famous definition: 'the sufficency of the laity hastening to the aid of the clergy's insufficency.' Especially the youthful recipients of this 'commission' have shown themselves vain, attached to exterior details and a hollow idealism. With no other mandate than their Christian fidelity, martyrs have managed to give the finest witness of apostolic charity. Their example should forewarn us against the initial pride of the novice.

Moreover, evidence of such abuse only serves to provoke ridicule. Each period of Church history finds mediocre minds misunderstanding the duties or titles gratuitously granted them. Prudent men shake their heads: depending on their temperament they are amused or hurt by fledgling bishops who reprimand their pastors and accuse them apparently (and sometimes more than apparently) of being lazy or old-fashioned. A specific mission demands self-sacrifice and zeal; still more does it require humble service. All the same, we can only regret a certain lack of simplicity that will not tolerate suggestions or information from serious minded laymen concerning pastoral practice. To all, Saint Paul recommends a mutual respect.

Pius XI did not hesitate before the term 'mandate,' nor what is more important, before its reality.[21] Certainly a mission received from authority does not supply for a lack of spiritual maturity. An illiterate person can deliver a letter for you, but you cannot ask a half-Christian to represent an integral Christianity. Official designation supposes a sufficiently refined religious sense. Carrying out the assigned task will strengthen this spirit, it is to be hoped, but it is unrealistic to suppose it can create the spirit. The excessive use of high-sounding phrases occasioned by a more or less artificial enthusiasm will not succeed in hiding the deficiency. Were it not so pitiful, such camouflage would be tantamount to profanation.

Mandate implies more than recommendation, less than institution. It supposes no power of orders since it is given to laymen, nor does it confer any power of jurisdiction since it imposes no obedience on others. The terms 'extra-' or 'para-' hierarchical have been proposed.[22] These terms are inaccurate. Though lacking strict delegation, 'mandate' nevertheless prolongs the hierarchy. Although supposing a free activity moved by the Holy Spirit, it can no longer be qualified as charismatic because it is in fact granted by the authority. Mandate is related both to institution and to charism; it is closer, however, to the first than the second. It constitutes a particular analogous application of the 'mission' given the Apostles by Christ. With the seal of ecclesiastical authenticity it gives a clear imprint to apostolic movement.

Thus in the apostolate, modern and ancient, priestly and lay, we must distinguish the hierarchical and the pneumatic aspects, while remembering that each is 'first' from its respective point of view. The hierarchical element is the mission confided by the bishop directly or indirectly. The pneumatic element is an intense, radiant spiritual life, or as Saint Paul puts it, the love of Christ which allows the apostle no rest. Above all else it is vitally important to know who Christ is.

Obviously no one is expected to be perfect before considering the apostolate. Otherwise, most of the laity would be condemned to silence, and who is the priest that would dare to speak? Every preacher bears witness against himself to the degree that he has not completely conquered sin. To boast a mantle of virtue only adds the sin of hypocrisy to our many personal weaknesses.

As long as the apostle-candidate fails to realize this doctrine, the hierarchical mission cannot take root in him. Though fitted with the finest credentials imaginable, all he would present would appear a poor counterfeit. It has been known to happen in Catholic Action that the mandate has been given too soon and too readily where spiritual maturity, and not merely technical competency, is lacking.

Eloquence and activity cannot mask interior poverty; they only reveal it. Mass movements especially run the risk of being deceived by such trickery. The result is most unfortunate when real life experience discourages an over-zealous youth just when he should be starting truly fruitful action.

We have all witnessed similar disappointments. In Belgium, the sad episode of the political Rexism is not yet forgotten, although most have forgotten that the title of Rex originally designated Christ the King. It offers us this serious warning: not too quickly should we grant approbations and official missions.

Still, an accidental setback and an individual abuse of the mandate does not warrant wholesale condemnation of Catholic Action. In this case, the highest ecclesiastical authorities could be arraigned each time a mission country's native clergy betrayed their hopes by the defection of those ordained too quickly. A paralyzing caution would prevent the Church from producing anything original in our times. True prudence does not lack the boldness necessary to seize unhesitatingly the inspirations of the Spirit.

The value of the mandate depreciates proportionately as it emphasizes hierarchical order at the expense of living and personal faith. This is externalism. And yet, to confide an authorized mission is a thoroughly Catholic method. We have Saint Paul's word that no one can preach without being sent (Rom. X, 15). Every apostolate is hierarchical; the Spirit quickens it within the framework of a Church governed by the bishops.

Obviously bishops are not the only ones who speak or who circulate set discourses. But whatever preaching is done must be done under their direction; and no one has the right to contradict their teaching. Whenever the Spirit of Christ 'opens the mouth' of someone, He does it *in medio ecclesiae*, in the midst of the hierarchical community which examines this testimony to see that it agrees with revelation and, therefore, with the Spirit. The mandate grants official recognition and guarantee to the witness. If this mission can sometimes be given tacitly, why hasn't the hierarchy also the right to grant it publicly and solemnly?

To dispense the Sacraments is the mission of priests alone. Others, however, have received from Church authority the mission of spreading the word. How many religious, men and women, and how many laymen were among the heralds that converted Europe to Christianity! Thus we need not reject the services of laymen to aid the mission and to revive the weakening life of our ancient Christian lands.

Viewed thus, the apostolate takes on a larger scope. No one disputes this. Its strength derives from Christ, the Apostle of the

Father, and though non-priestly, it still remains sacred. To emphasize this wider aspect, Fr. Congar once wrote that the layman possesses a parish *ex spiritu* in opposition to the *ex missione* apostolate of the clergy.[23] In his later publications he has not retained this terminology. Furthermore, the term has its difficulties.

If by the apostolate *ex spiritu* is understood simply zeal for the spread of Catholicism, we are in the presence of an excellent disposition but still no Catholic Action. According to pontifical documents this latter supposes that ecclesiastical authority guarantees and protects this zeal, declares it authentic and allows its exercise in the name of the Church. From this comes the characteristically strong attachment of Catholic Action to the hierarchy that places it under its direct and avowed responsibility.[24]

On the other hand, the apostolate *ex missione* exercised by the clergy presents us with a misleading pleonasm. Both words signify 'mission.' The one is Greek, the other Latin, and that is the only difference between them. What is more, the priestly apostolate is equally unrealisable without a minimum of 'spirit,' or interior vitality. Lacking this, it soon degenerates into formalism.

We, therefore, admit for Catholic Action a true 'mission.'[25] Fr. Congar grants to the organised laity 'a certain authority,'[26] certainly not a power in the strict sense, but nevertheless something more than simple prestige or a mark of honour. It is not only that the witness of Catholic Action is more impressive; rather it emanates directly from the Church, controlled and guaranteed by the hierarchy. Such appeals do not produce in the hearers any further obligations of submission; if that were the case, we would soon be overwhelmed by the number of our masters.

Still the fact remains that more than one theologian hesitates before extending the concept of mandate. However when non-ordained religious are sent into a pagan country, no one contests their title as 'missionaries' of the Holy See. Why then, under the same conditions, refuse it to the laity? Religious, it is true, remain subject to their constitutions and, keeping this in mind, Fr. Koester is of the opinion that a 'mission' can only be granted to laymen in case of necessity, where no one else is available. He adds a specious argument: if everyone is capable of assuming a mission and acting in the name of the Church's head, there will soon be no members. If everyone can command, authority will cease to exist.[27]

But Catholic Action cannot be compared to emergency baptism. It is not an appeal limited to a certain number, since the Pope appeals to all Christians to join its ranks. Moreover, there is no danger that everyone will rule, and none will remain to be ruled. One can certainly jest about the number of directors in our organizations; but as we have said, the Catholic Action mandate does not grant the power of authority in the strict sense. Besides, since its members act within the framework of limited missions, some will always be subject to others from different points of view. There will never be a lack of unbelievers and faint-hearted to wish to receive missionaries among the sinners that surround us and that we ourselves are. Such reciprocal influence is the ordinary law of every living organism whose functions are interdependent, one upon the other. Such is the earthly condition of a Church still imperfect but *en route* to perfection.

Legislation, too, ever dependent on the full life of the Church, is in the process of formation. Thus it is that the Code of Canon Law clearly admits a 'canonical mission' for laymen in the field of religious instruction. The concept is not, therefore, contrary to juridic principle.[28]

The bishops' conference held at Paris, in March, 1946, declared that the mandate of Catholic Action is conferred not on each of the members but on the Movement.[29] The Conference of Fulda in Germany made a similar observation. The Pope, too, intends primarily all the large associations of youths, workers, college graduates, and similar organizations. Nonetheless, the leaders of these groups are specifically designated or approved by the diocesan authorities. Obviously their function and their activities are only considered and approved by authority in so far as they fall within the organization's framework. The question, then, concerns an investiture given their person, and not simply their organization. This is the only possible meaning of the decree of the Council of Malines prescribing that leaders on the national, diocesan and even regional levels be installed by their respective bishops.[30] The Church never gives her directives and privileges to an impersonal group; she addresses herself to responsible persons within the collectivity. She does not administer to an anonymous mass: she addresses herself primarily to persons, as is manifested by her sacramental worship which always names the faithful by their individual baptismal names.[31]

Does all this end in the creation of an infinite number of miniature potentates, great admirers of their own self-sacrifice, yet unbearable to their fellow-men? Any of us is capable of misusing the best things to nourish our own narrow-minded vanity. Childishness is often too obvious for us to be troubled by it. We need only smile. Because the mandate itself is a designation for the apostolate, it is a very serious matter. It is not a privilege but a call to duty. We may laugh at the current mania for insignia and distinctions of rank and dignity—and it is not restricted to the young. The over-complicated organizations and the militarizing present in all positions and levels is equally amusing. A sense of humour will often encourage a beneficial, more balanced approach. The idea of personal responsibility is too precious to be mishandled. When it becomes preoccupied with foolish trifles, it loses its educative value. It must be purified without being destroyed.

More than once has the mandate been conferred on leaders coming from the working classes. Thanks to this call, simple young workers have realized a remarkable spiritual growth and sometimes discovered a higher vocation. Several have exchanged overalls for cassock or cowl. And so the worker apostolate has made itself felt even in the matter of priestly and religious vocations.

In giving a special mission to the young, one must proceed cautiously. They are easily fascinated by the footlights. It is correct to speak of Catholic pride but vanity is hardly Christian; and youth tend to confuse the two. Too much talk about personality will only produce arrogance.

Psychologists judge that before a certain age, the young are incapable of social thinking. Their realm of conscience does not extend beyond immediate experience and does not yet encompass an interest in their neighbour. Some even contend that religious motives have no hold on their minds and that many of them are ruined by an excessive 'apostolic' diet.

Progress in the mystery must be gradual. To jump intermediate stages can be dangerous in the domain of religion as well as that of education. Forced growth does not produce maturity.

Grace, however, is not destined exclusively for adults. In inaugurating early Communion St. Pius X did not yield to the scruples of the timid; as a result Christianity will be forever grateful to him. The Kingdom is for the little ones, and primarily for them. True, their horizon is limited; all the more reason not to turn them in upon themselves but to widen the scope of their understanding and of their charity. They should be habituated to giving rather than to receiving. For them God is not an empty word but a personal presence, as is their neighbour. They are capable, too, of a more sincere and direct prayer than the interested prayers of their elders.

If this is so, they can indeed be apostles; the word does not matter. But let us not hide from them the secrets of grace which are beyond the grasp of the narrow-minded, moralising sermonisers. These preachers, aware perhaps that they lack personal depth, can only talk about the mystery in an affected, unreal tone. But the public retains the right to claim from them words of life. For the young the strongest incentives are also religious ones. Far surpassing patriotic motives, religious incentives are too often used to brighten up the former so as to render them more compelling—a shocking use of sacred terminology.

The mystery of the apostolate, then, is to be touched only with pure hands, that is to say, with infinite respect and whole-hearted sincerity. To use it for a questionable human end would be sacrilegious. The call to the laity demands on the clergy's part a purification of which they have not hitherto been conscious. Detachment, humility and especially charity are required. In this little explored realm they will find another motive to seek virtue, and at the same time discover a safeguard against personal ambition. As for the commissioned layman, he will learn in his turn to guard against a sort of clerical pride which would be particularly offensive in him. The mandate of Catholic Action pre-supposes upright character, one without personal ambition. With men of such calibre, the work will be done more discreetly, undoubtedly more slowly, but with infinitely more fruit.

[1] The study of H. U. VON BALTHASAR appeared in German under the title *Der Laie und der Ordensstand*, in the series *Christ-Heute*, Einsiedeln, 1949. FR. E. BERNIMONT, O.P. presented it to the French speaking world with the title *Laïcat et plein Apostolat (Etudes Religieuses, n. 664-666)*, Paris, 1949, with explanatory notes on various debatable passages. See also: Z. SERRAND, *Pour une théologie du laïcat*, in *La Vie Intell.*, July, 1949, p.p. 37-42. M. D. KOESTER, O.P., *Theologie und Heiligkeit. Eine kritische Entgegnung*, in *Neue Ordnung*, 4, 1950, pp. 113-121.

[2] H. U. VON BALTHASAR-E. BERNIMONT, *o.c.*, pp. 14-15.

[3] See, for example, the discours of PIUS XII to Italian Catholic Action, May 3, 1951. *Docum. Cath.*, 48, 1951, col. 579. Under n. 2, the pope forcefully affirms that if the form is new, the reality is very old.

[4] E. MICHEL, *Von der kirchlichen Sendung der Laien*, cited in VON BALTHASAR-BERNIMONT, p. 25 ff.

[5] PIUS XII, Discours cited above of May 3, 1951, n. 4, *Doc. Cath., l.c.*, col. 580.

[6] For a thorough investigated analysis of the crisis of Catholic Action and its remedies, you will find very profitable A. HAYEN, S.J. *Le désintéressement de l'Action catholique* in the *Nouv. Revue Théol.*, 67, 1945, p. 810-827.

[7] PIUS XII, Address to the World Congress of the Lay Apostolate, Oct. 14, 1951. Eng. Trans. under the title *The Lay Apostolate—Its Need Today*, N.C.W.C., Washington, n. 22 ff.

[8] For an analysis of the idea of 'participation', consult R. SPIAZZI, *o.c., Missione dei Laici*, p. 234 ff. MGR. L. CIVARDI applied the same correction to many passages of his *Manuale di Azione cattolica*, as of the 11th ed., Rome, 1945.

[9] ST. THOMAS, *Summa Theol.*, III., q. 26, a.l., ad 1; *ib.*, q. 64, a.2, ad 3 and q. 72, a. 3, ad 3.

[10] Note that even the minor orders (lector, acolyte, etc.) and the sub-deaconate confer a certain power connected with the Sacrament of Holy Orders. Catholic Action is situated further on, beyond worship, in the sphere of Christian life.

[11] CF. P. TIBERGHIEN, *L'Action catholique. Expériences passées. Vues d'avenir*, Lille, 1945, p. 70.

[12] Cf. L. CIVARDI, *o.c., Manuale*, p. 21. Pius XI. explicitely invoked this text of St. Paul in an address to the priests of Latin America, Feb. 21, 1936.

[13] ST. THOMAS, *Summa Theol.*, III, q. 63, a.2, c.

[14] A propos of this, theologians oppose the *opus operatum* of the sacraments to the *opus operantis* of virtuous acts.

[15] PIUS XII, in his address to the World Congress of the Lay Apostolate also admits for Catholic Action the comparison of the instrument. An eminent orator had underlined

the expression during the course of the Congress. However the Pope explains it as a secondary cause which is free and responsible. Cf. Eng. Trans., *The Lay Apostolate —Its Need Today*, N.C.W.C., Washington, n. 30.

[16] Cf. J. LUZZI, S.J., *L'Appel de l'Amérique latine*, in the *Nouv. Revue Théol.*, 85, 1953, pp. 617-627.

[17] See above, p. 100.

[18] FR. CARPAY obviously exaggerates this duality, *o.c.*, *L'Action catholique*, pp. 49, 57, etc. Cf. *supra*, p. 40.

[19] Cf. the series of pontifical documents cited by MGR. L. CIVARDI, *o.c.*, *Manuale*, p. 107 ff. The aphorism cited is taken from an address of Pius XI. to Catholic nurses, April 27, 1935. Eng. Trans., C. C. MARTINDALE, London, 1935, pp. 78 ff.

[20] The same reproach could be stated against the Legion of Mary which is, however, very peaceful and very acceptable in its other aspects.

[21] PIUS XI., Letter to Card. Bertram, *Acta Apl. Sedis*, 1928, p. 385: 'Sacra ipsa hierarchia, quemadmodum *mandatum* impertit, sic incitamenta et stimulos adiicit.'

[22] FR. R. SPIAZZI, *o.c.*, *La missione dei laici*, p. 186 ff. and p. 213 ff. uses the words: mission 'ex Spiritu' for Catholic Action as opposed to a mission 'ex institutione' for the clergy. He uses a better sounding word when he calls it 'infra-hierarchical', p. 187. This distinction should be compared with that of 'ex Spiritu' and 'ex missione' as used by Fr. Congar. We will clarify his distinction further on.

[23] Y. CONGAR, *Pour une théologie du laïcat*, in *Etudes*, t. 256, 1948, pp. 42-54 and pp. 194-218. See esp. p. 204. Cf. the preceding note. In *Jalons*, p. 455 ff. Fr. Congar speaks more precisely of a mission *ex officio* for the clergy.

[24] Thence also for Catholic Action an equally characteristic restriction of its freedom of movement. In a certain way, it involves the Church in its activities.

[25] As does P. TIBERGHIEN, *o.c.*, *L'Action catholique*, p. 63 ff.

[26] Y. CONGAR, *l.c.*, *Etudes*, p. 32. Instead of *authority*, it would be better to speak of *authorisation*. Cf. chap. V., note 15. Cf. J. DE CASTRO ENGLER, *O Elemento formalmente constitutivo da Ação Católica*, in *Rev. Ecles. Brasil.*, 13, 1953, pp. 323-350.

[27] H. M. KOESTER, *o.c.*, *Die Magd des Herrn*, p. 441 and 443.

[28] Code of Canon Law, can. 1333, al. 1. Cf. *supra*, p. 80.

[29] The Assembly of Cardinals and Archbishops, 1946. See *Docum. Cath.*, July 21, 1946, col. 743.

[30] *Acts and Decrees of the 5th Provincial Council of Malines*, 1937. Appendix, n. 202-204.

[31] Consider baptism, confirmation, ordination and obviously marriage. For the Eucharist and confession the personal character is evident even though the name of the believer is not pronounced. Cf. F. SARTORI, *Fundamento sacramental do Apostolado dos Leigos*, in *Rev. Ecles. Brasil*, 13, 1953, pp. 298-322. B. DREES, *Die Berufung des Laien*, in *Documentos*, n. 13-18. 1953, pp. 108-114.

CHAPTER VIII

THE LAY APOSTOLATE
AND ALLIED CONTACTS

THE LAY VOCATION AND RELIGIOUS VOCATIONS

RELIGIOUS, too, enjoy an official status in the church and can receive a mandate from the hands of the bishop or Pope. Except for priests in parish work or education, they were until recently, the only ones to receive such a mission. But today a growing number of 'vocations in the world' is being added to their ranks. This includes in their own way the members of Catholic Action. More than a day or two will be needed for religious to become accustomed to these new fellow-workers. Some even wonder whether so much insistence on the lay apostolate is not having an unfortunate effect on the number of religious vocations.

Certainly a mandate that engages the whole personality and mobilizes all its resources is unthinkable for someone not free from all worldly cares and definitively consecrated to God. Furthermore, it supposes the practice of the evangelical counsels by vows taken either in religious life or in the world.

The term 'religious life' gives rise to great misunderstanding. It can signify an existence consecrated to the service of God or even simply a virtuous life; but generally today, the meaning is that of the Code of Canon Law: 'a state of community life in which besides the precepts, the evangelical counsels of obedience, chastity, and poverty are observed by means of vows.'[1] Without community life, therefore, one cannot be a religious, and still it is quite possible to pronounce vows while remaining in the world.

This is especially the case with the recently founded Secular Institutes. Juridically they constitute a 'state of perfection' comparable to that of religious, but their members are exteriorly indistinguishable from lay people in dress, general comportment, and professional occupations. The only thing that might attract the attention of those around them is that they voluntarily remain celibates.

In reality, the interior tenor of their life hinges entirely on divine charity. Their virginity, their detachment from all self-will and personal possessions are eminently positive. Because they wish to belong to God unreservedly, they renounce all the rest. And so their perfect liberty with regard to all worldly goods. To be at the service of God and His Church is their only mandate. From this point of view, they are the same as religious; but they do not recognize any separation from the world except a mental one, and this thanks to the intensity of a spiritual life that blooms in apostolic radiancy.

Such total consecration is conceivable not only outside the monastery but even apart from Secular Institutes. The vows of the people could be approved by the bishop, who would receive their possessions and persons in his hands as a holocaust; he would be satisfied in their regard with a minimum of restrictions and an individual rather than collective formation. The removal of juridical details would ensure an almost perfect mobility. The creative range of God's Spirit is unlimited.

In all the cases mentioned the mandate is identified with the man it absorbs, allowing his full development. But this complete form does not exclude the possibility of an apostolic realization of lesser scope; such would be the case where, owing to other obligations, especially family duties, a receiver of the mandate could only consecrate a part of his time and activity to the apostolate. What is better does not deprive what is good of its right to exist. Catholic Action does not pretend to be the vocation *par excellence;* yet that does not hinder it from dutifully engaging in less brilliant service. The 'all or nothing' theory ruthlessly crushes many praiseworthy efforts. If there is a difference between precept and counsel—and there is—the maximum degree cannot be imposed on all. At the lower level there is still room for more modest patterns of life.

Interpreted as a wholesale negation, the thesis of von Balthasar is thus untenable: the lay apostolate is possible even when it does not imply a total giving.[2]

But once this has been admitted, are we not endangering the novitiate enrolment? The same question arises, and even more heatedly, with regard to Secular Institutes. If they were to offer a vocation at a reduced price, as a sort of subsidy for mediocrity, they would not be deserving of any consideration. But, in fact, they in no way lessen the religious life for the use of the bourgeois and the slothful. They propose a vocation of another type that is only now beginning to take form in the Church. If we reduce it simply to an extramural monastic life, we strip it at once of all its originality; then it would constitute no more than an accidental variant. The complete lay vocation is not that of the religious temporarily secularized. It is definitely established—and happily so—in the very heart of the world. And that is its essential mark.

Catholic Action does not monopolize its member completely, body and goods; it leaves him certain temporal pre-occupations. In arousing aspirations of the spiritual order, however, there is danger that Catholic Action will betray his longings by making him self-satisfied, and so will turn him away from a total giving.

The danger is not an imaginary one. Still of its very nature, the deepening and the extension of Christian life cannot reduce the number of vocations. Many priests and religious have heard the supreme call because of their schooling in Catholic Action. Accidentally, and no doubt unconsciously, however, its vigorous activity can raise obstacles. We are thinking of the fever for works that it often occasions, the ideal of a living presence in the world that it reflects, the mysticism of marriage that it rates above virginity.

There is no need to disguise the fact that blundering propaganda about conjugal mysticism can lead many a hesitating mind and heart into error. On the other hand it would hardly be Christian to base a religious vocation on a more or less avowed contempt for marriage. To diminish one in order to extol the other is a device of the dishonest merchant. Only a shamefully false Christianity would hesitate to proclaim the transcendental beauty of virginal consecration.

In the midst of a dechristianized world the need for an apostolate is extremely urgent. It is vitally important for the world's salvation that some leave it; this is not to retreat. For others the task is one of staying where they are for the direct apostolate, total or partial. Often the very best will become victims of tortuous dilemma. For each the final decision rests with the Holy Spirit; it is He who calls and determines the type of vocation. Man does not have to mark the way for Him, but follow the particular way shown him.

Although the principles are clear, the psychological difficulties between the religious and the lay apostolate are not so easy to resolve. To say that Catholic Action ignores the importance of concerted action and the stable institution necessary to direct it is erroneous. Both movement and leaders are clearly aware that all must march together, that specialized organization must be foreseen. The coldness, the opposition, the mutual misunderstanding come from elsewhere.

The call to the apostolate had introduced much closer contacts between priests, religious and lay people. They brush shoulders, they get to know each other. More than before, rectories and religious houses are open and known. Without being in the least indiscreet, young lay leaders observe closely virtue or its lack in their clergy. Such an intimate association imposes greater demands on priests and religious if they are not to disappoint the expectations of the laity. Today youth has a highly developed critical sense that is often embittered by a flood of reformist literature. With all their heart they detest hypocrisy, formalism, show and affectation; they would experience genuine exhiliration in organizing iconoclastic groups in the midst of religious trappings. We should not regret this invitation addressed to the clergy and leaders of the Church to more manly virtue.

In last analysis, it is as always the spiritual intensity of a religious house that will assure it the opportunity of winning new recruits. Mediocrity creates a void that the most complex propaganda will never fill. More than ever before hypocrisy and bargaining with sacred things are abhorred. The strictest orders, the Trappists and the Carmelites, are still the least threatened.

Moreover, adaptation to legitimate needs of the times is necessary for religious houses. At the Congress for Regulars held in Rome in 1950, the Pope devoted a long passage of his discourse to this counsel. 'Three things,' he said, 'correspond excellently to the character and aspirations of our times; broadmindedness, unity in organization, promptness in execution.'[3] During the course of the same Congress, Cardinal Piazza proclaimed: 'Either adapt or perish.' The warning is a grave one. Let us not think that it refers to costume alone.

Young men and women who have given a part of their lives to youth work generally have a strongly marked personality when they come knocking at the door of the novitiate. They have learned to exercise responsibility and possess a skill for organizing. At difficult moments they are capable of deciding for themselves, and need not seek the superiors' counsel at every turn. Many of them have received a solid dogmatic and liturgical formation. Being far from ignorant when they present themselves for additional spiritual education, they hope to climb higher, not to compromise.

Novice-masters are often startled by their liberty of conduct and their slightly brutal frankness. Until now, they were used to handling more pliable matter. And if they try to pour all the candidates into the same mould, they expose themselves to bitter disappointment, and what is worse, in this depressing uniformity they risk the sterilization of immense resources. Unless they want to bungle their job badly, they must recognize that the situation has become more delicate. An understanding and spiritually refined mind that refuses to sacrifice life to the letter of tradition will aid them in cultivating and disciplining these difficult but rich temperaments. And, of course, spiritual direction should respect in every soul the work of the Holy Spirit.

Catholic Action applauds heartily when the best of its members enter the monastery or take the veil. It disapproves a systematic campaign of detraction against religious houses. A joke regarding the good sisters can be a mark of sympathy, but constant irony is unjust and even destructive. A bitter and sometimes malicious literature is replacing Taine's eulogy of heroic hospital sisters. This modern literature is no better, for it paints a false picture by demanding an impossibly angelic perfection. Obvious violations do not condemn a Rule but only attest to the weakness of those failing to observe it. Should religious houses become empty the loss for the church would be incalculable.

It can be that a lack of generosity or an hidden attachment to modern comfort and pleasure stops young people at the doorsteps of the monastery. In that case, to pretend an apostolic idealism would be the exact contrary of the sincerity so highly praised in our day.

Catholic Action and religious houses will not be in foolish competition if each remains loyal to its proper end. To the contrary, they will support one another.

YOUTH MOVEMENTS

Thus far, the work initiated by Pius XI has especially reacted upon our youth. Generally their organizational programmes envision more than the apostolate. Their religious action is part of a vaster movement.

'Youth movements' are a sign of the times. The surface has hardly been scratched and methods for rendering them productive are still in the experimental stage. Here again, the question is one of incarnation; here again, naturalists and supernaturalists confront one another. [4]

Were we to apply literally the motto: 'Health first, sanctity afterwards,' we would border on heresy. [5] To render man physically and morally healthy, grace is necessary.

Going to the other extreme, to make the young feed on pure spirituality is illusory. They cannot abandon their studies, their work, their recreation. On the contrary, they must learn to saturate all these with Christian vitality. A total disincarnation would cut them off from reality. The young can neither be split into parts, nor can they reach and influence their milieu by angelic means.

Free, yet involved, youth must seek an intelligent proportion in its programme: neither purely social and recreational nor purely religious.

This is the solution recently proposed by Pius XII for uniting religious aspirations and social preoccupations in the heart of Catholic Action.

'The activity of Catholic Action extends to the whole religious and social domain, that is, wherever the mission work of the Church is. Now, it is well known that normal growth and development of religious life supposes a certain measure of sound economic and social conditions.'

We may extend this observation to the hygienic and cultural conditions which concern our youth movements.

The Pope continues: 'Who does not feel his heart oppressed in seeing how economic misery and social evils have rendered the Christian life according to God's commandments much more difficult and how often heroic sacrifice is demanded. One cannot conclude, however, that the Church should begin by putting aside Her religious mission to attend to the healing of social misery first.'

'If the Church has always been solicitous to defend and foster justice, She has, from the time of the apostles even before the gravest social abuses, accomplished Her mission and, by the sanctification of souls and the conversion of inner sentiments, has sought equally to undertake the healing of social evils and distresses, convinced as She is that religious forces and Christian principles are more valuable than any others for promoting the healing.' [6]

Progressives in matters of social relief or in physical and intellectual improvement would do well to meditate on these carefully balanced words. Beginning with Her religious mission, the Church is interested in every kind of progress. She does not do things backwards, seeking first social relief or political action.

Youth movements need not hide their source of inspiration and their final end in order the more easily to penetrate the temporal and to garner further recruits. Such a sham would number among its earliest victims the young people themselves. They must learn that if Catholic Action promises them more happiness, it also demands a greater spirit of sacrifice. Otherwise, we will be forming mere profiteers who amass without giving.

It is obvious that schooling in generosity is progressive. What lad in a factory comes to inscribe in the Y.C.W. 'to extend the reign of Christ'? He seeks first the companionship and warmth of fellows of his own age and neighbourhood. Unconsciously, no doubt, he is urged on by a more profoundly human desire. He continues to come and does not refuse 'the other stuff.' Little by little he becomes aware that 'the other stuff' is the essential, and the only thing capable of solving his problems. At the beginning he only vaguely suspects it. If after years of patient formation he does not see the difference between the Y.C.W. and a sports club, he has simply failed to cross the threshold of Catholic Action.

Even after this discovery, he will not be transformed into a monk. The better part of his time not already consumed in the factory, will be spent in neighbourhood activities or on the athletic field and not in reciting Aves. Only a fool measures the value of anything by the number of hours consecrated to it. If it were otherwise, profane work, sleeping or pleasure-seeking as the case may be, would rank first.

Youth is aware both of team spirit and self-sacrifice. Why would it be opposed to the idea of the apostolate, if it is presented frankly, skilfully, and sanely, of course, and above all, straightforwardly?

Under penalty of sterility, the movement must capture the spirit of the completely unique milieu that is youth. As an object of sociological study the phenomenon is new. Only in our time have people become aware of the special character of the spontaneous grouping of adolescent outside the family or school and especially apart from untimely adult interference. By more careful observation, pedagogy, in its turn, is beginning to fix the symptoms of this transitional age.

Changes in living conditions, the break-up of the home, and the still greater confusion of war have accelerated the appearance of this movement especially among the ordinary classes. We are in the presence of a veritable 'third milieu', often more formative than a loosely formed family or school training. In the midst of this autonomous group, neither a gang of youngsters nor an association of adults, the young man under his own power first develops his personality. He learns to join comradeship with a sense of discipline, play with a sense of productivity, and solidarity with a new freely accepted authority. There are leaders and team mates; and all of this, lived in an environment that mixes the serious and the adventurous, in an atmosphere impregnated with feelings and imagination, which is too often labelled with the unfortunate name of romanticism.

We must not mock or try to ignore the phenomenon, and still less attempt to misuse. The temptation to do so will come to political agitators and sometimes to ecclesiastical leaders. An honest educator will respect its natural character and its rich potentiality. He will reckon its true value as immense and, scrupulously disinterested, will try to orientate it towards its real ends.

And so it is that we find a happy and unexpected contact between the youth movement and the organization of the apostolate. Both appeal to free and personal activity and a spirit of solidarity. Both oppose constraint, forced methods and paralyzing egoism. Both embody themselves in impressive captivating realisations. In both all is done for the young and by them.[7] An astonishingly fertile alliance can result if one observes the distinctions, the necessary balance and the laws of progressive growth.

This is why Catholic Action among the young does not reject but collaborates with the youth movement. It is careful not to monopolize it, for that is to destroy it. It does not use it as bait nor does it identify itself with the youth movement—to do so would give the apostolate an appearance of childishness. It neither lowers itself to mimicking the discoveries of Baden-Powell nor does it follow the findings of Nazi and Soviet pioneers. Here, too, the Church respects temporal values: and one of the most eminent among these values is the living milieu that is youth.

But this value has transitional richness. To wish to stabilize it renders it unreal and ridiculous. It is destined to be reabsorbed in a greater social good, by a gradually increasing contact with the cold realities of adult life. The accent will shift from 'the movement' to the 'apostolate' and views with a universal sweep will evolve. To impede this process is to fall victim to the excess of our age. With the stigmatising name of 'puerilism' the historian philosopher Huizinga has branded that excess.[8] We are witnessing, then, the march of the militarized masses under totalitarian régimes that produce grown men and women as intolerant and unmanageable as bad children and retarded youngsters.

Such pedantry, such leader-worship, such mania for parades, insignias and rally cries (of which the Nazis have given such a frightening example) sadly threaten to misguide personality in search of itself and to engulf him before he ever reaches reflection or moral maturity.

We are not blind to these troubling deviations that trap and entangle man's primitive instincts. Still it is wrong to forbid our young people to try their newly born strength within their own circles during this intermediary evolutionary stage, whose synchronization and harmonizing with youth's first collective religious reactions are so delicate. There is always an irreducible tension: even more than intellectual education, religious formation is received from above and it is mistaken to claim for oneself its accomplishment. Nevertheless, adolescence is admirably receptive; young people react eagerly to the sublime which presents itself to them, but does not impose itself, and they show themselves magnificently adaptable. Yet, once left to themselves, youth cannot unfold.

Catholic Action will find them an excellent testing ground provided it takes prudent care to cut away unhesitatingly all the dead branches of youthful vanity. Education of liberty is the art of arts and nothing demands a more unfettered and genuine liberty than the religious sense, and the apostolic service.

Although psychological adaptation is absolutely indispensable, it must not be allowed to degenerate into a false psychologism that is as disastrous as dogmatism. We stand now on grounds too lofty for psychology alone. The religious motive appears in exceptional terms: it touches the very aim of life. Man does not truly become man except before God. With social and moral categories alone one can never reach this level. Respect for the personality and society of youth contains something of the veneration experienced in the presence of the sacred, of grace, of a vocation.

The heavenly Father reveals to the little ones what he keeps hidden from the proud. Apostolic activity is an essential part of the mystery of the Church, the common gift of the Trinity in unity. The Spirit is not reserved to priests and monks alone. Provided they remain simple, lay people, even young men and women, gradually become men of the Spirit and propagators of His life. It is for them and for all like them that He sanctifies the hierarchy which rules the Body in His name. The Hierarchy owes it to Him to treat all as He Himself does, as free men, spontaneously labouring in the vital growth of their brothers. Such are the noble features of Catholic Action and the lay apostolate.

THE CATHOLIC'S TASK IN POLITICAL LIFE

Without losing sight of Catholic Action, we will go for the moment beyond this perspective to examine briefly what will be the Catholic's attitude towards politics.

The political field appears as an arena. There reigns an atmosphere of passionate struggle and a not infrequent reaction is to avoid it completely lest one's peace be lost. This instinctive aversion is unfounded. If politics is the sum total of the activities directing the organization called temporal society, then the affirmation of Pius XI is very understandable: 'One can say that no other field of action is so important, save religion itself.' [9] Politics deals with the good of the community that forms a perfect society independent in its own order, and regulates the acts and relationships of all its citizens in view of harmonious co-operation. No Catholic can refuse to serve the greatness of his country and its lesser communities—the family, cultural and social groups—which likewise are integrated into the universal community of nations by the introduction of obligations previously unsuspected. It is no exaggeration to speak of political justice, political charity and even of a true apostolate for the progress of the Christian profane order.

Today the juridically organized state exercises a much more

profound influence than formerly. It handles matters of real importance not only in social and economic relations but also in the most noble human activities, thus affecting their relationship with religion and the Church. The internal relations of public affairs are daily becoming more and more complex. Distance no longer exists; even continents are no longer strangers to one another. The universe has become a single, interdependent mass, a gigantic enterprise on the road to unlimited development.

The services of the State extend to labour organizations, commerce, the means of communication, technical and cultural projects, the family and education, health and recreation. In all these domains, the religious man ought to say to himself: *tua res agitur*, this is your business! We must not weep over the almost monstrous control of the modern state; we must vigilantly guard against encroachment upon the rightful territories of religion and of the state, and we must work to obtain respect for all rights.

Finally, the progress of democracy extends the responsibility for the common good to an ever larger number of individuals. Can it be said that these people are always the best and the most prepared? Realism and apostolic zeal, then, impose on believers an active vigilance. Indifference would be both a mistake and a sin: no one can claim to exert an effective influence from a distance.

Unfortunately, certain Catholics maintain a distrustful attitude, a complex of suspicion. They have seen so much abuse in public administration, so much egotism, ambition, corruption and bargaining that their impulse is to turn away immediately from so disheartening a spectacle. Some critics throw over moderation and even become unjust. As a result of bitter disillusionment, they suspect anyone who accepts a mandate of any kind. And in some lands is added to this an historical resentment against a state too long neutral or hostile to religion.

None of this furthers constructive agreement based on the clearly seen difference between the state and the Church and their complementary roles.

It is practically useless to recall that there is not only a difference between these two autonomous institutions as to the end but also a great difference as to the means of action. Because of the importance of the end to be attained in the ecclesiastical sphere, the means are fixed once and for all: faith, the sacraments and the hierarchy are valid to all and in the same way.

In the profane world how great are the differences of opinion and the different realisations achieved in the course of an evolving history and still more, how great the differences at any given moment among individual citizens! They are not forbidden to establish parties to support their preferences. Although a legitimate approach in political life, Saint Paul solemnly condemned a parallel attempt in the ecclesiastical society where perfect unity is the rule.

These parties set up programmes that are undoubtedly opposed yet, nonetheless, complementary. The problems to be resolved offer many aspects and it is only natural that different points of view will foster different solutions. As long as a violent party spirit does not replace solicitude for the whole country, the comparison of various groups can lead to a stimulating and balancing rivalry. This interplay of organized tendencies is foreign to the Church which is centered about a sacred power. The atmosphere in the state is very different. There freedom of opinion goes much further. Politics, it has been said, is the art of the possible and the compromise. It supposes practical foresight, vision, patience, dexterity and the sensitivity needed to recognize the opportune moment and to seize it.

Catholics receive their religious education in an altogether different atmosphere. Respectful of any immutable truth usually expressed by abstract principles, they are attached by preference to the thesis rather than to the hypothesis. As long as they are not politicians either by profession or by psychological preparation, the style of political action is something strange to their way of thinking. Their religious fidelity has not prepared them for close relations with dissidents, and when they move into the profane order, they fear compromise or even suppose too readily that their confreres are in bad faith. Their impatience often shows a lack of realism. Excess, whether to the right or to the left, conservatism or progressivism, could bring them to simple and almost always illusory solutions in which an enlightened active minority forcibly imposes its ideas on the masses.

They will need, therefore, a particularly thorough adaptation to avoid transposing absolute religious values to relative temporal contingencies. Considerable effort is required if they want to understand an adversary's point of view, a point of view that can often be perfectly honest. They must remember that, without recourse to the realm of concrete political and social claims, Christianity has contributed largely to diffusing a spirit of human dignity, universal fraternity, liberty and responsibility. Respect for the human person has especially prospered in Christian lands where it has found an ideology favourable to the growth of personal values. Nowhere else has the fundamental equality of all men and the respect for their inviolable rights found greater inspiration or more effective protection than in the religion of the heavenly Father and Christ, the universal

Redeemer. When the reigning Pope recommends democracy in the noblest sense of that term, he is not yielding to opportunism. It is enough to examine on which side of the famous barrier human liberty is most at ease.

If Catholics are to make use of this intellectual and moral influence of Christianity for the state's benefit, they cannot neglect a serious, persevering civic education. In some countries they must also learn the imperious duty to vote so that they may elect truly capable and conscientious citizens to positions of responsibility. Otherwise, they are wrong in complaining that the world is being built without them.

Their general formation should develop an ability to make essential distinctions, a sense of responsibility and civil courage.

And first of all let us once again underline the word *distinctions*. To confuse interests or mentalities will inevitably produce disorder. As Catholic citizens, their co-operation in both the communities to which they belong and the agreement between the two powers can only be obtained by a clear understanding of the differences in nature, spirit and method. In place of mutual suspicion, we must encourage mutual openness. Moreover, a firm goodwill must seek the wisest and the best practical arrangement of complicated problems, problems that so often resist solution. The Church and the Nation, each in its own place and in its own way, must be objects of a sincere and active affection for the Christian.

Catholic Action in particular, 'like the Church, whose helper it is, . . . of its very nature is above and outside of political parties, . . . it is preoccupied not with the particular interests of groups, but with the good of souls'.[10] 'It does not become involved in party competition nor is it reduced to the narrow limits of factions.'[11] The Popes have been lavish with similar recommendations to the faithful of every nation. Jealously must the apostolate preserve its proper character and its sacred atmosphere, and so respect the serenity and depth, the universality and eminence of the Church mystery.

Secondly, the *general formation* necessary in civic activity does not descend from heaven like revelation. It requires rigorous study of principles as well as knowledge of contingent circumstances. This includes, undoubtedly, a considerable amount of theology and philosophy, but also an art, a technique, a clear-sightedness refined by the careful observation of facts. Catholic principles are not coins to be inserted into a slot-machine for political solutions.[12] This type of work demands accurate judgment, inventive spirit and creative imagination. Without these, Catholic statesmen capable of introducing in national and international public life that active presence resulting from the union of undisputed ability and Christian wisdom will never arise.[13]

If the Christian community wants men of such calibre, it must be determined to offer them and then to prepare them. The lay apostolate, youth organizations included, has to concern itself with giving this formation to its members. It must be careful not to allow them to enter the arena of party battle prematurely; it must rather procure for them the armour of virtue needed to promote devoted service in the place of egoism.[14]

Lastly, Christians must have the *courage* of their responsibilities. Cowardice will not suffice; they must fight, defensively as well as offensively, know how to meet temporary defeat without moral capitulation, and maintain their ardour intact, ready to take up again the offensive. And should anyone be inclined to act the part of Nietzsche's bleating sheep, he is sure of one thing only—that he will make himself ridiculous in this combat of men.

'The youth of Catholic Action are to be taught how they can and should use their civil and political rights . . . ' says the Council of Malines.[15] Otherwise the desire to see lay people, mature adults, radiating their Faith and fashioning a new world, will remain indefinitely Platonic.

Pius XII has not hesitated to mobilize even women and young girls. For them, too, political duty is a form of Christian social charity, especially in the defence of the family's moral integrity.

In their service to the State, they are to introduce the specifically feminine notes of finesse and devotion, tact and perseverance.[16] In this discourse and others like it, the Pope shows a very real sense of the modern evolution which is changing the whole fabric of society. The Church will have to speak in time to obtain from her faithful, men and women, the Christian witness their vocation as baptized souls and citizens imposes on them. And if the lay apostolate does not become entangled in party rivalries, it does not work the less effectively to better governments by breathing something sacred into political life and by extending it to the disinterested and magnificent service of the community of men.

---

[1] *Codex Juris Canonici*, can. 487.
[2] H. U. VON BALTHASAR, *Der Laie und der Ordensstand*. Cf. Chap. 7, note 1.
[3] PIUS XII, *Address to the Congress of the States of Perfection*, Dec. 8, 1950. *Acta Apl. Sedis*, 43, 1951, p. 26-36, esp. p. 35. French trans. and commentary in the *Nouv. Rev. Théol.* 73, 1951, p. 179-192.
[4] See above, Chap. III, on temporal values, p. 44.
[5] P. TIBERGHIEN, *o.c.*, *L'Action catholique*, p. 87.
[6] PIUS XII, Address of May 3, 1951, n. 3. *Docum. cath.* 48, col. 579 ff.
[7] This is a case where the words of Pius XI. should be applied: 'The first and immediate

146

THE ROLE OF THE LAITY IN THE CHURCH

apostles of the (young) working-men must themselves be (young) working-men'. Encyc. *Quad. Anno.* Eng. Trans., *The Social Order*, Cath. Truth Soc., London, 1931, n. 141.

8 See esp. the important work of J. Huizinga, *Homo Ludens*, which consecrates a very stimulating chapter to this phenomenon. French Trans., C. Seresia, in the series *Les Essais*, n. 47, Paris, 1951, p. 327 ff.

9 Pius XI., Address of Dec. 18, 1927, *To University Students in Catholic Action.* Cf. L. Civardi, *o.c.*, *Manuale*, p. 286; Eng. Trans., Martindale, p. 183 ff. See also L. Sturzo, *Coscienza e Politica*, Brescia, 1953.

10 Pius XI, *Letter to the patriarch of Lisbon*, Nov. 10, 1933. *Actes*, Ed. Bonne Presse, p. 176.

11 Pius XII, *Letter to the President of the Youth of Italian Catholic Action*, March 12, 1943. Cf. L. Civardi, *o.c.*, *Manuale*, p. 276 ff.; Eng. Transl. Martindale, p. 193 ff.

12 Cf. M. Romme. *Katholicisme en Politiek*, in *Documentatie*, 8, 1952, p. 145.

13 On this point the *Conclusions* of the World Congress of the Lay Apostolate are very noteworthy. See *Actes*, I, p. 183 and ff., esp. nos. 4, 6 and 8.

14 Cf. the prescriptions of the Provincial Council of Malines concerning the Catholic Action of youth, *Actes*, n. 116.

15 Council of Malines, *l.c.*

16 Pius XII, *Address to Members of various Catholic Women's Associations*, Oct. 21, 1945, Cath. Truth Soc., London.

CHAPTER IX.

TOWARDS A LAY SPIRITUALITY

IT IS A SIGN OF THE TIMES, and in this instance a very happy one, that even outside Catholic Action circles the layman, no longer content with a respectable mediocrity, is seeking to realize religious aspirations within the framework of profane life itself. Does that justify our speaking about a 'spirituality of the layman'?[1]

Some answer with a blunt 'No!' In a recent inquiry, a militant Catholic woman found the expression 'stupid' and a theologian added that the layman as such has juridical, but not theological existence.[2]

A QUESTION OF PRINCIPLE

We must begin, obviously, by grasping the meaning of the words. Spirituality refers to the way in which the mystery of faith is lived, to the general atmosphere of Catholicism as piety, to the ensemble of concrete and particular aspects that are found in the ideas, sentiments, reactions and prayers of a determined group of believers, a totality that varies from one group to another.[3]

Obviously there are neither two kinds of sanctity, nor two kinds of grace or faith. There is only one divine life that the common Father communicates to all through His Incarnate Son, the sole Mediator, through the out-pouring of the one, unique Spirit. No one is condemned to a diluted Christianity that would in reality no longer be the true religion of the Father. God shows no preference among men; He takes His elect from all the varying spheres of life.

And yet in the history of the Church we speak with good reason of different forms and even schools of spirituality, each having its proper physiognomy. The desert fathers practised the same Catholicism as our priest-workers, but they practised it in a different way. The difference is not so much in the material conditions of their lives; both worked untiringly. The first to assure the salvation of their souls and the glory of God, fled as far from the world of men as possible; the second, on the contrary, sought to come as close to the world of men as possible for the glory of God and the salvation of souls. The emphasis is obviously not the same.

147

Scholars distinguish between oriental and occidental piety; they delineate Benedictine, Cistercian, Franciscan, Dominican schools, the mysticism of the Netherlands, the Rhineland, Spain and France, and so on. The national character is not the principal differentiating factor, and the colour of the frock or the cut of the habit is quite secondary. Still there is a certain way of ordering the different elements which make up the richness of our Christian life, of emphasizing this mystery or that virtue or this particular religious attitude without in the least neglecting other values. Thus a great variety of original compositions can present the theme in different forms. [4]

The end is always the same, of course, and the essential means remain the same for all: revealed doctrine, the Church, the work of grace, sacramental rites, and the infused virtues especially the theological ones. Their adaptation, however, can be worked out in an infinite number of ways. From this point of view, too, there are many mansions in Our Father's house. Nowhere can one meet so much variety as in the gallery of the saints. In their unanimous imitation of Christ, each has his own vision. Holiness is multiform in its creation; there are no serial editions on that shelf.

The 'schools' of spirituality take their origin from the extraordinary success of some saint who has stamped his influence on an entire region or epoch. The geniuses and giants of the Christian life had not the least intention of founding a school to transmit to their followers one element of holiness to the exclusion of all the others. [5] Often their spiritual sons undertook this work and elaborated conceptions or even scholarly formulas. Yet the pioneers are always universalists especially when, under the guidance of the Spirit, they are fired by a grace intense enough to transmit a powerful current. Leave the arrangement of the categories to the theologians and historians of spirituality. The field is theirs, and a useful one it is, if it does not become too narrow. Personally, we thank heaven for the gift of St. Francis but also for the blessing of Franciscanism.

Not all saints are founders or reformers of orders. Moreover, the question that occupies us is a little different; may we speak in general terms about a particular spirituality for large groups in the Church, the clergy, religious, and the laity?

At present we are not considering schools in the strict sense, but rather a kind of style or diversity arising from differences in living conditions.

The liturgy recognizes only one formula for a canonization and yet she delights in honouring the elect by different categories; and on the feast of All Saints, she presents them in an orderly procession, each group with its particular attributes, a procession such as we find in the magnificent Van Eyck triptych *The Adoration of the Mystic Lamb*. The Little Office of the Blessed Virgin also distinctly prays 'for the people, the clergy and the choirs of monks.'[6]

Priests are sanctified chiefly by the exercise of their ministry: preaching the word of God and of His Church, the celebration of the sacrifice and the Sacraments. Monks form a community of prayer, an oasis of life absorbed in God in the midst of a worldly desert unmindful of God. And laymen? They lead the Christian life in the heart of the world by trying to exalt and christianize it from within. If they are the immediate apostles of their brothers, as Pius XI has proclaimed, how can they be forbidden a corresponding piety? Theirs is certainly not the devout clerical or monastic life transplanted to the home or factory. Their spirituality cannot be to have no spirituality, nor to have one that has no theological foundation. It cannot live only on the regret that its subjects do not wear the cassock and are unable to take refuge in the monastery. That would be purely negative and far too meagre.

But does that imply a genuine 'lay spirituality'? Not quite, for we must first be able to uncover a striving towards perfection in the group viewed as a component part of the Church. The question is one of the universal call to holiness rather than to the determination of a particular school of spirituality. The problem is certainly one of tremendous importance. Moreover, sufficient attention must be given to the lay 'situation' as such in connection with the purpose of the Church. And, finally, a systematic study of the whole issue must be undertaken. Today we are witnessing this great progress.

The practice of Gospel truths among ordinary Christians dates evidently to the preaching of apostolic times although it did not form a specific center of interest for early scholars. In fact for a long time we note a certain disdain for the worldly condition in which most of the baptized unfortunately have to work out their salvation. Such reserve is understandable when compared to the superior value of the professional devout life of the cloister.

Compared with the life of the cloister even priestly piety seemed to pale. True, the Latin clergy was obliged to celibacy and was not unaware of the practice of obedience and a more or less compulsory poverty. But as a general rule, they were not bound by vows nor were they organized into separate communities. As for the lay form of life, that was even further removed from the cloister.

Still, it would be wrong to consider the spirituality of clerics as a diminished monastic spirituality and the spirituality of the layman, as a reduction of that first reduction. What would remain would be rather negligible. Moreover, this whole process fails to regard the facts.

If religious are professionals in the pursuit of perfection, it does not follow that all the others must be amateurs. Groups differ not in their concept of Christian life but in the particulars of a special vocation and the circumstances of concrete existence. This ensemble involves and works upon the soul so profoundly that a particular kind of spiritual life is born. To underestimate the religious vocation is something that will always be foreign to the true Catholic mind. Religious forsake all temporal goods, in this sense, that they despise but they do not condemn. [7] They renounce all in view of a greater good but they willingly acknowledge that laymen have to sanctify themselves not without but within their daily programme of life and its framework of natural values.

They are to remain faithful to the duties of their state in life; let us take, as an example, self-sacrifice for their families and work for the prosperity of the community. They must not look on such duties as necessary evils or as subject for resentment but as sacred obligations. They do not live simply in the midst of their own but also a little, we hope, 'for their own,' sharing their anxieties, helping them to carry their burden courageously. Christ has provided for this by the sacrament of Matrimony and it is not to be considered in any way suspect. [8] And still even the immediate union to the Heavenly Spouse by virginal consecration can be destined by God for the people of the world: it surely surpasses in value the imitation of the union between Christ and His Church found in Christian marriage.

Lay spirituality is not confined to the mysticism of marriage; it is broader than that. Nor when compared to the ideal of the religious is it to be imagined something like an article at reduced price. Rather lay spirituality is something different, namely, a special way that is not the highest or most perfect but that nonetheless retains its value, so long as it does not lead to self-worship and narrowness.

Let us not forget that convent life not only permits spiritual retreat but also a special and physical separation that is made possible by the enclosure. As mild as this may be in our days, its spirit remains; furthermore, if all the walls were torn down, there would be no more cloister. In this regard, lay brothers and sisters, whom Canon Law considers as 'laici,' are numbered among the religious whose dwelling they share. As for lay people, their Christian condition in the world, their existence and activity in the age in which they live determine their manner of loving and serving God and neighbour, and so too their spirituality. Such spirituality is not characterized by the *object* which would be exclusively or for the most part profane; it depends on the *subject* involved totally in the secular situation, the lot of the vast majority of men. [9]

A propos of this, we quote the commonsense observation of a religious: 'We would commit an error in judgement were we to propose to the people of the world as an ideal for their spiritual life a more or less monastic sanctity *ad usum laicorum*, that is, a formula of cloistral sanctity mercifully adapted to the layman's use and sweetened with a large dose of condescendence. To look at the situation this way fails to recognize the type of sanctity proper both to the religious and to the layman.'[10]

A certain historian of spirituality excuses himself for also consulting as documentation of his work, the lives of secular priests and laymen.[11] To us his precaution seems superfluous; we freely admit that sanctity does not depend on the costume. What is more, no religious pretends, and it is said to his honour, that the perfection of his state is in fact repeated in each member. Without tonsure or cowl there still exists a way to rise to heroic virtue even amidst occupations for the most part profane.

By this we do not mean that by adding pious intentions the layman compensates for the inherent imperfection of his 'secular' works. Faith demands that he sanctify them directly and from within. Workers, doctors, mothers of families must not face daily tasks as unavoidable evils from which they are to salvage whatever scraps they can use for a higher end. Young men in the Y.C.W. are taught to consider their work bench as an extension of the altar and so to sanctify their labour in union with the sacrifice of Christ.

Sometimes people try to compare from the viewpoint of merit the concrete life of a layman and of a religious. The monk, they say, takes the vow of poverty but his life has more security than that of the common labourer who does not know whether tomorrow will find him work and bread for his family. The religious too has his activities determined for him; but what workman can choose trade and factory as he likes? Monks and nuns renounce marriage, but how many are there in the world, both unmarried and married, who must practise continence![12]

Any such superficial comparison should not be taken literally. If the plain life of the convent were so wondrously attractive we would soon be faced with the problem of over-crowding in religious houses. The greater number of religious congregations today have not reached such a stage; in Europe they are closer to being empty.

Complete and irrevocable detachment remains the requirement for all who wish to enter into the religious state. Most men, whether workers or not, recoil before this radical renunciation; they seek a less steep path to heaven. Frequently they undergo the anxieties of destitution and an uncertain lot. But they have not renounced forever the right of possession and the right of personal liberty, and they certainly have not rejected the hope of acquiring and keeping these rights. The religious can no longer even desire them. If it is necessary, the layman will submit to and suffer these mortifying restrictions; the religious embraces them, not for themselves obviously, but for the love of God. To avoid any sharing of his life, he prefers the radical solution; instead of parting from his goods one by one, he abandons them all at once and without a backward glance.

In the last analysis it is the religious who enjoys the greatest liberty; the layman is generally not disposed to pay the price for such independence. God has marked out other paths for him, paths equally Christian and well sown with trials. To fortify his kingdom once he has entered it, the religious realizes that he needs to strengthen his spirit of sacrifice by voluntary mortifications. Penitential exercises are a part of his programme. Married people do not have to look so far to find occasions for conquering and mortifying themselves: opportunities come to them in abundance. No need of a bell to sound the hour for Matins: at all hours the babies 'chant' their own plaintive nocturns. And the whole day long—children to raise, a mother to comfort, a foreman to satisfy—demands whether we like it or not a self-sacrifice not catalogued in a Rule, yet nonetheless burdensome.

Living a well ordered way of life, professed religious are tempted to establish themselves in the ways of perfection with a subtle self-sufficiency. Semi-Pelagianism was born in monasteries. The monks of Lerins lacked humility, not fervour: they had too much confidence in their works of piety. That condemns their pride, not their vocation. Clerics and monks can only take pride in their superiority in serving others. They remain subject to the word of Christ which they preach and which can become the principal indictment laid to culpable weakness.

Nonetheless, preaching is required of them. The faithful especially need the witness of their lives. Without the example of these daring souls who have sacrificed all for the Gospel, the layman in his profane life situation would be even less inclined to risk living the full Christian life. It is not without cause that the fathers of today's families have been called 'the great adventurers of modern times.'

Courage born of faith leads to authentic sanctity even outside the cloister. As long as it does not give rise to the caste spirit a greater differentiation tokens an enrichment. This specialization is an especially modern phenomenon, and leads us to inquire what picture our age paints of a saint. We will try to determine the typical traits while carefully considering the layman's views and his more or less explicit aspirations, though we will not limit ourselves to this aspect. We will find many excellent characteristics but also with the light of faith we must be on guard against the dangers of possible deviation. We deem it useful to arrange our considerations, admittedly incomplete and provisional, under three principal headings : in his conception of sanctity, the modern Christian wants an absolute sincerity, a profound community sense and a realistic desire for adaptation.

MODERN SANCTITY AND SINCERITY

Did the sanctity of former days lack sincerity? such an assertion would be untenable. However, in comparison with the devout life at the end of the last century, the contemporary ideal emphasises a severe purification of exterior forms which, in its eyes, will remove us further from the danger of formalism.

Modern man wants these forms simplified so that they may be more authentic. The exigence has something fierce about it. The reaction is completely understandable : the whole world is infested with lying, it applies the art of deception with scientific rigour. Thus, in the religious domain, truth's sole refuge, man asks for radical honesty, deep-rooted and followed to its final consequences. It is expressed in the desire for complete purity in principle and uncompromising fidelity in execution.

From this particular viewpoint, the piety of fifty years ago was less troubled, more confident; we could even say mediocre.[13] Our grandparents cultivated respectability and distinguished manners. Going to church for them was something of a formal parade; they 'assisted' at Mass without any liturgical preparation. Communion was reserved for the more important days. Their books of piety presented prayers and sacramental practice as the great means of individual sanctification. They did not hide an instinctive horror of exaggeration, mysticism included.

Their sermons had a more moral tone than those of today, emphasizing the sense of duty, respect for laws, and the value of obedience. Equally popular was the 'devotional' sermon that extolled pious practices, the veneration of the saints and indulgences, and hardly showed any familiarity with Sacred Scripture and dogma. For the more advanced, there was emphasis on the necessity of systematic meditation and a detailed examination of conscience.

In all of this, a certain freshness and openness was wanting. Apologetic and defensive reflexes were more hold than the missionary spirit, apostolic zeal or oecumenism, movements which were all, and particularly the last, in an embryonic stage. It would nevertheless be wrong for us to disregard the solid qualities of this slightly bourgeois

spirituality with its attachment to duty and tradition, its high evaluation of morality, its faithfulness to the practice of fatiguing penances.

Be that as it may, the sense of God today has a different tone. We
sense more vividly the distance between a rationally elaborated concept of the divine, and the living, personal God, and this imposes on
us a more interior spirituality. Now it would certainly be pretentious
to attempt to define a programme to which the saint of our days
should conform; the Spirit Himself fixes the norms without referring
to our opinion. In every case, the true Christian will be a living witness
to the mystery. They will be 'men of God,' that is, men who have
seen God and in whom God can be seen. To see God makes a man
like God: there is no question of theoretical contemplation but rather
one of genuine transformation.

By opposition, the sense of God determines the sense of sin. Today
the sense of sin is no longer the flagrant transgression of positive precept it once was, no longer a kind of ecclesiastical police regulation.
Nor can sin, despite what is said about it today, be reduced to psychological illness, a matter exclusively reserved to doctors and special
institutions. Its essential dimension consists in opposing the personal
love of God and the fundamental law of the dependent creature who
is the expression of that love.

This pronounced God-centeredness does not by-pass the Mediator;
rather, it works quite explicitly through Him. The light of the Father
is reflected in the face of Christ, and the Saviour's glory effects a meta-
morphosis in us through the power of the Spirit (II. Col., III,18). The
imitation of Jesus is no longer interpreted as a human, purely moral
attempt 'to do as He did'; it is precisely the creation of the new man,
the old self being destroyed by mystical identification with the crucified
and glorified Redeemer. It is precisely in this mystical union that one
finds the full meaning of the imitation of Jesus. Herein lies the deeper
understanding of this primal truth, which gives it that aspect of
newness so noticeable in the lives of the saints.

And Christ touches us through His Church which continues His
life and work. Christ-centeredness, then, will be either ecclesiastical
in character or inauthentic. This is another value of which our immediate predecessors were hardly conscious, and only a return to
sources has awakened us to it.

By sources we mean Holy Scripture and living Tradition. These
we find in the teachings and directives of the Magisterium, in dogmatic theology, and in the liturgical celebration which is the living
doctrine of prayer. The piety of the faithful is profiting immensely
from this Biblical and patristic revival as well as from their initiation
into the mystery of worship.

Their devotion unhesitatingly favours the sober taste of the gospel to the sentimental ramblings of gilt-edged prayer books. Their sweet, romantic formulas evoke images similar to the statues of Saint Sulpice that disfigure our European churches, and so do violence at once to religious truth and to our sense of beauty. Baroque at least had something heroic and conquering about it.[14] We are still awaiting an acceptable statue of the Sacred Heart. It would grieve today's Christian to see a decline in devotion to the human Heart of the Saviour, that Heart opened by the lance to give birth to the sacramental Church; but he repeatedly demands a more biblical, more dogmatic and more liturgical presentation. Obviously it would be wrong to be offended by these demands.[15]

In the language of the Bible, the 'heart' does not signify tearful emotion. It is the whole interior man with his thoughts, his decisions, his wilful passions, his cowardice or his spirit of sacrifice, such as God with His infinite vision sees him. There is no 'honey' in the 'sweet' Heart of Jesus if we retain the bitter taste, the word had in Roman usage, which found it 'sweet' to die for a country : 'sweet' signifies that which is uplifting and irresistibly attractive. The ardent and sorrowful Heart of Christ, suffering the malice of the world's sinners is certainly something for us to 'console', but not to overwhelm with sentimental affection. The spirit of faith desires to learn from serious theology what this consolation really means. The thought of the Man-God passes beyond time and space. He has truly suffered agony, weighted with all human crimes accumulated upon Him, the expiatory victim; and the virile fidelity of loving souls, past or future, was present to Him in the garden through the angel of comfort.

Today's Christian also asks for a liturgical expression that respects the noble and deeply engraven lines of the Gospel and of dogma. The *improperia* or 'reproaches' of Good Friday, so charged with the piety of both Testaments, impress him more in the mouth of the suffering Christ than the reproaches of the visions of Saint Margaret Mary; and the preaching of the twelve promises would accomplish more in his eyes if it followed the style of the promises of the Messianic alliance. On the other hand, he appreciates the grandeur of the Mass of the Sacred Heart, *Cogitationes*, constructed as it is with some of the most sober and monumental passages of the Bible.

The same change has come about in Marian devotion. Never has it been so theological. The Middle Ages delighted in beautiful legends and miracles. Now brocaded capes are disappearing from old, blackened statues, and more study is devoted to what the Gospel says about Our Lady, as well as to the beautiful writings of the Fathers on the New Eve.

The key words of our times, says M. Folliet, are: *experience, existence, history* and *sociology*.[16] We must immerse such values in the totality of faith. The concrete fact, really present and livable, merits all our respect; fantasy, myth and 'the system', none of it: the gospels present nothing of this kind. The abstract analysis of a rationalistic age leaves us completely cold: We venerate the mystery of *existence*, especially the existence of the Man-God and His work: We will heartily welcome *historical* criticism and *psychological* introspection provided they respect the transcendence of the Saviour and His saints. The Gospel 'fact' continues to dominate our religious life and to nourish our spiritual contacts. As to the *social* resonances, we will touch on them later in speaking about the community spirit.

Now Gospel devotion demands of us simplicity, vigour, charity and realism.

Simplicity is majestic when its grandeur proceeds from interior richness and not from accidentals. To ornament the Gospel is to profane it. Our age's choice in hagiography is a modern, simple style. Accounts of wondrous happenings designed to produce wide-eyed amazement are regarded with suspicion. The central fact of mystical union with the Saviour is infinitely more important than the attendant phenomena of visions and ecstasies. The former commands respect, the latter astonishes the public. The distance between Christine the Admirable, who rose from death on two occasions, and Therese of Lisieux is considerable. The astonishing thing this time is that a life so drab could attain to such a rare interior richness. Her smallness is not in the least bourgeois: her ascent was like the flight of an eagle. If she brings sanctity closer to us, it is not by diminishing it, but by enlarging our means of attaining it.

It can be said that the spiritual life has passed from the plural of abundance to the singular of intensity. Objects can be multiplied; personality remains one. The modern Christian prefers piety to exercises of piety that form a complicated gymnastic programme far removed from life's core. The value of prayer does not hang on the number of formulas recited; devotions can smother true devotion, which is the sense of God. Consciousness of sin as an offence against Love is more indispensable than any enumeration of faults well catalogued and categorized. The various commandments only explain the great precept of charity, just as multiple graces only prove the benevolent grace of God. For if there are many gifts, there is but one, eternal Spirit who remains the gift *par excellence*. The 'little virtues' we envision as a kind of retail business whereas genuine virtue demands heroism. Living faith is much more than the sum of articles to be believed and of practices to be observed. Willingly would we forego excessive casuistry to be compensated by a greater union with God in the theological virtues.

To realize this programme, an unusual *vigour* is required. Today's Christian is confused when he hears it asked whether or not Christianity is just 'a pseudonym for the coalition of the weak and fearful'? Why has Christianity been reduced to 'a code of moral and religious propriety whose principal anxiety seems to be to discourage enthusiasm, to avoid risks, excuse any boldness . . .'?[17] Has Christianity really emasculated man? This is not to say that woman has a diminished personality. The weaker sex often show more force, determination and courage than many of those males whom Nietzsche whipped and drove like a pack of slaves.

His waves of insults fail to touch Christianity: the message of the New Law is not the stupid resignation of the herd but a self-domination for the service of God and neighbour, a victory that far surpasses the conquest of any empire. The strength of Nietzsche's superman is mere violence at the service of pride. Before the pastor who, incapable of true energy, cozily settles back into indifference or even sometimes into cowardice, the parishioner shows himself a severe judge. And basically, he is right; his biting criticism is still another homage to the sublimity of the priestly vocation.

Modern literature has made popular a new type of saint. He might be called the 'scandalous saint,' a sinner, weak and fearful, troubled and passionate, retrieved by grace in spite of himself, finally realising the supreme sacrifice with a heroism not his own.[18] Such decadence in saints seems to bring them closer to us. Again, we must avoid relegating courage to inaccessible heights. Strength of soul comes as a gift of the Spirit to transform even the most shattered nature.

The force that raises the heaviest weight is *charity* which seeks nothing for itself and gives itself without recompense. In France, work freely given is held in honour. Still, that is no reason to look askance at duty accomplished without show. Even obligatory work can assume an authentic beauty, and many are the humble souls who know no other work. Contrary to what some fear, love is not opposed to duty: love transforms duty.[19] If we give preference to the supererogatory, to 'the extras,' we are victims of an illusion. Before we can think of the luxury of unrequired sacrifice, we must carry out the orders that have been given us. Nor does difficult obligation look to any return involved; it accompanies the charity of Christ obedient even unto death.

When a healthy *realism* tackles work in all its concrete disagreeableness or even in its materiality, then all self-illusion disappears. A false idea of religion leads some to replace effort with an untimely cry for supernatural help. Such people are concealing culpable laziness under the guise of piety and when their enterprise collapses because of their neg-ligence or stupidity they speak of the trials that Providence sends them, they assume the attitude of martyrs.

All that is false if not sacrilegious. In Catholicism, rash con-fidence without virtuous works is labelled a sin against the Holy Spirit. Prayer is not an insurance policy guaranteeing against the inevitable effects of inactivity. God gives the increase, but He does not dispense Paul or Apollo from the work of planting and watering. You do not dismiss the physician once the novena begins. 'Recourse to God does not purpose to render effort superfluous . . . Some requests are in reality refusals to co-operate.'[20] True prayer arouses, supports, purifies effort.

In all the apostolic writings there are severe admonitions that reveal active mutual aid as the touchstone of true love of God. The modern saint, especially among the laity, will be a 'social saint' serving and loving Christ in all the persons who make up His Body.[21]

COMMUNITY SPIRITUALITY

It is obvious that without *diffusion* the idea of a community is un-thinkable. The basic tendency toward universalism is manifested in the increasing number approaching the ideal of sanctity. People talk of the *turba magna*, the great crowd climbing the spiritual mountain, and even of a democratization and secularization of spirituality. Spirituality is advancing beyond the cloister and sanctuary to gain recruits from an ever wider circle of profane society.

In processions and in biographies saints habitually appear to us in ceremonial dress. They have a rather aristocratic allure and reveal a somewhat distant nobility. We find it difficult to separate them from their halos and jewelled cloaks. All that is symbolism. The secrets of the heavenly life inaugurated on earth are equally destined for the disinherited and despised. In Van Eyck's famous painting, *The Adora-tion of the Mystic Lamb*, among the choirs of the elect streaming with gold, the bourgeois have a place only because they represent the artist's patrons, and the poorest of the poor do not appear at all. Present day hagiography recognizes proletariat saints and heroic labourers next to canonized university professors. Such a motley assemb-lage in no way diminishes the solemnity of former saints.

Let it be said without prejudice to Charles de Foucauld, the time of the desert fathers is gone. In fact, the Little Brothers of Father de Foucauld have established themselves in the very heart of the masses.[22] We no longer think of stylites: the column has become simply the pedestal of the statue. Formerly ascetics in quest of solitude bade adieu to the agitation of the crowds and even to the splendours of the liturgy. Face to face they met the violent demons, for in their hearts they had brought part of the world with them; but for society their flight was a harsh sermon on the passing nature of earthly goods and the urgency of saving one's soul from perdition.[23]

It would be unjust to deny the anchorites any apostolic influence. Thousands of disciples followed Anthony and Pachomius to their desert solitude and later, Benedict and Cassien to their monasteries. The man of the world, however, seemed excluded from higher religious aspiration. The third orders which grew out of the Franciscan and Dominican movements dreamed of the ideal of perfection found within monastery walls.[24] The laity had no access to the cloister; therefore, they gathered round the sacred enclosure and dutifully kept their nostalgia.

During the course of the centuries, it can be generally said that monastic life and lay life have sought to come closer together. The Middle Ages no longer built monasteries on the mountain peak or in the depths of the forest, but in the center of the city. Isolation became less rigorous; first men's and then women's congregations permitted their members to come in contact with the people of the world. Where Saint Francis de Sales had failed, Saint Vincent de Paul succeeded: the Visitation nuns have remained strictly cloistered, but the Sisters of Charity, with the conspicuous white cornette of the Breton peasant, walk the streets of crowded quarters and enter the homes of the poor.

The gentle Francis succeeded in interesting people of the world in the devout life. These women, it is true, had the time to apply themselves to pious meditations. Nonetheless, the movement soon spread to all levels of society.

Diffusion alone, however, does not create the community. The majority could still be scattered in many different directions; they must next concentrate in *unity*.

The Mystical Body, however, is not a religious replica of social unification which, in the face of liberal individualism, accents the natural interdependence of persons and groups. In the religious society, there is something besides organization and the reciprocal influence of members. An intimate bond exists with the Leader, Jesus Christ, the Source of life and unity. The faithful are united among themselves first of all because each of them is mystically identified with Christ and becomes a part of the Body animated by His Spirit. Their wills do not produce the unity of the Body by some sort of social contract in the spiritual order. Rather, they are the manifold fruits of a single organism. The unity, therefore, is not merely in the final term: it springs from the source.

In this way, Church society, the creator of Christian personalities, more easily avoids the collectivism that absorbs people in a monstrous biological entity. Her means of action are adapted to her nature: she does not force herself upon the world with waves of propaganda that provoke mass psychosis and frenzy; she rather invites man to liberty that leads him to self-reflection before Christ.

Everything begins with Him. Only when their union with the center is sufficiently conscious can the members think of propagation without the attendant danger of activism. To unite oneself to the mass and remain 'glued' there is not enough; we must have the substantial bread in our hands to satisfy the starving. Cardinal Suhard warned apostles against the deception of 'contact without current.'[25] Once immersed in the populace, once free of prejudices the bearer of the message must beware of losing the treasure he was sent to give.

In order to have goods to exchange in the Mystical Body, we must first receive them from the Leader and take the time to assimilate them. Not all are aware that they are merely ministers in the hands of Christ; some claim to do the work in His place. It is not astonishing if their results show evidence of this.

Community life reaches its greatest intensity in the liturgy. The eucharistic celebration of the Redemptive mystery diffuses a current of grace. That is why the apostle's starting point is the altar. There all become brothers. Liturgical prayer expresses itself with complete naturalness in the plural, Christ serving all by His existence and His earthly work.

We said above that the simplification of the spiritual life goes from the plural to the singular. The movement is inverted, because we are no longer considering things, we are speaking of persons. Amalgamating human beings is the great error of collectivism. In Sacred Scripture the Mystical Body is also called the City and Family of God. Within this group, all have value in and for themselves and each retains his own name. The liturgy is a choir of many voices singing in harmony.

Alas, parish worship is often a somewhat disfigured image of the heavenly liturgy. Many of the faithful complain about it; more do not even think to complain—and that is more deplorable. And in spite of everything, in the village church with its pastor who sings off-pitch and its sacristan who hastens the proceedings, the Mystery is celebrated as really as in a Benedictine abbey. The destitution of Christ assumes, so to speak, a still baser form: those responsible should see that the ignominy is repaired quickly.

In this regard, it does not suffice to multiply exercises of worship.

In our schools students are often obliged to assist at Mass, even during the week and the simple result, it appears, is that they become disgusted with it. Educators have become alarmed, but still have not sought where the remedy is to be found. This problem will not be solved by intensifying physical education. When a child has no appetite, his mother tries to excite in him a beneficial hunger; in this case that hunger will be spiritual. Some claim such a means is outmoded and no longer effective. You could also reduce rations to a minimum; but there is little chance, with such a war-time diet of restoring a languishing organism or of rearing a robust generation.

We greatly underestimate the resources of to-day's youth if we believe they are indifferent to every ideal, and treat them accordingly. They have no sympathy for superficial religion; it irritates them. But this is no reason to distribute to them parsimoniously the living faith, the sense of liturgy, and apostolic zeal. Modern man rejects narrow, individualistic piety, but responds to the abundant inspiration of the Communion of Saints.[26]

THE PROBLEM OF ADAPTATION

This problem is not posed only a propos of foreign missionaries; the call of the laity to sanctity urgently demands intelligent adaptation.

An adapted 'lay' spirituality, some have said, would be characterised by its active nature in opposition to the contemplative forms of monastic piety. Such an affirmation is, we think, inexact. The layman, also, eagerly seeks hours of recollection. The significant success of *Moral Rearmament* proves this. The people affected by this movement have especially discovered in it the importance of interior silence and contemplation. At the Caux center, this is called 'quiet time' and not meditation; it is a question of adjusting the vocabulary to the contemporary mind. Likewise, intense reflection on the 'four absolutes' is preferred to the old-fashioned asceticism of the theological and cardinal virtues.[27] Here again, the sense intended is more important than the terminology. In every case, a purely active life will soon be emptied of resources and will die of exhaustion; it absolutely needs the regular nourishment of contemplative prayer.

Indeed, those who insist on the active nature of lay spirituality hope the experience of human insufficiency in the apostolate will force the soul to have recourse as they say to supernatural means. Not everyone shares their optimism. Furthermore, it would be a grave error to use prayer only as a corrective or complement: it is *the* source of apostolic dedication.[28] Prayer which binds us to heaven is a cord that should not be cut; it would be difficult to re-tie the severed ends.

The ordinary Christian must serve God without leaving the world; therein is the great difficulty of all lay spirituality. Saint Paul says the married man is 'divided'. As for the layman, God attracts him and the world attracts him, but in opposite directions. A distressing tension arises and becomes unbearable until that moment when the soul releases its hold on the world and launches out to God. Then, renewed to its very depths, the soul returns to creation to accept it joyfully, welcomes it as it has come forth from the creative thought of God and no longer as it appears disfigured by sin. For Christ has restored this perverted world and made it His Kingdom that in it God might finally be all in all.

Let us again cite Cardinal Suhard: 'The Christian is not called upon to destroy or vilify the world, but to assume it, to sanctify it, to offer it in homage to God. In such a process lies the true incarnation; it is the invasion of mankind by the power of God in order that mankind may be uplifted and introduced into the realm of divine life.'[29]

And further: 'The return to God in action does not require a greater amount of activity. It merely supposes—and that is a life task—that the Christian place at the very heart of his commitments a passionate belief in the transcendence of God and the firm conviction that such a faith will bring about the necessary adaptations. The apostolate, as established by Christ, requires a living faith as much as method. Prayer is as necessary as the knowledge of how to proceed—or rather, the latter must be based on the former. We must go to souls by God. It is in this sense that it has been said that the apostolate is beyond contemplation.'[30]

The Cardinal, note well, is writing for laymen. In his opinion, contemplation is possible for them also. He does not at all mean to treat them as seminarians with a well-ordered schedule. He is taking them in their hum-drum, everyday existence, but with the intention of determining for them a programme of action destined spiritually to transfigure their environment.[31]

Apostolic action, therefore, will begin in God, and contemplation will be the 'propelling dynamism.' If not, adaptation will be lost in illusion.

One of the most subtle forms of this error resides, we fear, in what is called *the prayer of action*. By this is meant that the modern apostle, priest or layman, submerged in work, makes these very occupations a prayer. For does he not undertake them solely for God's glory? And so Saint Teresa, without ever ceasing to contemplate, accomplished the great work of establishing her Foundations in fulfilment of the divine will to which she was identified.

Were the prayer of action this supreme transformation, we could only admire such a genuine marvel. But alas! more than one who has tried this widely heralded method is still far from the seventh mansion of the Carmelite saint. Moreover, she herself was admitted to the mystical marriage only because she adhered unshakeably to pure contemplative prayer.

But, one may say, the intention sanctifies the exterior work and charity infuses it with a transcendent value. That is true. And nevertheless, that it might be true prayer, something else is needed. During the work the mind must remain free to grant a minimum of attention to the Lord Himself and not be totally occupied with the work undertaken for His glory. Otherwise, it will perform an action of eminent merit, maybe, but not one of true prayer. Prayer is defined as an uplifting of the soul *to God*, or, according to Saint Augustine: *affectuosa attentio ad Deum.*

Work accomplished in Church-like recollection with a suppliant soul—and that is truly called prayer—is a most excellent thing. But the disturbances of modern life impede this fixing of the soul on higher realities except for those who have endured the demanding asceticism of contemplation, a daily renewal of their souls.[32]

Action does not replace prayer. The more his burdens overwhelm him, the more the modern apostle has need of prayer if he does not wish to be swept away by the tide. The fever for works can cause a certain dizziness. For most of us the 'prayer of action' risks the loss of both prayer and action, substituting for them an agitation often intoxicating, always unproductive.

If this danger awaits priests and religious, what can be said for laymen? If they wish to keep alive the thought of God amidst all the world's turmoil, they cannot often neglect to seek His face, as the psalms say, in contemplation. It is a part of their adaptation to the time and place that Providence determines for them, not by means of some kind of oracle, but by the course of history and the push of social contingencies.

The *voice of the times*, said Cardinal Faulhaber, is the voice of God. *Vox temporis, vox Dei.*[33] The saints are always rooted in their age. 'All follow their century and protest against it,' says Folliet.[34] They accept it that they might be able to correct it. They say 'yes!' to the world, the work of God, that they might say 'no!' to the world of sin. They are passionately in love with their age, but with the love of God. With as strong a passion they hate the vices of their times: but they do not curse their age; they rather wish to redeem it and they are strong enough not to become exasperated, or to capitulate before the delays which are opposed to their zeal.

They willingly accept *their place* on this earth and, if they are laymen, this will be where the waters churn turbulently and not in the calm of the hermitage. They do not submit to their situation amid the temporal with a resigned heart; they welcome it as a gift and a mission from Christ. They do not flee contact with the profane world; they rather refuse obstinately to let themselves be monopolized by it; they use their liberty, which is their strength and joy, to uplift it. That is their humanism. It is not moral decadence that is profoundly human as modern literature would have us believe; it is the hope of divine redemption.

Such optimism in the face of the world is sometimes misunderstood. In the enquiry already mentioned concerning the type of modern saint, certain answers described the end to be attained as 'the free flowering of every human value,' or 'the union of the highest spiritual life with all human joys, sin alone excepted.'[35] Is it not disconcerting that Christians try to define sanctity without ever breathing a word about God or Christ? On a close examination one wonders if their conception does not put the last end in man, subordinating religion to social good. Christianity is incapable of admitting such a reversal.

Optimism, then, cannot possibly be maintained without suitable asceticism. Nobody wishes a return to the terrifying macerations of the ancients. Such an ideal could only appear suspect. Asceticism is merely a tool in the service of divine love.[36] What is more, our psycho-biological conditioning has greatly evolved, general culture is transformed, sensitivity has become complicated and even unsettled to the point of nervosity. Because of this, voluntary suffering can become ambiguous, uncertain. 'When the psyche of the individual ceases to be of a sufficiently hardy and simple constitution . . . , corporal affliction opens the door to deception and morbidness. From the moment when, because of general neurological reasons basically quite simple, bodily macerations tend to become indirect occasions of hedonism, they are no longer of much value for Christian penance.'[37]

Should we complain about this or become indignant before the shamelessness of psychiatry? A wiser course would be to adapt penitential exercises to our modified reflexes. The age of renunciation is never past; Christian humanism is a crucified humanism.[38] The social asceticism spoken of today is no less profound, but takes other forms. Under the impulse of charity it seeks perfect interior detachment the better to obey—that is, more freely, and the better to love—that is, to love disinterestedly and more divinely. In ordinary dealings love purifies the 'natural' virtues: respect for personality, thoughtfulness, sincerity, inviolable integrity, tact and discretion. These many victories cannot be won without a great fight. The field of exercise extends to all the social relations: work, economics, science, politics, family life. Do spouses no longer need to master themselves ? And if money is an evil master, so too technical civilization can become tyrannical and finish in slavery.

Detached love will be the redeeming feature. The Christian will walk upon the earth as a pilgrim, refusing to become 'settled' here below. While resisting captivating seductions, he will still take his human work seriously. If he only touches it with his finger tips and with a mercenary spirit, he betrays his vocation of bringing this terrestrial 'home' to its definitive state.

If the faithful recognise this duty the dream of an enclosure of Christian virtue in the midst of surrounding paganism vanishes. The winds of the world blow across its imaginary frontiers. Christ sends His sheep among the wolves that the wolves might be converted. He does not ask that His Father take His disciples from the earth, but that He preserve them from evil. A trembling flock, fleeing the light of day and enclosed upon itself, can hardly be a sign raised on high in the midst of the nations.

The modern Christian must carry the message even to the miserable who are stagnating in the filth of our industrial quarters. All theory gives way before the sacrifice of priests and laymen who live their lives in the hell of slums and mines. Their witness has no need of eulogy. Men respect such total generosity; all spirit is not dead in Christianity.

In the ivory tower of our bourgeois culture, we are no longer in a position to understand the profound aspirations of a dehumanized mass. And this mass, for its part, will no longer let itself be conquered except by the total gift of oneself.

With this in mind, it is easy to see that the attempt at adaptation has not yet reached its definitive form. The priest who does not 'play at' work but 'becomes' a worker is still, for all the effort, unable to become a member of the proletariat. He carries a religious and human culture engraved on his being, a culture that he cannot possibly forsake. He can understand the disaster of complete insecurity, the crushing burden of a personal home and the grief of youngsters; he can never experience them in his own body. It is not enough to descend to the Marxist workers; they must be raised and helped to rediscover their true dignity for themselves. If it is extremely difficult to live one's faith amidst the dregs of society, it is a hundred times harder to make despairing souls believe, not in the final revolution, but in the Father's religion as preached by Jesus Christ. Perhaps today the folly of the cross is forced to undergo its greatest abasement before it can begin again its ascent.[39]

The responsibility of Church leaders and those directing consciences is graver today than it has ever been before. Each and every method

is liable to questioning. Laymen possessed of religious and apostolic aspirations rightfully expect more than vague exhortations and honeyed
discourses. They are worthy of counsels suitable to real men. Pastoral
work presents unexpected but exalting tasks.

Here the priest of average virtue and bookish knowledge will not
suffice. Saint Teresa and Saint John of the Cross have little sympathy
for confessors of mediocre theological formation. Even exemplary
piety cannot compensate for such a lack.

True theology, moreover, does not spend itself on theoretical
distinctions, 'pulling apart divine things with an indiscretion that
sickens the heart.'[40] It is fired with an interior flame that is the very
sense of mystery. The intellectual layman does not rigorously demand
that his pastor attain the level of his own university culture, but he
objects—and rightly so—if the priest is not a man of God.

On the other hand, if he wishes to reach to the heart of the matter,
the priestly minister must be sufficiently initiated in the concrete
problems of lay existence. If he remains in the abstract he will render
no service. He will not charge with lowered head into the profane
arena, but he will also avoid looking down on it from on high. He will
especially guard against dictating solutions, yet always aid in the
finding of them. Theologians, especially moralists, must also look to
the earth and the history of man: conservatism and progressivism,
each in its own way, come from an underdeveloped sense of the
real and of history.

Only under such conditions is an honest adaptation possible. The
adaptation: not mere adjustment of revelation to man's free will,
but rather sustained effort to speak intelligibly to each generation
and to find concrete forms of life suitable to the situation at hand.
First the apostle has to adapt himself to God Who determines his
mission for him, and then to the men to whom he is sent. To unite
these two terms he will not appeal to the superficial in man, but to
those profound desires that open him to God.

The sanctity of the laity then will not be a dream but a magnificent
reality. It is with this end that the spirituality of the laity is now in
formation.

---

[1] In speaking of a *lay spirituality* there is danger of equivocation. It must be understood
in the same way that we understand *priestly* or *monastic* piety, that is, lived with certain
particulars proper to laymen, priests or religious. Cf. Y. CONGAR, *o.c., Jalons*, p. 559 ff.
A. Z. SERRAND, O.P., *Sur une 'spiritualité' des laïcs*, in the *Vie Spir.* Suppl. n. 15, 1950,
p. 393-415. J. GRANGETTE, O.P. *Autour d'une spiritualité des laïcs*, in the *Vie Spir.* Suppl.,
1952, p. 49-65. A. PLE, O.P., *Mises au point et suggestions*, ib., p. 91-100. G. WULF,
Grundfragen einer Laienaszese, in *Geist und Leben*, 23, 1950, p. 311-315. This particular
number of the Review is consecrated to *The Layman faced with Christian sanctity*. J.
B. LOTZ, *Laienchrist und neue Frömmigkeit*, ib., 26, 1953, p. 304-308. J. M. PERRIN,
L'Heure des laïcs (Le Rameau), Paris, 1954.

[2] J. DELFOSSE, *La Parole est aux laïcs*, in the *Revue Nouvelle*, Dec. 15, 1952, p. 501 and 502. Cf. ID., *La Spiritualité des laïcs*, in *Documentos*, n. 13-14, 1953, p. 140-142.

[3] Cf. W. GROSSOUW, *Katholiek Réveil en Spiritualiteit* (*Te elfder Ure*, n. 2), Laren, 1952, p. 12.

[4] J. DE GUIBERT, *En quoi diffèrent réellement les diverses écoles catholiques de Spiritualité*, in *Gregorianum*, 19, 1938, p. 263-279. G. CANTINI, *Le Scuole cattoliche di spiritualità*, in the *Scuola Cattolica*, 78, 1950, p. 103-125.

[5] An objection given in one of the responses to the above mentioned questionnaire *Revue Nouvelle*, p. 502.

[6] The antiphon '*Ora pro populo, interveni pro clero, intercede pro devoto femineo sexu*' is of monastic origin. The brothers pray for the people, the priests and the religious sisters.

[7] Thus the sense of the formula frequently used in the liturgy, *terrena despicere*, must not be misunderstood. Compared with heavenly goods, the goods of earth are nothing. In the Gospel, however, Christ does not condemn riches which are good, but the rich who misuse them.

[8] See the doctrine of St. Paul on Christian marriage, *Eph.*, V, 32 ff.

[9] In reality laymen also must exert a religious influence. See above, p. 35.

[10] H. SCHILLEBEECKX, O.P., *Theologische grondslagen van de lekenspiritualiteit*, in *Tijdschrift voor Geestelijk Leven*, 5th year, t. I, 1949, p. 147. The entire issue is consecrated to the layman's spirituality. See also, M. SMITS VAN WAESBERGHE, *De Grondslagen van de lekenspiritualiteit*, *ib.*, 9, 1953, p. 423-473.

[11] S. AXTERS, *o.c.*, *Geschiedenis van de vroomheid in de Nederlanden*, I., p. XVIII.

[12] R. SCHERER, *Ordens-und Laienaszese*, in the number cited from *Geist und Leben*, p. 299-309.

[13] This description is inspired by W. GROSSOUW, *o.c.*, *Katholiek Réveil*, p. 9 ff., omitting what is specific to the Netherlands. See also E. MASURE, *Les tendances de la spiritualité contemporaine*, in *Documentos*, n. 13-14, 1953, pp. 117-139.

[14] E. MOUNIER is less understanding for Baroque, but he is justly indignant at such excessive pomposity. 'The parishioners learn beauty from gaudily painted plaster figures, sincerity from false marble, simplicity from gesticulating and inordinately gilded Virgins, mystery from hyperbole, military hardiness from the silly smiles attributed to sanctity . . .' E. MOUNIER, *L'affrontement chrétien*, Les Cahiers du Rhône, 58, 1945, p. 68.

[15] A. DERUMAUX, *Crise ou évolution dans la dévotion des jeunes pour le Sacré-Coeur*, in *Etudes Carmélitaines*, Le Coeur, Paris, 1950, p. 296 ff. This article has been the object of much unjust criticism.

[16] J. FOLLIET, *Les Chrétiens au carrefour*, Lyon, 1947. The author compares Christian thought with modern thought. See p. 123 ff. esp. p. 133.

[17] E. MOUNIER, *o.c.*, *L'affrontement chrétien*, p. 12 and 26. This small volume which pours forth a continuous flow of indignation, is very strongly influenced by the author's fascination with Nietzsche.

[18] I. F. GOERRES, *Die Leibhaftige Kirche. Gespräch unter Laien*, Frankfurt a.M., 1950. 6. Brief: *Die Kirche der Heiligen*. We are thinking also of the novels of GR. GREENE, in particular of the Whisky-priest in *The Power and the Glory* and of Scobie in *The Heart of the Matter*. Cf. his *Catholic Essays*.

[19] A. PLÉ, *Conclusion à l'enquête 'Vers quel type de sainteté allons-nous?* in the *Vie Spir.*, 74, 1946, p. 250, on the primacy of evangelical charity.

[20] R. THIBAUT, S.J., *La prière et l'effort*, in the *Nouvelle Revue Théol.*, 74, 1952, p. 1078 ff. -The 'realism' of the laymen's spirituality should also be applied to their profession. In regard to this, see: *Spiritualità cristiana nell'esercizio della professione* (VI, Settimana di Spiritualità), Milan, 1951, in particular the pages consecrated by G. LAZZATI to the spirituality of the politician, p. 143-167.

[21] Even dogma, it has been said, presents social aspects. See the fine work of FR. DE LUBAC, *Catholicism*. Eng. Trans., L. C. SHEPPARD, London, 1950.

[22] Cf. R. VOILLAUME, *Au coeur des masses. La vie religieuse des petits frères du Père de Foucauld* (*Rencontres*, 33), Paris, 1950. M. D. CHENU, O.P., *Dimensions collectives de l'ascèse*, in *L'Ascèse chrétienne* (*Cahiers Vie Spir.*), Paris, 1951, p. 209.

23 R. DRAGUET, *Les Pères du Desert* (*Bibl. Spir.*), Paris, 1949, p. XX. ff.

24 Cf. J. BONDUELLE, *Les Tiers-Ordres séculiers*, in the *Vie Spir.* Suppl., W. 15, 1950, p. 423-457.

25 CARD. SUHARD, *o.c.*, *The Meaning of God*, pp. 13-14.

26 Cf. *Communion des Saints* (*Cahiers de la Vie Spir.*, 4-5), Paris, 1945.

27 The four absolutes are absolute honesty, absolute purity, absolute disinterestedness, absolute love. The exercise is carried out in teams and a length of one hour is recommended. For the Catholic reservations about this movement, see the book of BISHOP L. J. SUENENS, *The Right View of Moral Re-Armament*, London, 1954.

28 Read the beautiful text of RUYSBROECK on the error of those who want to launch out into the apostolate without being men of contemplation: *Blinckende Steen*, Conclusion. *Ruusbroec-Genootschap* edition, III, Tielt, 2nd. ed., 1947, p. 41. Eng. Trans., *The Sparkling Stone* in *John of Ruysbroeck*. Trans. by C. A.WYNSCHENK DOM, New York, 1916.

29 CARD. SUHARD, *o.c.*, *The Meaning of God*, p. 32.

30 CARD. SUHARD, *ib.*, p. 30.

31 Consult A. M. GOICHON, *La Vie contemplative est-elle possible dans le monde?* Paris, 1952. D. DOHEN, *Vocation to Love*, New York, 1950. This book is a fine example of doctrinal solidness presented with a completely American vivacity.

32 P.M. E. BOYLAN, O.C.R., *Difficulties in Mental Prayer*, (10th impression) Dublin, 1953, p. 35 ff. The thesis of the book is the necessity of affective prayer in the sense of contemplation. Chapter 8, however, is a little optimistic regarding the transformation of work into prayer. It is true that the author is thinking of monks rather than people in the world.

33 CARD. M. VON FAULHABER, *Zeitrufe*, *Gottesrufe*, Fribourg-en-Brisgau, 1932.

34 J. FOLLIET, O.C., *Les Chrétiens au Carrefour*, Chap, entitled *Sainteté d'aujourd'hui*, p. 158.

35 A. PLÉ, *a.c.*, *Conclusion à l'enquête*, p. 237 ff.

36 P. M. ALLÈGRE, O.P., *Vers les conclusions*, in *L'Ascèse chrétienne et l'homme contemporain*, p. 354 ff. See also p. 360.

37 D. DUBARLE, O.P., *Le conditionnement anthropologique des actes de pénitence*, in the same *Cahier de la Vie Spir.*, p. 262.

38 P. M. ALLÈGRE, *a.c.*, p. 355.

39 Early in 1954, the Roman authority published express reserves about the modern experiment of the priest-workers. According to good theology, they should above all else remain priests. Only on this condition can the essential distinctions and proper character of the indispensable and irreplacable apostolate of the laity be safeguarded. See the joint letter of the French bishops in *Les Problèmes de l'Apostolat ouvrier*, Doc. Cath. 51, 1954, col. 263 ff. Since that time, Rome has given the seminary of the *Mission de France* a new supra-diocesan statue; and thanks to this it is hoped that this distressing problem can be resolved without stifling any generosity. For a summary of the Apostolic Constitution *Omnium Ecclesiarum*, see *Esprit*, 22, 1954, pp. 636-639.

40 E. MOUNIER, *o.c.*, *Affrontement chrétien*, p. 28.

CHAPTER X.

CONCLUSION

THE generous reader who has patiently followed us thus far will feel that many questions about the laity's role in the Church require more precise formulation before one can give them a speculatively satisfying answer. Fortunately, life works out a solution, if only a temporary one, to a host of problems without waiting until theoreticians are ready with their syntheses. Moreover, theologians are obliged to draw their principles from Revelation as it is communicated to them by the living Church. Since this Revelation has attained its fulness in Christ, a theology which has studied it can give ecclesiastical life firm directions about the road to follow. But because it is also true that our knowledge of Christ's doctrine increases in richness and depth in the measure that religious experience itself increases, the life of the Church will, in its turn, indicate to theology the orientation of its research. The director in this double work is the Spirit of Christ.

That is why, in the course of our exposition, we have lent an attentive ear to the Word of God in the Gospels and in tradition, but have also heard the witness of the Spirit speaking in the directives of the Magisterium and in the lived response of the community of the faithful to them. If then our work lacks a certain completeness, it is because of the very nature of the subject. We cannot afford the luxury of waiting until all these problems have been brought into full light before we interest ourselves in them; the laity are still earnestly seeking instruction about their own vocation despite the gropings of theology.

THE NOTION OF THE APOSTOLATE

We have purposely left this analysis for the end of the book. It would be impossible to outline the evolution of the word and idea of the apostolate by relying on ancient documents alone.[1] Here, if ever, we must examine the great life of the Church if we are to determine the development of this conception and its extraordinary destiny.

Is the notion perfectly unequivocal? Already, the New Testament authorizes an enlarged definition : it recognizes the charismatic Apostles and certainly the missionary preachers, not to mention the many

169

kinds of collaborators who served to spread the Gospel. Subsequent evolution, however, did not lead to equivocation. For the apostolate of the laity always retains its reference to the Biblical type of the Twelve to which it is analogous. This analogy is not something arbitrarily extended or metaphorically employed. No one asks modern lay apostles to sacrifice themselves for a metaphor; they are called to serve the most sublime realities, even when the profound meaning of their vocation can only be expressed with the aid of comparisons and images. In its most beautiful pages the Bible, too, has recourse to anthropomorphisms in speaking of God.

Christ Himself is called 'the Apostle' and the Pontiff in Whom we profess our belief: it is He Who brings us a 'heavenly calling' and the first fruits of salvation (Heb., III, 1). Has He not called Himself a hundred times 'the One Sent' of the Father?

He Himself gave the name 'apostle' to *the Twelve*. He had freely and individually chosen these faithful companions to be with Him that He might send them to preach with authority. Destined to become His witnesses, they were to see Him and hear Him intimately, were to accredit His Resurrection, were to receive from Him their full powers.[2] Afterwards, once enlightened and strengthened by the Paraclete, they would have to found and direct His Church. And finally, they would seal with their blood the truth of their witness, put to death as 'martyrs,' that is, witnesses whom it is impossible to silence.[3]

For Catholics the Apostles have *successors*. It is evident that the qualities of the companion of Christ, founder of the Church and possessor of the fulness of power are untransmittible.[4] Similarly, with the death of the last Apostle, the deposit of Christian revelation has been fixed and completed. But the ruling office that the Twelve exercised toward the community was instituted to endure, and they have communicated it to lawfully-consecrated successors. These are our *bishops*. By divine law, they are the supreme members of the hierarchy and cannot relinquish their authority.[5]

To share their pastoral cares, the bishops call upon *priests* of a lower rank; to such is communicated a power of orders and jurisdiction essentially subordinate.[6] But *laymen* are not admitted to this sacred 'function.'

To a certain extent, however, the bishops can share their role as 'witness' and even as 'one sent' with those who have received only the initial consecration of Baptism and Confirmation. Actually, Christ charged all his disciples to bear witness to Him before men. Obviously this extension suppresses neither the sacerdotal power nor the hierarchical institution, just as the latter in no way destroys the predominance of the great founders nor the authority of revealed sources. The bishops continue to depend on the Body of the Twelve, their writings and their traditions. In the same way, priests remain faithful to their bishops, and the simple faithful who bear witness especially by the splendour of their charity will never be able to exempt themselves from the direction and control of their shepherds or to do without the priestly ministry.

Laymen, however, can be entrusted with more than simply giving witness to their Faith. They can also receive, as we have said, a special mission, a canonical designation or mandate that is a type of official recognition for a more determined ecclesiastical task.[7] In this case, as limited and dependent as it may be, their title to the apostolate nevertheless carries greater weight than the universal vocation of all Christians.

In the measure, then, that one descends in the organization of the Church, the concept of apostle diminishes without ever becoming completely diluted. In final analysis, it is neither restricted to the power of ruling properly speaking nor to the ministerial function of distributing the Sacraments : in every case it keeps some element relating to the orderly diffusion of the message of Faith. As a matter of fact, every Christian remains personally responsible for the salvation of his brothers. The law of charity which is the soul of the Church, designates the Christian as a bearer of salutary grace for all the present members of the Body of Christ and for all its future members. From the highest leader to the most humble of the baptised, the line of descent that starts from the Incarnate Word and guarantees the transmission of heavenly gifts is never broken.

No doubt the average Christian is only slightly conscious of his duty of social charity. All the more reason then to awaken in him a sense of his responsibilities.[8] Furthermore, as he grows in the vision of Christ and in fidelity to the inspirations of the Spirit he will feel himself pushed more irresistibly to bear witness to his faith and his love, and the hierarchical Church will be able, should she so wish, to entrust him with further authorized missions.

Even then, he does not enter orders : he remains a layman.

We must remember that the layman is also a part of the Body that incarnates the divine word of salvation. In Baptism, the very least of the chosen undergoes a complete transformation. 'Undergo' is not accurate : it is a joyous acceptance. How wondrous it is ! No longer does the witness carry the message, but rather the message carries him, stimulates him and assures him astonishing success. Salvific power is in the Word; if it is faithfully announced, it is enough to move the listeners. The apostle is not a vulgar propagandist nor a recruiter of proselytes. He does not bind himself to a personal or partisan activity. He consecrates himself to the Lord of every work, to the Master of the whole apostolate.

During the ages of Christianity, to live as a believer did not require exceptional courage; it was the unbeliever who appeared revolutionary. Today, as in the very beginning, it is the convinced Christian, faithful to his vocation, who is the witness and instrument of the great liberation.

The Antinomy of the Catholic Synthesis

If a dissident Christian were reading this book he would certainly be struck by the hierarchical tone that surrounds the description of the laity. If a Protestant, he would wonder whether in the presence of such extensive authority there remains any liberty for the harassed and stifled Catholic. Perhaps he would be surprised to learn how resolutely the Roman Church affirms the eminent dignity of lay people and how earnestly she appeals to their whole-hearted co-operation. Her affirmation and appeal are the most direct answer to his accusation of clerical obscurantism. If he persists in his scepticism, only contact with a truly 'adult' layman—let us rather say one who is conscious of the noble exigencies of his state—will be able to overcome that misunderstanding. Here the Catholic laity can discover for themselves an oecumenical mission of the greatest importance.

But as long as the Protestant fails to grasp the spirit of Catholicism, he will stumble again and again, always on the antinomy of authority and personal faith. He sees himself faced with a choice whereas the Catholic embraces the two. He will see in Catholicism a *complexio oppositorum*, a bundle of contradictions, instead of recognizing the higher synthesis in it. [9] The fullness of the mystery, it is true, does not find its perfect human translation in that synthesis but there all its complex richness is unreservedly assumed. The Church refuses a choice that will impoverish her; she will neither sacrifice authority to vitalism nor the liberty of her sons to the instinct of domination.

It is common to all life and, therefore, to divine life in the midst of the human community, to admit tension and an uninterrupted exchange of currents. Any unwarranted stress of one of the factors breaks the equilibrium, disturbs communications, and endangers life itself. If the clergy and the laity were to battle for supremacy, the Church of God would cease to exist. The grandeur of one makes the grandeur of the other since far from rivalling one another they complement each other.

In 1950, Rome summoned a World Congress 'for the apostolate of laymen' and not an assembly of lay deliberators. The entire Church, clergy and faithful, needed to reflect on the sense, extent and methods of action of her transcendent mission. The hierarchy does not impose a silent and hateful submission, it calls for obedience, 'that inseparable mixture of renouncement and initiative, privation and transfiguration.'[10] Were the laity to transfer to the clergy all their religious and apostolic tasks, they would not prove themselves submissive but rather rebellious by their gravely culpable apathy. In such matters inferiority or superiority complexes have no place.

And once again we are at the mystery's center. The hierarchy, a sacrament of grace, is not a screen between souls and God. It is the connection and transmission of life and as such the base of Christian liberty. To non-believers the rites, the definitions, and especially the laws of the Church will appear as restrictions. But in the heart of these institutions is the Spirit, who augments all to the unlimited dimension of God.

Grace is truly incarnate in the mystery of the Church. Human material however is not yet perfectly spiritualized. The Church in the process of growth is familiar with work, pain, conflicting influences, and even sometimes with the scandal of sin as it reappears among laity or clerics.[11] Victory is in the power of Christ who will ultimately triumph over every obstacle.

THE INSTITUTION AND THE INTERVENTION

The 'new man' is born of the Church by the unceasing renewal of the miracle of Faith. But the miracle is not an argument browbeating our reason; it is a sign that only the clear eye of the Gospel can behold.

Protestantism claims to be alone in respecting the *Intervention* by which the Word continually raises up sons of Abraham from the stones. The Catholic Church tries to capture the divine power in Her *Institutions*, thence to dispose of it as she sees fit.[12] Whereas the Reformation bows before the inaccessible majesty of God, Rome substitutes itself for God and claims His powers.

To the eyes of Catholicism, the institution of the Church is the continued intervention of God. God is constantly at work in the ecclesiastical organisation. He does not speak through the Church occasionally : as prolongation of the Word, she is rather His permanent witness. She is not an idol raised in opposition to the grace of God. She is an instrument of salvation in His hands, by which He, and not she, works redemption.

His power descends in a vertical line from heaven as long as under His impulse the institution continues to fulfil its task. The creative act does not hurl the world into space and abandon it to its own forces.

The conservation of beings is a creation that continues; for every minute of its existence, earth literally depends on heaven. If all creatures are solidly bound to one another on the horizontal plan of secondary causes, each link on the chain remains perpendicularly fastened to the first Cause.

Providence, however, does not treat us like marionettes on strings; it invites us to a generous co-operation that changes subjection to adherence. And if the weight of sin hinders our ascent, the grace of the Saviour brings us the freedom of Sons of God. Every redeemed soul is responsible before Him, but during the earthly phase of the Church He has submitted individuals one to another not to remove from anyone the need for personal effort, but to engage all in the organic growth of the whole Christ.

Far from lost, the miracle of faith is even more resplendent here. The hierarchical institution in the very act of its commanding is executing the perfect obedience that transmits the salvific intervention. We have more than the dotted line of Christ's interventions; we have the firm, straight line of His permanent dynamism. The mystery is uninterrupted.[13]

Neo-protestantism recognizes with us the parallelism between the Church and the Virgin Mary. For us, both answer 'Yes!' in words and in acts to the divine invitation, but for the Reform, the answer is 'No!' on both sides, because in practice the creature is sin.[14]

The Mother of Christ is a type of the creature who through Faith accepts the gift of God and co-operates with grace and by grace to achieve the world's Redemption. By its receptivity—which is neither passivity nor personal justice, but rather spontaneous collaboration received from on high—the Communion of Saints glorifies with her the Author of Salvation. The Church recognizes in Mary Her perfect model; we might say Her essence, Her epitome. But in honouring the Virgin, She does not honour Her own value : She recognizes joyfully the marvels with which omnipotent Beauty has—in Christ— filled both the Virgin and the community which is Her crown.

After the hierarchy, then, it is the layman in the Church who receives all so as to give all. The Word, the Sacraments, the law of liberty—the layman benefits from all these in a total act of living Faith : they are not his to imprison in his own egoism but to radiate in charity.

In serving God humbly, ardently, and in the place determined for him, he will be, with Our Lady, a cause of great joy for the whole society of the elect.

---

[1] For the New Testament notion of an apostle, cf. A. MEDEBIELLE, art. *Apostolat*, in the *Supplément au Dict. de la Bible*, I, Paris, 1928, col. 533-588. K. H. RENGSTORF, art. *Apostolos*, in the *Theologisches Wörterbuch* of G. KITTEL, I, Stuttgart, 1933, pp. 406-448.

2 Mathias and Paul also saw Christ and received from Him their doctrine and their personal mission, though under different circumstances; they are assimilated to the Twelve.

3 Later the sense of the word *martyr* was inverted: the Christian becomes a martyr because he is put to death.

4 Cf. R. M. SPIAZZI, o.c., *Missione dei Laici*, p. 76.

5 Concerning the origin of the episcopate, consult L. MARCHAL, art. *Evêques*, in the *Supplément du Dict, de la Bible*, II, Paris, 1934, col. 1297-1333.

6 Concerning the priesthood cf. A. MICHEL, art. *Prêtre*, in the *Dict. Theol. Cath.*, XIII, 1936, col. 138-161.

7 See above, Chap. VII, p. 125 ff.

8 On the spirituality of the apostle, cf. A. PLE, O.P., *La sainteté de l'apôtre*, in the *Vie Spir.*, 78, 1948, pp. 198-226. ID., *Les Mystères de l'apôtre, ib.*, 79, 1948, pp. 407-434.

9 This theme of Catholicism as a *complexio oppositorum* is a favourite one with, among others, K. BARTH. Protestantism, for its part, nearly always takes an extreme position either to one or to the other side; hence a very characteristic fluctuation.

10 E. MOUNIER, o.c., *Affrontement chrétien*, p. 75.

11 The 'scandal' of the Church has been the subject of many works. Cf., among others, K. ADAM, *Kirchenmüdigkeit. Vom Aergernies zum sieghaften Glauben*, Paderborn, 1940. P. SIMON, *The Human Element in the Church of Christ*, Trans. by M. BOOTH, Cork, 1953. J. VIEUJEAN, *Difficultés tirées de l'histoire de l'Eglise*, in the Encyclopédie *Apologétique* of M. BRILLANT and NÉDONCELLE, Paris, 1948, pp. 1228-1284.

12 The formula 'Institution and Intervention' was popularized by the well known work of J. L. LEUBA, *L'Institution et l'Evénement*, Paris-Neuchâtel, 1952. For an idea of the repercussions of this book, cf. A. MINON, *L'Eglise, Institution et Evénement*, in the *Revue Eccl. de Liège*, 39, 1952, pp. 268-287, and R. AUBERT, *L'Institution et l'Evénement*, in the *Ephem. Theol. Lovan.*, 28, 1952, pp. 683-693.

13 K. BARTH's theory of the 'vertical miracle' (das senkrechte Wunder) does not recognize this fact.

14 See the objections of K. BARTH against Catholic Mariology and ecclesiology in his *Kirchliche Dogmatik*, 1, 2, 3rd. ed., Zollikon, Zurich, 1945, 153-160.